MARY BERRY
COOKS TO PERFECTION

MARY BERRY
COOKS TO PERFECTION
STEP BY STEP

Penguin
Random
House

Senior Editor Polly Boyd
Art Editor Tessa Bindloss
US Editor Karyn Gerhard
US Consultant Kate Curnes Ramos
US Executive Editor Lori Hand
Editorial Assistant Kiron Gill
Design concept Louise Brigenshaw
Jacket Designer Nicola Powling
Jackets Coordinator Lucy Philpott
DTP Designers Satish Gaur and Anurag Trivedi
Senior DTP Designer Tarun Sharma
Pre-Production Manager Sunil Sharma
Senior Production Editor Tony Phipps
Senior Production Controller Luca Bazzoli
Creative Technical Support Sonia Charbonnier
Managing Editor Dawn Henderson
Managing Art Editor Marianne Markham
Art Director Maxine Pedliham
Publishing Director Katie Cowan
Recipe consultation Angela Nilsen and Jeni Wright
Recipe photography William Reavell and Stuart West
Author photography Georgia Glynn Smith

NOTE: The author and publisher advocate sustainable food choices, and every effort has been made to include only sustainable food in this book. Food sustainability is, however, a shifting landscape, and so we encourage readers to keep up to date with advice on this subject, so that they are equipped to make their own ethical choices.

First American Edition, 2021
Published in the United States by DK Publishing
1450 Broadway, Suite 801, New York, NY 10018

Text copyright © 2014, 2021 Mary Berry
Copyright © 2014, 2021 Dorling Kindersley Limited
DK, a Division of Penguin Random House LLC
21 22 23 24 25 10 9 8 7 6 5 4 3 2
002–322328–Mar/2021

A catalog record for this book is available from the Library of Congress.
ISBN: 978-0-7440-2909-3

Printed and bound in China

For the curious
www.dk.com

MIX
Paper from responsible sources
FSC™ C018179

This book was made with Forest Stewardship Council ™ certified paper—one small step in DK's commitment to a sustainable future. For more information go to www.dk.com/our-green-pledge

CONTENTS

INTRODUCTION

Welcome. I'm very excited about this recipe collection. Some of these recipes are brand new—some are my tried-and-tested favorites given a refreshing twist; others contain a selection of new ingredients or flavor combinations. I have included a variety of recipes for the whole family to enjoy, quick suppers for you to rustle up after work, and impressive dishes for when you're entertaining. I'm sure you'll find much to tempt you.

One of the most exciting things about this book is that it's given me the opportunity to crystallize the knowledge and experience I've gained over so many years of cooking for my own family and friends, and to pass them on to you in a way I hope you'll find useful.

For each recipe, I identify the "key to perfection"—that is, the crucial part that you need to get right to guarantee excellent results. Sometimes it's a case of preparing some of the ingredients correctly, or you might need to be aware of a technical step during the cooking process or learn to recognize when a dish is done. Whatever it is, the step-by-step photographs and guidance make it easy to understand what you need to do to get the recipe perfect. Imagine I'm in the kitchen, cooking alongside you. I might just gently say in your ear, "Ah, watch out for this bit" or "Keep an eye on that." Well, that's what I'm doing here, while sharing with you a host of techniques that I've honed over the years. Some of the recipes may look a little longer than my usual ones—but it's not that they're complicated, it's just that I'm giving you more detailed information than I ever have before.

The more you cook these recipes and master the keys to perfection, the more they will become second nature. And who knows, perhaps you will then become the one whispering gentle advice into the ear of a less experienced cook! Just read through the recipe and keys carefully, and cook with care, and you, too, will achieve perfect results—time and time again.

Wishing you happy cooking.

SOUPS

SERVES 4

4 tbsp (50 g) butter

1 onion, coarsely chopped

*1 stalk of celery,
coarsely chopped*

*3 cups (750 ml)
chicken stock*

1 lb 2 oz (500 g) frozen peas

2 tbsp snipped fresh chives

*7 oz (200 g) roast ham off
the bone, excess fat
removed*

*salt and freshly ground
black pepper*

For the croûtes

*2 tbsp (scant 1 oz) butter
(room temperature)*

1½ tsp Dijon mustard

*16 slices from a
baguette loaf, cut
about ½ in (1cm) thick*

PEA AND HAM SOUP WITH MUSTARD CROÛTES

*Soup is one of my favorite weekday lunches, and this one
is quick and nutritious. I buy ham from the deli because you can have it
cut thickly and it has a good flavor, or use leftover roast ham.*

1. Melt the butter in a large pan. Add the onion and celery and fry for 8–10 minutes over medium heat, stirring often, until softened but not browned. Pour in the stock and bring to a boil over a high heat. Stir in the peas and quickly bring back to a boil, then reduce the heat and simmer for 3 minutes or until they are just cooked (see below: *Bright green color*).

2. Using a blender or food processor, purée the soup with the chives until smooth. Return the soup to the pan.

3. Shred the ham into small pieces (see below: *Bite-sized pieces of ham*) and drop it into the soup. Set aside.

4. Make the croûtes: preheat the broiler to its highest setting. Beat the butter and mustard together with a palette knife or spoon. Lay the baguette slices on a baking sheet and toast on both sides under the broiler until golden. Spread the mustard butter on one side of each slice of toasted bread. (See below: *Crispy croûtes*.)

5. Reheat the soup briefly over low heat. Season with salt and pepper, then serve with the mustard croûtes on the side.

KEYS TO PERFECTION

Bright green color

Add the peas to the boiling stock and start to time the cooking once it returns to a boil. Fast cooking makes the peas soft enough to purée easily without losing color.

Bite-sized pieces of ham

You are aiming for bite-sized pieces of ham for this soup. Use two forks to shred the meat—one to hold the ham steady and the other to pull it apart.

Crispy croûtes

Watch the slices of bread carefully during broiling to make sure they don't burn. Spread the mustard butter on the bread while it's still slightly warm, so it soaks in.

SERVES 4

1¾ lb (800 g) small,
ripe vine tomatoes

½ small red onion,
coarsely chopped

3 garlic cloves, sliced

2 tbsp olive oil

freshly ground
black pepper

½ tsp granulated sugar

1¾ cup (400 ml) vegetable
stock or chicken stock

1 tbsp tomato purée

small handful of fresh
basil leaves, plus extra
small leaves to serve

salt (optional)

4½ oz (125 g) ball Italian
mozzarella cheese, torn
into small pieces

ROASTED TOMATO SOUP

*I've made many versions of tomato soup, but roasting
the tomatoes really brings out their rich, sweet flavor.
Add the cheese at the last minute, so it doesn't melt too quickly.*

1. Preheat the oven to 400°F (200°C). Scatter the whole tomatoes, onion, and garlic into a large, shallow roasting pan. Drizzle the oil over and toss all together. Season with pepper and sprinkle the tomatoes with the sugar. Roast for 30–35 minutes (see below: *Sweet, soft tomatoes*).

2. Remove the roasting pan from the oven and add the stock, tomato purée, and the handful of basil leaves, stirring gently to combine them with the syrupy juices in the pan.

3. Transfer the mixture to a blender or food processor and purée until smooth, then press it through a sieve (see below: *Really smooth texture*).

4. Pour the soup into a pan to reheat. Check the seasoning (you may not need salt), then ladle into warmed bowls. Scatter some of the mozzarella, a few small basil leaves, and a grinding of pepper on top of each serving.

KEYS TO PERFECTION

Sweet, soft tomatoes

1 A sprinkling of granulated sugar over the tomatoes before roasting helps to draw out their sweetness and make the flavor of the soup more intense.

2 You will know the tomatoes are fully roasted when they are soft, starting to burst, and turning brown at the edges. They will have produced tasty, syrupy juices.

Really smooth texture

Sieving the soup gives it a smooth texture and bright color. Set a fine sieve over a bowl and press the soup through, a little at a time, using the back of a wooden spoon.

SERVES 4

2 tbsp (scant 1 oz) butter

1 stalk of celery, thinly sliced

8 scallions, trimmed: 6 thinly sliced, 2 finely chopped

1 tsp chopped fresh thyme, plus extra to garnish

1 bay leaf

2 tbsp all-purpose flour

2½ cups (600 ml) fish stock

⅓ cup (90 ml) white wine

12 oz (350 g) fluffy potatoes, such as russet, peeled and cut into 1 in (2.5cm) cubes

12 oz (350 g) salmon fillet, skinned and cut into slices 1 in (2.5cm) thick

salt and freshly ground black pepper

½ cup (100 ml) heavy cream

3½ oz (100 g) cooked, peeled large shrimp

SALMON AND SHRIMP CHOWDER

*When served with warm, crusty bread, this makes
a perfect main meal soup. It's a combination of two types of
chowder—fish and shellfish—gently simmered in a creamy, fragrant broth.*

1. Melt the butter in a large pan. Add the celery, sliced scallions, thyme, and bay leaf and cook gently over medium heat for 2 minutes, stirring, until softened but not browned. Stir in the flour and cook for 1–2 minutes.

2. Gradually blend in the stock, then add the wine and potatoes. Bring to a boil over high heat, still stirring, and cook until the liquid has slightly thickened, then reduce the heat to medium and simmer for 10 minutes or until the potatoes are just tender.

3. Season the salmon with salt and pepper, then carefully slide the slices into the pan. Reduce the heat and simmer very gently, covered, for about

4 minutes or until almost cooked. Remove from the heat, pour in the cream, and scatter the shrimp over the top. Cover again and let sit for 5 minutes. (see below: *Tender salmon and shrimp.*)

4. Remove the bay leaf and, if necessary, heat the chowder through gently but very briefly, for no more than 1 minute. Ladle the chowder into warmed bowls. Scatter the chopped scallions and extra thyme on top, plus a grinding of pepper if you wish.

KEYS TO PERFECTION

Tender salmon and shrimp

1 After adding the fish to the pan, don't stir the chowder. The salmon will cook better if left undisturbed and won't break into smaller pieces that could become overcooked.

2 As you add the cream, swirl the soup around so it mixes in; don't stir. Leaving the pan off the heat enables the salmon to finish cooking gently and the shrimp to warm through.

MARY'S TOP TIPS

Read the recipe

Read through a recipe carefully a couple of times: first to check you have the ingredients and equipment, and identify what you need to buy, then again before you start so you're familiar with the order of work.

SERVES 4

9 oz (250 g) shelled fresh
or frozen fava beans

4 tbsp (50 g) butter

4½ oz (125 g) shallots,
finely chopped

3 garlic cloves,
finely chopped

1 large zucchini,
about 7 oz (200 g)

7 oz (200 g) small new
potatoes, such as baby
reds, scrubbed, halved
lengthways, and sliced
thinly across

3¾ cups (900 ml) vegetable
stock or chicken stock

4½ oz (125 g) thin
asparagus, sliced into
2in (5cm) lengths

salt and freshly ground
black pepper

chopped fresh tarragon,
to garnish

chopped fresh flat-leaf
parsley, to garnish

SUMMER VEGETABLE SOUP

Early summer offers so many different vegetables and herbs, and this soup is a great way to make use of them. Brief cooking of the beans and asparagus keeps the soup looking and tasting fresh.

1. Cook the fava beans in a small pan of simmering water for 3 minutes (or up to 5 minutes if using large, fresh beans), then drain and rinse under cold running water. Peel the beans and set aside (see below: *Peel the beans*).

2. Heat the butter in a large pan. Add the shallots and garlic and fry over low heat for about 10 minutes, stirring occasionally, until well softened but still quite pale. Meanwhile, grate the zucchini down its length to create long strands (see below: *Grate the zucchini*).

3. Add the potatoes to the pan and cook for 3–4 minutes, stirring often, without letting them brown. Increase the heat, then add in the grated zucchini and stir for about 1 minute to start to let it soften and take on the buttery juices. Pour in 3 cups (750 ml) of the stock and simmer for about 8 minutes or until the potatoes are tender.

4. Add the asparagus and the remaining stock, or less if you like a slightly thicker soup, then simmer for 2–3 minutes or until just tender. Stir in the peeled fava beans to warm them through. Season with salt and pepper.

5. Ladle the soup into wide, warmed bowls and serve sprinkled with tarragon and parsley.

KEYS TO PERFECTION

Peel the beans

1 Very brief simmering ensures the fava beans retain their color and flavor. As soon as the beans are cooked, drain them in a sieve under cold running water. This will cool them quickly, making them easier to handle.

2 Squeeze one end of each bean so it pops out of its skin. Removing the skins from the shelled beans may seem rather labor-intensive, but it shows off their bright color and accentuates their tender texture.

Grate the zucchini

Grating the zucchini gives variety of texture. Run the zucchini down the coarse side of a box grater for long strands. Using the coarse side ensures the zucchini won't disintegrate easily when added to the soup.

SERVES 4

Special equipment
*3in (7.5cm) plain
round cutter*

*2½ cups (600ml) full-fat
or low-fat milk*

2 bay leaves

2 sprigs of fresh thyme

¼ tsp grated nutmeg

*salt and freshly ground
black pepper*

3 tbsp (45g) butter

*1 large fluffy potato,
such as russet, about
10 oz (300g), peeled and
cut into 1in (2.5cm) cubes*

*2 large leeks, trimmed
and finely sliced*

*1¾ cups (400ml) vegetable
stock or chicken stock*

*3 oz (85g) Dolcelatte
cheese, cut into
small cubes*

heavy cream, to serve

For the Parmesan crisps

*1¾ oz (50g) Parmesan
cheese, coarsely grated*

DOLCELATTE AND LEEK SOUP WITH PARMESAN CRISPS

This is a rich version of a popular classic—leek and potato soup.
The accompanying Parmesan crisps are easy to make and
add a nice touch for a special occasion.

1. Pour the milk into a small pan and add the bay leaves, thyme, nutmeg, and a grinding of pepper. Bring just to the boil, until you see tiny bubbles appear around the edge of the pan. Remove from the heat and set aside to infuse for 20 minutes. (See p22: *Infuse the milk.*)

2. While the milk is infusing, make the Parmesan crisps: preheat the broiler on its highest setting. Line a baking sheet with parchment paper. Separate the grated Parmesan into 8 mounds, each about 2½in (6cm) in diameter, on the parchment paper. Place the cutter over each mound and spread out the cheese so it fills the cutter. Place the baking sheet under the broiler and cook for about 4 minutes or until the cheese is melted and pale golden. Transfer the crisps to a wire rack to cool. (See p23: *Make golden brown Parmesan crisps.*)

3. Melt 2 tbsp (25 g) of the butter in a large pan, add the potato cubes, and cook over very low heat for 5 minutes or until starting to soften but not turn brown.

4. Increase the heat, add the rest of the butter and the leeks, and cook for 3–4 minutes, stirring often, until almost tender. Pour in the stock and strain the infused milk into the pan. Bring the liquid to a boil, then simmer for 8–10 minutes to finish cooking the vegetables. (See p22: *Gently simmer the vegetables.*)

5. Using a blender or food processor, purée the soup until smooth. Pour it back into the pan.

6. Reheat the soup and stir in the cubes of Dolcelatte. Remove from the heat and season to taste. (See p22: *Add the finishing touches.*) Serve topped with a drizzle of cream and the Parmesan crisps on the side.

KEYS TO PERFECTION
See pp22–23

KEYS TO PERFECTION

Infuse the milk

Infusing the milk with herbs and spices gives the soup a lovely, subtle flavor and aroma. It's important to use full-fat or low-fat milk rather than skimmed, which doesn't have the required strength of flavor and richness. You will need to strain the milk before adding it to the soup in order to remove the flavorings.

Gently simmer the vegetables

Sautéing the leeks briefly over high heat initially enables them to soften and take on the flavor of the butter without losing their color. As soon as the leeks have wilted down, stir in the stock and milk. Reduce the heat as soon as they have come to a boil. The soup should simmer gently. If it boils vigorously, it will become too thick and the vegetables will overcook, which will impair the flavor.

Add the finishing touches

After puréeing the soup, reheat and stir in the cubes of gorgonzola cheese over very low heat. As soon as they start to melt, remove the pan from the heat. If the cheese is melted over too high a heat or left over the heat for too long, it will overcook and spoil the texture of the soup. Taste the soup before seasoning with salt; with the stock and cheese, which are both salty, you may not need much.

ABOUT DOLCELATTE CHEESE

Dolcelatte is a blue-veined soft cheese that is ideal for this soup, as it has a smooth, creamy texture, mild, slightly sweet taste, and it melts easily. If you can't find Dolcelatte, the texture and taste of Gorgonzola makes it the best substitute, or you could also use Stilton.

Make golden brown Parmesan crisps

1 It's important to line the baking sheet with parchment paper, because it will prevent the crisps from sticking while they bake. When making the Parmesan circles, you don't have to make them really neat initially: just make sure they're all roughly the same size and that they're far enough apart so that they won't touch when broiled.

2 After laying out all the Parmesan circles, place the cutter over each and spread the cheese as evenly as possible within the cutter. The cutter will help to make the crisps neater and more uniform in size and shape so they cook evenly. After you've neatened the circles, put the baking sheet under the broiler.

3 When the crisps are golden, remove the baking sheet from the broiler and let them sit for 1 minute on the sheet. Lift the crisps off with a palette knife and place them on a wire rack to cool completely—they will crisp up as they cool. It's best to eat the crisps while they're fresh, as they soften if stored for too long.

WATCH THE CRISPS CLOSELY!

When broiling the Parmesan crisps, watch very closely, as they can quickly become too brown. The baking sheet should be about 3in (7.5cm) from the heat. If it's too close to the element, the cheese will burn; if too far away, it won't brown well enough to turn crisp. Broil until the cheese has melted and turned pale golden, about 4 minutes.

SERVES 4

2 tbsp sunflower oil

1 onion, finely chopped

2 carrots, diced

2 garlic cloves, crushed

1½ tsp peeled and grated
fresh ginger

¼ tsp ground turmeric

2 tsp garam masala
(see box, opposite)
or mild curry powder

5 oz (140 g) dried red lentils

3¾ cups (900 ml) chicken or
vegetable stock

⅔ cup (150 ml) tomato juice

salt and freshly ground
black pepper

1¾ oz (50 g) fresh spinach,
finely chopped

plain, full-fat yogurt,
to serve

CURRIED LENTIL AND SPINACH SOUP

This is one of those really warm, comforting soups made with just enough spice to add interest without being overpowering. To complement the flavors, serve it with warm Indian bread.

1. Heat the oil in a large pan. Add the onion and carrots and fry gently over a medium heat for 8–10 minutes, stirring occasionally, until the onion is very lightly colored. Increase the heat to medium–high, add the garlic and ginger to the pan, and fry for 1 minute more. Stir in the turmeric and garam masala.

2. Add the lentils and pour in the stock and tomato juice. Bring to a boil over high heat, then reduce the heat and simmer gently for 15–20 minutes or until the lentils and carrots are tender (see below: *Al dente lentils*). If the soup looks like it is thickening too quickly, pour in a little more stock. Season with salt and pepper.

3. Remove the pan from the heat. Just before serving, stir most of the spinach into the soup (it should just start to wilt). Ladle the soup into warmed bowls, top with a scattering of the reserved spinach, and swirl a dollop of plain yogurt into each bowl.

KEYS TO PERFECTION

Al dente lentils

1 While the lentils are cooking, taste them occasionally to see if they're tender. They should be soft but still retain their shape and bite. Overcooking breaks up the lentils and makes the soup too sloppy.

2 After 15–20 minutes, when the lentils and carrots are cooked (and not before), season the soup with salt and pepper. If salt is added too early in the cooking process, it can make the lentils tough.

ABOUT GARAM MASALA

Garam masala, a blend of aromatic spices used in Indian cooking, is really handy to have in your spice rack. It instantly adds an authentic Indian flavor without the need for buying and storing lots of different spices.

FIRST COURSES

SERVES 6

12 diagonal slices from
1 long white baguette,
cut about ½in (1cm) thick

3 tbsp extra virgin olive oil

⅓ cup (85g) mayonnaise

1 garlic clove, crushed

½ tsp Dijon mustard

1 tsp lemon juice

freshly ground
black pepper

4 oz (115g) cooked
chicken breast

8 leaves of romaine lettuce,
root ends trimmed

4–5 canned anchovies,
drained and chopped

1½ tbsp finely grated
Parmesan cheese

CHICKEN CAESAR SALAD CROSTINI

These crostini are creamy, crisp, salty, and crunchy—all in one delightful mouthful. For informal occasions, you can pass them around with drinks rather than serving them at the table.

1. Preheat the oven to 375°F (190°C). Brush both sides of the bread with the oil and place the slices on a large baking sheet. Bake for 10 minutes. Flip the bread and bake for another 4–5 minutes (see below: *Crunchy bread*). The bread can be baked up to 1 day ahead and will keep crisp if wrapped in foil or stored in an airtight container.

2. Meanwhile, in a small bowl, stir together the mayonnaise, garlic, mustard, and lemon juice, and season with pepper. Set aside. Finely shred the chicken into small pieces using two forks—one to hold the meat, the other to pull it apart. If it does not shred easily, cut it into fine strips.

3. Just before serving, finely shred the lettuce leaves (see below: *Crisp lettuce*) and put in a bowl with the chicken and anchovies.

4. Spread just a little of the mayonnaise mixture on one side of each slice of bread. Lightly stir the rest of the mayonnaise into the chicken, anchovy, and lettuce mixture in the bowl. Season with pepper. Pile up a little lettuce, chicken, and anchovy mix on each slice of bread, then sprinkle some Parmesan over the top (see below: *Perfect timing*). Serve immediately.

KEYS TO PERFECTION

Crunchy bread

Flip the bread when it's just starting to turn golden. This gives a wonderful crispy texture to complement the topping. Keep a close eye on the crostini, as they can quickly become too brown.

Crisp lettuce

Roll up each lettuce leaf like a cigar and slice it across into fine shreds. Don't do this too early, or the lettuce may wilt, and stir in the mayonnaise at the last minute, otherwise the lettuce will lose its crunch.

Perfect timing

Spread each crostini with the mayonnaise mixture and spoon the lettuce, chicken, and anchovy mix on top just before serving. If assembled too far ahead, the crostini will lose its crispness. Finally, sprinkle with Parmesan.

SERVES 4

4½ oz (125 g) ball Italian
mozzarella cheese

6 slices Parma ham

salt and freshly ground
black pepper

12 fresh basil leaves

1 ripe mango
(see box, opposite)

For the marinade

2 tbsp extra virgin olive oil

2 tsp lime juice

1 small garlic clove, crushed

2 tsp chopped fresh
flat-leaf parsley

For the dressing

5½ oz (150 g) carton plain,
full-fat yogurt

2 tsp honey

finely grated zest and juice
of ½ lime

MANGO, PARMA HAM, AND MOZZARELLA PLATTER

*This is a very easy first course that doesn't require any cooking,
just assembling lovely fresh ingredients. If you don't have time to marinate
the wraps, simply put it all together at the last minute.*

1. Cut the mozzarella into 6 slices, then cut each slice in half lengthwise. Cut each slice of Parma ham in half lengthwise. You should have 12 slices of mozzarella and 12 of ham. Season each slice of mozzarella with pepper and lay a basil leaf on top. Wrap a strip of the ham around each piece of mozzarella and basil.

2. Make the marinade: mix together the olive oil, lime juice, garlic, and parsley, then season with salt and pepper. Pour this into a shallow dish. Put the mozzarella wraps in the dish and turn to coat well. Set aside for 1–2 hours, but no longer, as the Parma ham can soften and lose its brightness.

3. Make the dressing: spoon the yogurt into a small bowl and stir in the honey, lime zest, and lime juice. Set aside.

4. Remove the pit and skin from the mango and cut the flesh into thin slices (see below: *Attractive mango slices*). To serve, arrange the mango slices on a platter. Place the mozzarella wraps on the mango slices, with the seam on the bottom, and drizzle the marinade on top. Serve with the dressing on the side.

KEYS TO PERFECTION

Attractive mango slices

1 The pit runs flat through the center of the mango, so using a sharp chef's knife, cut the fruit vertically down either side of the stone to give you two mango "cheeks." Peel the mango cheeks and remaining mango.

2 Place a mango cheek on your cutting board, flat-side down, and cut it lengthwise into thin slices. Repeat with the other half. Finally, slice off any flesh clinging to the pit into neat wedge shapes.

BUYING AND USING MANGOES

Choose a mango that is fully ripe, as that will give the best flavor, color, texture, and shape. To test for ripeness, press the fruit at the tip of the stalk end; it should have a bit of give. Also, it should have a perfumed aroma.

SERVES 4

Special equipment
*Ridged cast-iron
grill pan*

*2 tbsp olive oil, plus extra
for drizzling and frying*

1 tbsp lemon juice

*1 eggplant, sliced into
rounds ¼in (5mm) thick*

*salt and freshly ground
black pepper*

*4 oz (115g) firm
Spanish chorizo*

*1 onion, halved lengthwise
and thinly sliced*

*1 red bell pepper, seeded
and cut into small pieces*

*2 garlic cloves,
finely chopped*

*4 oz (115g) cherry
tomatoes, cut into
small pieces*

*14 oz (400g) can butter
beans or canellini beans,
drained and rinsed*

*2 tbsp chopped fresh
flat-leaf parsley*

EGGPLANT, BUTTER BEAN, AND CHORIZO TAPA

Spicy and colorful, this Spanish-style appetizer can be served hot or at room temperature. If you're preparing it ahead, keep the butter bean mixture moist by drizzling it with a little olive oil.

1. Mix the oil and lemon juice in a bowl. Preheat the grill pan over high heat for 5–10 minutes. Brush one side of the eggplant slices with half the oil mixture. Grill for about 3 minutes. Oil the other side and grill for 2 minutes (see below: *Soft, grilled eggplants*). Transfer to a large, shallow dish, season, and drizzle with some olive oil. Set aside.

2. Slice the chorizo very finely (see below: *Crisp chorizo shavings*). Heat a large, nonstick frying pan and add the chorizo slices. Fry for 2–3 minutes over high heat, turning often, until crisp. Using a slotted spoon, transfer the chorizo to a paper towel to drain. Leave the oil from the chorizo in the pan.

3. Reduce the heat to medium–high and add the onion, red pepper, and garlic. Fry for 6–8 minutes or until softened and starting to brown, adding extra olive oil as needed. Increase the heat to high, add the tomatoes, and cook until softened. Stir in a few tablespoons of water, then add the butter beans to warm through. Season well with salt and pepper, remove from the heat, and stir in the parsley.

4. Spoon the butter bean mixture onto 4 plates, top with folded slices of eggplant, and scatter the crisp chorizo shavings over the top.

KEYS TO PERFECTION

Soft, grilled eggplants

1 When you add the eggplant, the pan must be very hot and the slices must fit in a single layer. Place the slices oiled-side down and grill for 3 minutes or until soft. While grilling, brush the tops with the remaining oil.

2 When the undersides of the eggplants are starting to look soft and juicy, and the markings from the ridged pan have become a dark golden color, flip the slices. Cook for another 2 minutes or until soft.

Crisp chorizo shavings

Slice the chorizo, using a very sharp knife, as thinly as possible on the diagonal. The thinner the slices are, the more the chorizo will create interesting curly shapes and become crisp when fried.

SERVES 8

Special equipment
*1 lb (450 g) loaf pan,
7½ x 3½in (19 x 8.5cm)
and 2¼in (5.5cm) deep,
with 3-cup (750 ml) capacity*

*7–9 oz (200–250 g) smoked
salmon in long slices*

*freshly ground
black pepper*

*3½ oz (100 g) roasted
salmon flakes*

*8 oz (225 g) full-fat
cream cheese*

*8 tbsp (115 g) butter
(room temperature)*

1 tbsp lemon juice

*1 tbsp hot
horseradish sauce*

*4 tsp finely chopped
fresh dill, plus small
sprigs to garnish*

*baby salad leaves,
to garnish*

CHILLED SALMON TERRINE

Having an elegant first course that can be made ahead and kept in the fridge until needed is really handy when entertaining. Top this terrine with a few pretty leaves and serve chilled with toast.

1. Dampen the bottom and sides of the loaf pan using a pastry brush dipped in water. Line the pan with plastic wrap so that it overhangs the sides. Cut 3 slices of salmon into long strips about 2½in (6cm) wide. Line the bottom and sides of the pan with the slices, allowing a 1½–2in (3.5–5cm) overhang. (See below: *Firm, well-shaped terrine*, steps 1 and 2.) Sprinkle with pepper.

2. Make the pâté: put the salmon flakes, cream cheese, butter, lemon juice, and horseradish sauce in a food processor. Purée the mixture until smooth and season with pepper (you shouldn't need salt, as the salmon is salty).

3. Spoon one-third of the pâté into the salmon-lined pan and spread evenly to level the surface. Scatter 2 teaspoons of the chopped dill on top. Continue with another third of the pâté, the remaining dill, and then the last of the pâté. Bring the smoked salmon overhang over it to cover (see below: *Firm, well-shaped terrine*, step 3), then the plastic wrap overhang. Chill for at least 6 hours, preferably overnight, to firm up.

4. Serve the terrine straight from the fridge, as it will be easier to slice. Turn it out of its pan onto a serving plate. Peel off and discard the plastic wrap and garnish the top with dill sprigs and baby leaves. Slice with a sharp knife.

KEYS TO PERFECTION

Firm, well-shaped terrine

1 Lining the pan with plastic wrap makes the terrine easier to remove and helps to keep its shape. Dampen the pan first and smooth the wrap over the bottom and sides, and allow some overhang. Don't worry about wrinkles.

2 Line the pan with the salmon as neatly as you can. Since the size of the slices can vary, you may need to trim or overlap them and patch up any gaps with leftovers. Lightly press the salmon strips so they stick together.

3 After adding the layers of pâté and dill, fold in the smoked salmon overhang, filling any gaps with leftover salmon and folding over the ends. Cover the terrine tightly with the plastic wrap overhang before chilling.

SERVES 4

2–3 tbsp olive oil

3½ oz (100 g) asparagus
tips, cut into long, thin,
diagonal slices

12 king (large) shelled
scallops, trimmed
(see below, box)

salt and freshly ground
black pepper

For the dressing

3 tomatoes

1 small shallot,
finely chopped

1 garlic clove,
finely chopped

¼ cup extra virgin olive oil

1 tbsp lemon juice

1 tbsp finely chopped
fresh parsley

1 tbsp finely snipped
fresh chives

PAN-FRIED SCALLOPS WITH WARM TOMATO DRESSING

King scallops are always a treat, as they are particularly large and succulent.
Here, dainty asparagus tips make the perfect base for them to sit on;
like the scallops, they are cooked very briefly.

1. Make the dressing: peel the tomatoes and remove their seeds and juice (see below: *Seed the tomatoes*). Cut the flesh into small dice. Put them in a small pan with the shallot, garlic, extra virgin olive oil, and lemon juice, and set aside.

2. Heat 2 tablespoons of the olive oil in a large, nonstick frying pan. Add the asparagus tips and stir-fry over medium–high heat for 2–3 minutes or until just tender and starting to brown. Remove from the pan and keep warm.

3. If necessary, add a little more oil to the pan. When the oil is very hot, add the scallops. Season and cook briefly for 2–3 minutes (the cooking time depends on their size),

turning once halfway through cooking (see below: *Tender, golden scallops*). When done, they should be opaque and browned on both sides. Remove from the pan and keep warm.

4. While the scallops are cooking, warm the dressing over medium heat for 2 minutes, then take off the heat and stir in the parsley and chives. Season with salt and pepper. Divide the asparagus among 4 plates and top with the scallops. Spoon the warm dressing around the scallops and serve.

KEYS TO PERFECTION

Seed the tomatoes

To ensure that the dressing is not too watery, remove the seeds and juice from the skinned tomatoes. Over a small bowl, scoop out the insides with a teaspoon, or gently squeeze with your hand, and discard.

Tender, golden scallops

The scallops must fry quickly, as they can soon become tough and rubbery. Get the oil very hot and press them down with a fish slice; the outsides should be golden brown, the centers slightly rare.

BUYING AND USING SCALLOPS

Scallops must be very fresh, so be sure they smell sweet and their flesh is plump, soft, and creamy. Trim them using sharp kitchen scissors to cut off the crescent-shaped muscle found on the side of the body, as this can be slightly tough. If the scallops have their orange coral attached, you can leave it on, if you wish, as it is a delicacy.

SERVES 4

16 raw peeled tiger shrimp (with tails left on), deveined

3 tbsp olive oil

4 garlic cloves, finely chopped

1 tbsp chopped fresh cilantro

For the mayonnaise

2 large egg yolks

1 tsp Dijon mustard

1 garlic clove, crushed

salt and freshly ground black pepper

5 fl oz (150 ml) olive oil

2–2½ tsp lemon juice

½ tsp finely grated lemon zest

1 tbsp chopped fresh cilantro

a generous splash of Tabasco

pinch of granulated sugar

CRISPY GARLIC SHRIMP WITH LEMON AND CILANTRO MAYONNAISE

This makes a lovely light, piquant first course. The tails are useful for dipping, so if you can't find peeled, tail-on shrimp, buy shell-on shrimp and peel them yourself, leaving the tail ends on.

1. Make the mayonnaise: place the egg yolks, mustard, garlic, and some salt and pepper in a bowl and combine using a hand-held blender. With the blender still on, add the oil very slowly, blending all the time, until it has all been incorporated and the mixture has thickened (see below: *Creamy, smooth mayonnaise*). Stir in 2 teaspoons of the lemon juice, the lemon zest, cilantro, and Tabasco. Check the seasoning, adding a little sugar and more lemon juice if desired.

2. Season the shrimp with salt and pepper. Just before serving, heat the oil in a large, nonstick frying pan over high heat, add the garlic and shrimp, and stir-fry for 1–2 minutes (see below: *Tender shrimp*) until the shrimp are just cooked and the garlic is golden and crisp. Do not let the garlic burn, or it will have a bitter taste.

3. Toss the cilantro into the shrimp, then pile the shrimp onto 4 plates, spooning the crispy garlic and any juices over the top. Serve immediately with the lemon and cilantro mayonnaise.

KEYS TO PERFECTION

Creamy, smooth mayonnaise

Pour in the oil, drop by drop at first, then in a slow, steady trickle, and blend continuously until the mixture thickens. If you add the oil too quickly at the beginning, the mayonnaise will start to separate.

Tender shrimp

Fry the shrimp over high heat and keep them moving. If cooked too slowly or for too long, they can become tough and chewy. Take them off the heat as soon as they turn from opaque to pink all over.

MY TIPS FOR CURDLED MAYONNAISE

If the mayonnaise separates, try beating in 1 tablespoon of hot water. If that doesn't work, you may need to start again by combining 1 fresh egg yolk and ¼ cup (75 ml) oil as before. Once the eggs and oil have thickened, gradually stir in the curdled mayonnaise.

Special equipment

Six 5 fl oz (150 ml) ramekins, about 3¼in (8cm) diameter and 1¾in (4.5cm) deep

4 tbsp (60 g) butter, plus extra for greasing

5½ oz (150 g) crimini mushrooms, chopped into small, even-sized pieces

salt and freshly ground black pepper

3 tbsp (45 g) plain flour

1¼ cups (300 ml) full-fat hot milk

3 large eggs, separated

3½ oz (100 g) Camembert cheese, cut into small cubes

arugula, to garnish

For the sauce

1¼ cups (300 ml) heavy cream

4 tsp grainy mustard

TWICE-BAKED MUSHROOM AND CAMEMBERT SOUFFLÉS

The beauty of this recipe is that the soufflés can be baked ahead and kept for several hours, then just before serving they can be re-baked and will come out of the oven all puffed up again.

1. Generously butter the ramekins. Melt 1 tablespoon (15 g) of the butter in a large, nonstick frying pan over medium–high heat, add the mushrooms, and fry for 3–4 minutes or until they start to turn brown and all their juices are reduced (see p42: *Fast-fry the mushrooms*). Remove using a slotted spoon, drain on paper towels, season with salt and pepper, and set aside to cool. Preheat the oven to 425°F (220°C).

2. Make the soufflé base: melt the remaining butter in a large pan over medium heat. Stir in the flour and cook, whisking continuously, for 1 minute. Remove the pan from the heat and whisk in the hot milk very gradually. Return to the heat and bring to a boil, whisking all the time, until thickened. (See p42: *Make a thick, smooth soufflé base.*)

3. Cook for a few seconds, still stirring, then remove the pan from the heat. Beat in the egg yolks, one yolk at a time, then stir in the mushrooms and cheese and season with salt and pepper. Let the mixture cool slightly.

4. Whisk the egg whites until they form soft peaks. Stir about 1 tablespoon of the egg whites into the egg-yolk mixture, then carefully fold in the rest of the whites. (See p42: *Lighten the mixture.*)

5. Divide the mixture evenly among the ramekins. Place them in a small roasting pan and pour enough boiling water into the pan to come halfway up the sides of the ramekins. Bake the soufflés for 15–18 minutes. (See p43: *Bake light, fluffy soufflés.*) Carefully remove the ramekins from the pan. Let the soufflés sit for 5–10 minutes.

6. Butter a large, shallow baking dish. Carefully unmold each soufflé and sit them in the dish (see p43: *Re-bake the soufflés*). (The soufflés can be made to this point several hours ahead and chilled in the dish covered with plastic wrap.) Return the soufflés to the oven and bake for 10–12 minutes, or up to 15 minutes for chilled soufflés.

7. Meanwhile, make the sauce: heat the cream and mustard in a small pan over medium heat and season with salt and pepper. When bubbles appear at the edge of the pan, lower the heat and simmer gently for 3–4 minutes (see p43: *Make a creamy sauce to finish*). To serve, spoon and drizzle a little sauce into the center of each plate and place a soufflé on top. Garnish with arugula and serve the rest of the sauce separately.

KEYS TO PERFECTION
See pp42–43

KEYS TO PERFECTION

Fast-fry the mushrooms

It's important to use very high heat when frying the mushrooms, so the juices are drawn out and reduce quickly. If the heat is too low, the mushrooms will steam rather than fry, which can create a lot of liquid and make the soufflés heavy.

Make a thick, smooth soufflé base

Add the milk to the flour and butter mixture ("roux") a little at a time, and whisk vigorously so it mixes in well and to prevent lumps from forming. When all the milk has been added and comes to the boil, the sauce should be very thick, similar to the consistency of mayonnaise.

Lighten the mixture

1 Whisk the egg whites in a large bowl using an electric hand mixer on a high setting, or a hand-held balloon whisk, until they form soft peaks (but are not dry) and resemble fluffy clouds. Make sure the bowl and whisk are completely clean and free of grease, and don't under- or over-whisk the whites, otherwise they will lose their power to make your soufflés as light as air.

2 Stir just a little of the whisked whites into the cooled base before adding the rest. Fold in the rest of the egg whites using a large metal spoon or spatula rather than a wooden spoon, which can quickly deflate the egg whites. Gently stir the whites through the base in a figure-eight motion. This keeps the lightness of the whites and prevents the soufflés from sinking while cooking.

Bake light, fluffy soufflés

1 Fill the ramekins to the top with the mixture, so when the soufflés bake they will rise above the ramekins. To allow the soufflés to have the perfect "lift" and not catch on the ramekin sides, run your thumbnail around the inside of the rims to remove any excess mixture.

2 The soufflés are ready when they are risen and golden, and feel springy when touched. Never open the oven door while the soufflés are cooking or they are likely to sink. After the soufflés have rested they will shrink by about one-third, but don't worry. Once they have been re-baked they will become puffed up again.

Re-bake the soufflés

To make it easier to turn out the baked soufflés, run a palette knife around the inside edge of each ramekin to loosen the sides. Then turn out the soufflé onto the palm of your hand and place it right side up in a buttered baking dish. Make sure you butter the dish well, so the soufflés don't stick, and don't put them too close together, as they will expand. Re-bake the soufflés until puffy and golden.

Make a creamy sauce to finish

The simmering cream and mustard sauce will gradually thicken, so keep checking to see if the consistency is as you want it. When the sauce is thick enough to coat the back of a wooden spoon, take the pan off the heat. If you have the heat too high or cook for too long, the sauce will become very thick; if not cooked for long enough, it will be too thin.

MARY'S TOP TIPS

Buy good equipment

Kitchen equipment is a long-term investment. Buy the best you can afford: good-quality pans, ovenware, knives, and other utensils all make preparation and cooking easier and more enjoyable, and will last longer.

2–3 thick slices white bread (preferably 1 day old) or ¾ cup (50 g) fresh white breadcrumbs

2 tbsp (30 g) butter, plus extra to serve

¼ tsp paprika

salt and freshly ground black pepper

1 lb (450 g) asparagus spears

4 large eggs (see p49, box)

ASPARAGUS WITH SOFT POACHED EGG AND BUTTERY CRUMBS

*Hollandaise sauce is traditionally served with asparagus,
but there's no need for it here, since the poached eggs give a light texture
to go with the rich, buttery crumbs. Serve with brown bread.*

1. Make the breadcrumbs: cut the crusts off the bread. Tear the bread into large pieces, put them in a food processor, and process until they make fine crumbs. You will need ¾ cup (50 g) of breadcrumbs. Heat the butter in a nonstick frying pan over medium heat, add the breadcrumbs, and fry until evenly brown and crisp (see p48: *Evenly crisp breadcrumbs*). Add the paprika and a little salt and pepper. Remove from the pan and set aside.

2. Trim the asparagus spears and lay them in a wide-based sauté pan or frying pan. Pour enough boiling water over just to cover the asparagus and bring to a boil, then reduce the heat slightly and simmer for about 3 minutes or until just tender. (See p48: *Tender-crisp asparagus*.) Drain and keep warm.

3. Poach the eggs gently in a pan of simmering salted water over low heat for about 3 minutes. Remove using a slotted spoon and drain on paper towels. (See p49: *Soft poached eggs*.)

4. For each serving, lay some of the warm asparagus on a plate and dot with a small knob of butter. Carefully place a poached egg on top, season with a little salt and pepper, and scatter the buttered breadcrumbs on top.

KEYS TO PERFECTION
See pp48–49

KEYS TO PERFECTION

Evenly crisp breadcrumbs

1 Use the pulse button of a food processor until the bread is reduced to same-sized crumbs. If the bread forms big lumps it will be more difficult to get the breadcrumbs evenly crisp.

2 When browning the breadcrumbs in the frying pan, you must keep stirring them with a wooden spoon or spatula, so they cook evenly and don't burn.

Tender-crisp asparagus

1 It's important to buy asparagus that is all the same width, so each spear cooks at the same rate. Before cooking the asparagus, trim the spears by removing the woody ends. Rather than using a knife to cut off the ends, snap them off with your fingers; the asparagus breaks off at the point where the stalk naturally starts to get tender.

2 A large, wide-based sauté pan or frying pan is good for cooking asparagus, as the spears can lay flat. Timing is key: if left to boil for too long, the asparagus will lose its color and crisp texture. Test for doneness by inserting the tip of a sharp knife into a stalk. If it goes in easily and the asparagus feels tender but still firm, it is just right.

Soft poached eggs

1 Use a slotted spoon to swirl the simmering water in the pan to make a vortex, then crack an egg into a small bowl or cup (this ensures the whites stay contained and won't spread in the water). Slide the egg into the water. Poach only 1 or 2 eggs at a time, so they have room to gently move around without touching each other.

2 As soon as the egg touches the water, turn the heat to low and set the timer for 3 minutes. Swirl the water around the edge of the egg white to gather it in and give the egg a neat shape. Keep the water at a gentle simmer to ensure the egg doesn't get too hard.

3 When the egg is done, the egg white will look set and opaque and the yolk will look slightly cloudy with a bit of a wobble. Carefully lift out the egg using a slotted spoon and lay it on a paper towel, so the excess water can drain away. Place the egg with the best side uppermost, in preparation for transferring it to the plate.

BUYING, CHECKING, AND USING EGGS

When buying eggs, check them carefully to be sure they're fresh and that they don't have cracked shells. Always use eggs before their "best before" date. This is vital from a safety point of view, but also because stale eggs have flat yolks and watery whites, which spoil both texture and taste.

Special equipment
4-cup Yorkshire pudding tin

1 large red onion

2 tbsp (20g) butter

2 tsp olive oil

1 large egg

⅔ cup (150ml) heavy cream

salt and freshly ground black pepper

½ oz (15g) arugula leaves

scant 1 oz (25g) Parmesan cheese, coarsely grated

scant 1 oz (25g) mature Cheddar cheese, coarsely grated

For the phyllo dough shells

2 tbsp (25g) butter, melted

2–3 large sheets shop-bought phyllo dough (see p53, box)

4 tsp fresh thyme leaves

CARAMELIZED RED ONION AND ARUGULA TARTLETS

These tartlets are easy to make with phyllo dough—there's no rolling out, and its crisp texture makes a great contrast to the soft, creamy filling. You can prepare the tin and filling ahead.

1. Finely slice the onion. Heat the butter and oil in a large, nonstick frying pan until the butter has melted. Add the onion slices and fry over medium–low heat for about 15 minutes, stirring only occasionally, until soft and caramelized. Remove the onion, drain on paper towels, and set aside to cool. (See p52: *Caramelize the onion.*) Preheat the oven to 375°F (190°C).

2. Prepare the phyllo dough shells: brush a little of the melted butter in the hollows of the Yorkshire pudding tin. Using a sharp knife, cut 16 squares, measuring 4½ x 4½in (11 x 11cm), from the phyllo sheets (how many you get from each sheet depends on the brand of phyllo). Layer up 4 phyllo squares per hole, each at an angle to the previous squares, brushing melted butter and sprinkling thyme over each one. Scrunch up the dough edges to add a bit of height. (See p53: *Make crispy phyllo shells.*)

3. In a small bowl, beat the egg, then stir in the cream and some salt and pepper. Roughly chop the arugula, setting aside just a few leaves for garnish. In a separate bowl, combine the two cheeses.

4. Carefully spoon the onion into the phyllo shells. Scatter half the cheese and the chopped arugula on top. Pour in the egg mixture, then top with the rest of the cheese.

5. Bake for 15–20 minutes or until the filling is just set and starting to turn golden brown at the edges. Remove from the tin and serve warm, garnished with the reserved arugula leaves.

KEYS TO PERFECTION
See pp52–53

KEYS TO PERFECTION

Caramelize the onion

1 Peel the onion. Using a sharp chef's knife, quarter the onion lengthwise. Cut the hard root from the base, then slice down each quarter lengthwise into thin slices. This will give small, delicate pieces that are suited to the scale of the tartlet shells.

2 It's important to fry the onion in a mixture of butter and oil. The butter adds flavor and the oil helps to stop the butter from over-browning during the long cooking time needed to caramelize the onion. Fry the onion very slowly to bring out its sweetness. Stir occasionally to prevent it from burning, but not too often, as you want it to start browning where it's in contact with the pan.

3 As the onion starts to turn brown and gets a bit sticky, stir so it doesn't burn and to bring the paler bits of onion to the bottom of the pan so they can also get brown. Scrape up the browned bits at the bottom of the pan using a spatula.

4 When the onion is done, it should be well reduced and evenly caramelized to a rich deep brown color. Its flavor will become sweeter and more intense during the cooking process. Remove it using a slotted spoon and drain on paper towels.

Make crispy phyllo shells

1 Stack the phyllo dough sheets on a board and cut out the 16 squares, each 4½ x 4½in (11 x 11cm), using a sharp knife in order to prevent the dough from tearing as you cut. Phyllo dough dries out and becomes brittle very quickly, so keep the phyllo covered with plastic wrap or a damp dish towel until you start lining the tins, which you should do as soon as possible.

2 For each shell, brush one square of phyllo with butter and lay it in a cup in the buttered tin; the edges of the square should extend over the rim. Sprinkle with thyme. Repeat for the three remaining squares, laying each at an angle to the previous ones so they overlap, and buttering and sprinkling thyme over each layer. Layering the phyllo like this strengthens the pastry shells.

3 To add a bit of height and interest to the shells, ruffle up the edges. Use your thumb and forefinger to bring up the sides so they're upright, then turn over the edges in small, soft folds, keeping the sides raised to maintain height. A bit of irregularity with the folds is fine and adds character to the shells.

BUYING AND USING PHYLLO DOUGH

This paper-thin dough is not easy to make, but it's widely available in packets containing a number of ready-made sheets. Sizes of phyllo sheets can vary according to the manufacturer, so for this recipe you may need more than the number of sheets specified to be able to cut out enough squares. Careful handling is important. The sheets are extremely thin, so try not to split or tear them, as it may allow the filling to leak. If the dough does tear, patch it up with another piece of buttered phyllo.

FISH AND SHELLFISH

SERVES 6

Special equipment
*2-quart (1.7–2 liter)
baking dish, about
10 x 7in (25 x 18cm)
and 3in (7.5cm) deep*

5 tbsp (75 g) butter, plus
extra for greasing

1 large leek, trimmed
and cut into ¼in (5mm)
thick slices

½ cup (50 g) plain flour

2½ cups (600 ml) hot,
full-fat milk

1½ tbsp chopped fresh dill

finely grated zest
of ½ lemon

salt and freshly ground
black pepper

14 oz (400 g) cod fillet,
skinned and cut into
1in (2.5cm) cubes
(see p59, box)

14 oz (400 g) salmon fillet,
skinned and cut into 1in
(2.5cm) cubes

7 oz (200 g) fresh spinach

For the topping

1¾ lb (800 g) new potatoes,
such as baby reds,
scrubbed

2 tbsp olive oil, plus 2 tsp
for drizzling

FISH PIE WITH CRUSHED POTATO TOPPING

The filling for this fish pie is a tasty blend of spinach, salmon, and cod. Instead of putting a classic mash on top, I've used quickly crushed potatoes, drizzled with olive oil to make them crunchy.

1. Grease the baking dish with butter. Melt 4 tablespoons (50 g) of the butter in a large pan over medium heat. Add the leek and fry for 3 minutes or until softened but not browned. Stir in the flour and cook, stirring, for 1–2 minutes. Remove from the heat and gradually pour in the hot milk. Return to medium heat and stir until boiling, thickened, and smooth. Stir in the dill, lemon zest, and some salt and pepper. Add the cod and salmon to the sauce. Cook over low heat for 2 minutes, stirring gently twice, just to start cooking the fish. (See p58: *Make a smooth, creamy filling.*)

2. Pour the fish mixture into the buttered baking dish and set aside to cool (see p58: *Let the filling cool down*). You can prepare up to this point 1 day ahead and refrigerate overnight.

3. Melt the remaining butter in a large, nonstick, deep-sided frying pan or sauté pan over medium heat. Add the spinach and cook, stirring, for 1½–2 minutes or until it wilts. Drain thoroughly in a colander, pressing down with the back of a wooden spoon to extract excess moisture. Roughly chop and set aside. Preheat the oven to 400°F (200°C).

4. Meanwhile, make the topping: put the potatoes in a large pan of cold salted water and bring to a boil. Cover and simmer for about 15 minutes or until tender. Drain well. Return the potatoes to the pan and, using a fork, break up the potatoes into rough, chunky pieces. (See p59: *Make a crispy topping.*) Stir in the olive oil and some salt and pepper.

5. Scatter the spinach on top of the cooled fish mixture, then spoon the potatoes over the spinach layer (see p59: *Carefully add the topping*). Drizzle the remaining 2 teaspoons of oil over the potatoes and bake for 30–40 minutes or until the pie is bubbling at the edges and the topping is golden and crispy.

KEYS TO PERFECTION
See pp58–59

KEYS TO PERFECTION

Make a smooth, creamy filling

1 The leek should look wilted before you stir in the flour. However, you don't need to cook it completely, as it will finish cooking in the sauce. Stir the flour constantly for 1–2 minutes, making sure it is combined thoroughly with the butter. Don't let the butter or flour brown. You're aiming for a pale gold paste, or "roux."

2 I like to add hot milk when making a white sauce, as I find it blends into the roux more easily than cold milk and helps to prevent the sauce from turning lumpy. Bring the milk to a gentle simmer, then remove it from the heat. If you keep it simmering for too long, it will start to reduce in the pan. Add it gradually to the roux, stirring continuously.

3 After adding the dill, lemon rind, and seasoning, add the fish to the sauce. Don't stir too much, or the fish may start to break up; you want to keep it in chunky pieces. Just give a couple of gentle turns using a wooden spoon so the fish is well coated with the white sauce.

Let the filling cool down

Let the fish and sauce cool in the baking dish. This will provide a firmer base for when you spoon the potatoes over the top, so they won't sink in. Spoon the spinach over the sauce before adding the topping. The spinach must be well drained so the sauce doesn't get watery.

Make a crispy topping

1 Put the whole potatoes in a pan of cold water (if very large, cut them in half) and start the timing once the water comes to the boil. Reduce the heat slightly and let the water simmer gently. They will take about 15 minutes to cook. To test if the potatoes are done, insert the tip of a sharp knife; it should go in easily.

2 To crush the potatoes, use a fork to break each one into several chunky pieces. You don't want to break them down too much, and they don't need to be completely uniform in size. By crushing them the oil will be absorbed into the potato pieces, which will improve their flavor and make them golden when baked.

BUYING AND USING COD

Cod has a delicate flavor and, although it has a soft and flaky texture, if handled lightly it's still dense enough to work well and not break up in a fish pie. As when buying any fish, try to choose cod that has been responsibly sourced. Look for the MSC (Marine Stewardship Council) ecolabel, which means the fish has come from a sustainable fishery.

Carefully add the topping

Spoon the potatoes loosely over the top of the filling, rather than packing them down, so the broken edges can become crisp.

SERVES 4

8 single sole fillets, each about 2½–3¼ oz (75–90 g), or 4 double fillets, each about 5½–6½ oz (150–180 g) (see p84, Slice and skin the fillets, step 1)

⅓ cup (45 g) plain flour

salt and freshly ground black pepper

2 tbsp olive oil

1 tbsp (15 g) butter

For the sauce

2 tbsp (20 g) butter

7 oz (200 g) small white button mushrooms, thinly sliced

1 garlic clove, crushed

½ cup (120 ml) dry white wine

¾ cup (170 ml) heavy cream

finely grated zest of 1 lemon

juice of ½ lemon

2 tbsp chopped fresh dill

fresh dill sprigs, to garnish

PAN-FRIED SOLE WITH A CREAM AND MUSHROOM SAUCE

This is a special occasion dish. The cooking is more or less last-minute, so it's useful for times when you've invited guests but haven't time to cook ahead. Serve with mashed potatoes and broccoli.

1. Prepare the sole fillets: if they have their skin on, remove it; if you purchased double fillets, cut them in half lengthwise first (see p84: *Slice and skin the fillets*). Rinse the fish, if necessary, and pat dry with paper towels. Sprinkle the flour onto a plate and season with salt and pepper. Coat both sides of the fillets with the seasoned flour.

2. Heat 1 tablespoon of the olive oil with the butter in a large, nonstick frying pan over medium–high heat. Add 4 sole fillets and fry for 1½–2 minutes or until golden (see below: *Keep the fillets flat*). Turn over and fry the other side for 1½–2 minutes. Do not let the butter brown. Transfer the fillets to a serving platter, cover with foil,

and keep warm. Heat the remaining 1 tablespoon of oil and fry the remaining 4 fillets; transfer them to the platter.

3. Make the sauce: melt the butter in the frying pan. Add the mushrooms and fry over medium–high heat for 2–3 minutes, then add the garlic and fry for 1–2 minutes. Pour in the wine, stir, and bring to a boil over medium–high heat. Simmer for 1–2 minutes, then pour in the cream. Simmer, stirring, until the sauce thickens. (See below: *Make a thick, creamy sauce.*)

4. Stir in the lemon zest and juice, salt and pepper, and the chopped dill. Spoon the sauce over and around the fish and garnish with dill sprigs.

KEYS TO PERFECTION

Keep the fillets flat

Fry the unskinned side of the fillets first, as it will be the "presentation" side. Press down with a fish slice if needed to prevent curling.

Make a thick, creamy sauce

1 Fry the mushrooms until their juices run and they become tinged golden brown. Let the wine evaporate before adding the cream.

2 After the cream has been added, the sauce should simmer until it has thickened enough to coat the mushrooms (about 3 minutes).

Special equipment
*Parchment-lined foil
(see p64, box)*

4 scallions

1 small carrot

*4 small bok choy, each
2½–3 oz (75–85 g)*

*4 pieces skinned cod loin
or fillet, each about 7 oz
(200 g)*

*2 tsp sesame oil,
for brushing*

4 tsp dark soy sauce

*salt and freshly ground
black pepper*

*1 fresh, mild red chilli,
seeded and thinly sliced
lengthwise*

1 tbsp rice wine

*2 tsp finely grated
fresh ginger*

*2 garlic cloves, finely
chopped*

½ tsp granulated sugar

1 tbsp sesame seeds

ASIAN-STYLE FISH PARCELS

Cooking fish in parcels (or "en papillote") is such a delicate way to cook fish; it's healthy, too. All the flavors are trapped inside the bag, so as you open it you're treated to a tempting aroma.

1. Preheat the oven to 450°F (230°C). Trim and thinly slice the scallions, slice the carrot into matchsticks, and cut the bok choy into quarters (see p64: *Slice the vegetables uniformly*). Pat the fish dry with paper towels. Set aside.

2. To make the parcels, cut four 12in (30cm) squares of parchment-lined foil. Lay them foil-side down and brush a little of the sesame oil in the middle of each square.

3. In the center of each square, lay 4 bok choy quarters, scatter one-quarter of the carrot sticks on top, pour ½ teaspoon of soy sauce over the vegetables, and place a fish fillet on top. Brush the fish with a little more of the sesame oil and season with salt and pepper. Scatter the scallions and chilli on top. (See p65: *Make tightly sealed parcels*, step 1.)

4. In a small bowl, mix the remaining 2 teaspoons of soy sauce with the rice wine, ginger, garlic, sugar, and 2 teaspoons of cold water. Spoon over the fish. Bring the parchment-lined foil up over each fish portion, fold over, and seal very tightly. (See p65: *Make tightly sealed parcels*, steps 2–4.)

5. Lay the parcels on a baking tray, with the folded ends facing up, and bake for 12–15 minutes (depending on the thickness of the fish).

6. Meanwhile, toast the sesame seeds: heat a small, heavy-based frying pan over medium heat. Pour in the sesame seeds and dry-fry for a few minutes, moving the seeds around in the pan so they don't burn, until they are toasted to a golden brown color. Tip the seeds out of the pan and set aside.

7. Open up one of the parcels to test if the fish and vegetables are cooked. Do so carefully, as the contents will be very hot. When the fish is done it will look opaque and feel firm but tender. If you insert the tip of a small, sharp knife into one of the carrot sticks it will feel tender. When the fish and vegetables are cooked, remove all the parcels from the oven and let stand, unopened, for 5 minutes before serving.

8. Serve the fish, vegetables, and juices from the parcels on plates and sprinkle each portion with toasted sesame seeds. Alternatively, put the unopened parcels on plates and place the sesame seeds in a bowl so that diners can unwrap the parcels and help themselves.

KEYS TO PERFECTION
See pp64–65

KEYS TO PERFECTION

Slice the vegetables uniformly

1 Using a sharp knife, trim the ends from the scallions and slice the onions thinly on the diagonal. Sliced this way, they cook quickly and absorb other flavors easily.

2 Slice the carrot into uniform matchsticks. This will help them to cook evenly with the bok choy, scallions, and fish. To make matchsticks, cut the carrot lengthwise into 4 slices, then cut each slice in half widthwise. Slice again, lengthwise, into sticks no more than ¼in (5mm) wide.

3 Select small bok choy and cut them uniformly to ensure even cooking. Using a sharp chef's knife, trim the root ends of the bok choy very slightly to neaten, but make sure you don't cut too far in or the leaves will start to separate. Cut each bok choy lengthwise into quarters to give you 16 similar-sized pieces.

ABOUT PARCHMENT-LINED FOIL

This useful product is perfect for this recipe. Being double-sided, it combines the properties of both foil and baking parchment in one. The parchment protects the food and holds its shape better than foil alone, while the foil insulates the contents and promotes even cooking. It is strong enough not to tear and flexible, too, so it is easy to fold over tightly and seal. If you can't find it, a layer of foil on a layer of ordinary baking parchment will work well—it's just a little fussier.

Make tightly sealed parcels

1 Wrapping and sealing the parcels tightly and securely will enclose all the flavors and aromas and keep the steam trapped inside, so it can cook the fish and vegetables efficiently. Lay the vegetables and fish in the middle of the parchment-lined foil square. There should be plenty of paper all around to bring up to create a parcel.

2 Carefully spoon the soy sauce and other flavorings over the fish and vegetables, distributing it evenly. This will create steam inside the parcel, which will gently cook the fish, making it very moist and tender. You don't need much liquid, as the fish and vegetables will release some of their own juices, too.

3 For each parcel, bring up the 2 long sides of the parchment-lined foil to meet in the middle over the fish. Using both hands, hold the 2 edges firmly together, and fold them over tightly 2 or 3 times to secure. Press the central fold down onto the fish to seal.

4 To seal the ends of the parcel, fold in the corners of one end to almost meet in the middle and make 2 triangles, as if you were wrapping a present. Fold over the end 2 or 3 times to secure tightly. Repeat at the other end so that the parcel is completely sealed.

SERVES 4

6 tbsp (85 g) butter
(room temperature)

1 tbsp chopped fresh dill,
plus 4 large sprigs for
stuffing and a few small
sprigs to garnish

salt and freshly ground
black pepper

1 oz (30 g) sliced almonds

4 whole trout, each
about 10 oz (300 g) with
head and tail left on,
gutted, cleaned, rinsed
inside and out, dried,
and small fins removed

2 small oranges: 1 cut into
8 thin slices and each slice
halved; 1 cut into wedges,
to garnish

3 small heads of Belgian
endive, damaged outside
leaves removed and
quartered lengthwise

½ tsp granulated sugar

2–3 tbsp fresh orange juice

BROILED TROUT WITH
ENDIVE AND ALMONDS

*Endive really complements broiled trout, especially when
it's caramelized. Serve with new potatoes, so you can enjoy the buttery
juices that gather in the broiler pan and around the endive.*

1. In a bowl, mix 3 tablespoons (45 g) of the butter with the chopped dill. Season and set aside. Heat a small, nonstick frying pan until hot, pour in the almonds, and dry-fry over medium heat until golden all over, turning often. Remove from the heat and drop a quarter of the dill butter into the pan. Set aside.

2. Preheat the broiler. Remove the grid of the broiler pan and line the pan with foil. Cut slashes across one side of each trout. Spread the remaining dill butter over the tops and undersides. Lay the trout in the broiler pan, slashed-sides up, and stuff the cavities with the orange slices and large dill sprigs. Season. Broil the fish about 4in (10cm) from the heat. After 5–7 minutes, turn the fish over and broil for another 4–5 minutes. (See below: *Moist flesh, crispy skin.*)

3. Meanwhile, melt the remaining butter in a large, nonstick frying pan over medium–high heat. Add the endive, cut-sides up, sprinkle with the sugar, turn, and fry until the undersides start to brown. Reduce the heat slightly, then turn again and add 2 tablespoons of the orange juice. Simmer until tender; add extra orange juice if needed. (See below: *Sweet-tasting endive.*)

4. Gently reheat the almond and dill butter mixture. Serve the trout slashed-side facing up, topped with the almonds, with the endive alongside and the juices drizzled over. Garnish with the orange wedges and small dill sprigs.

KEYS TO PERFECTION

Moist flesh, crispy skin

1 Make 3 or 4 long, diagonal slits in the flesh, ½in (1cm) deep, using a sharp knife. Spread dill butter over the top, into the slashes, and underneath. This will keep the trout moist and give more flavor.

2 It's vital to preheat the broiler for at least 5 minutes, so the fish starts cooking right away. Turn the trout carefully so it doesn't break, using a fish slice. When cooked, the flesh should be moist and the skin crisp.

Sweet-tasting endive

Caramelizing endive takes away its bitter taste. Just as the sugared leaves start to brown and caramelize (about 5 minutes), turn them over and add orange juice so the thicker undersides can finish cooking (2–3 minutes).

SERVES 8

3 tbsp olive oil

3 shallots, finely chopped

7 oz (200 g) crimini mushrooms, finely chopped

3 garlic cloves, finely chopped

1 tbsp lemon juice

4½ oz (125 g) watercress, chopped

salt and freshly ground black pepper

2 tbsp full-fat crème fraîche

1lb 10 oz (750 g) store-bought puff pastry (preferably all-butter)

2 pieces skinned salmon fillet, each 1lb 2 oz (500 g)

1 tbsp hot horseradish sauce

1 egg, beaten

For the sauce

2 tbsp (20 g) butter

1 shallot, finely chopped

2 tbsp (15 g) all-purpose flour, plus extra for dusting

1¾ cups (400 ml) vegetable stock

3½ oz (100 g) frozen peas

3½ oz (100 g) watercress, chopped

5 tbsp full-fat crème fraîche

1 tbsp finely chopped fresh mint

SALMON EN CROÛTE WITH WATERCRESS SAUCE

This is an ideal dish for entertaining, as you can assemble the croûte ahead and chill it before baking. The combination of crisp pastry, succulent salmon, and watercress sauce is a real winner.

1. Heat 2 tablespoons of the oil in a large, nonstick frying pan. Add the shallots and fry over medium heat for 3–4 minutes or until softened, stirring occasionally. Increase the heat to high, stir in the mushrooms and garlic, and fry for 4–5 minutes or until the liquid has evaporated. Add the lemon juice. Take the pan off the heat and mix in the watercress until wilted. Season, transfer to a bowl, and set aside to cool, then stir in the crème fraîche. Preheat the oven to 425°F (220°C).

2. Roll out half the pastry on a lightly floured surface. Trim to a rectangle 2in (5cm) larger all around than the salmon. Wrap the pastry trimmings in plastic wrap and set aside. Place the rolled-out pastry on a large piece of parchment paper that will fit on a large baking sheet or in a shallow roasting pan. Lay one of the fillets in the middle of the pastry. Season and spread the horseradish sauce on top, then the mushroom and watercress mixture. (See p70: *Make a well-sealed parcel*, steps 1 and 2.) Lay the other fillet on top. Season.

3. Roll out the remaining pastry to a rectangular shape that is about 3in (7.5cm) wider and 2in (5cm) longer than the bottom pastry layer. Brush the edge of the bottom layer with the beaten egg. Lay the pastry over the salmon and trim off the excess to give a ¾in (2cm) edge

all around. Press, score, and crimp the edges. Reroll the pastry trimmings thinly and cut them into strips. Brush the croûte all over with egg, lay the strips on top in a decorative pattern, and brush these with egg. (See p70: *Make a well-sealed parcel*, steps 3 and 4.)

4. Carefully lift the croûte onto a large baking sheet, with the parchment paper still underneath. Bake for 30 minutes or until the pastry is golden brown. (See p71: *Bake the croûte to perfection*.)

5. Meanwhile, make the sauce: melt the butter in a medium pan. Stir in the shallot and fry for 2–3 minutes or until softened but not browned. Stir in the flour and cook for 1 minute. Take the pan off the heat and slowly stir in the stock. Return the pan to the heat and cook, stirring, over medium–high heat, until the sauce has thickened slightly. Add the peas. Simmer for 2 minutes.

6. Remove the pan from the heat and stir in the watercress. Purée in a food processor until smooth. Pour the sauce back into the pan and set aside. When the croûte is done, remove it from the oven and let it rest for 10 minutes. Meanwhile, stir the crème fraîche and mint into the sauce, season, and reheat. (See p71: *Make a bright green sauce*.) Transfer the croûte to a board or serving platter and serve in slices with the sauce.

KEYS TO PERFECTION
See pp70–71

KEYS TO PERFECTION

Make a well-sealed parcel

1 It's important to roll out the pastry so it's not too thick, as it needs to cook in the same time as the fish (the fish will become dry if overcooked). Roll it out so it's about ¼in thick—that way, it will bake up light and crisp. The first piece of pastry (for the bottom of the croûte) should be 2in (5cm) larger all around than the size of a salmon fillet.

2 Spoon the mushroom and watercress filling carefully over the length of the bottom salmon fillet, then spread it out using a palette knife or round-bladed knife. Go almost up to the edge but not quite all the way, otherwise when you place the second fillet on top the weight of it may cause the filling to ooze out. Place the second fillet on top of the filling and season.

3 To make sure you don't stretch the pastry while covering the top of the salmon, lay it over a rolling pin to make it easier to lift and lower onto the fish. Press down the pastry edges well, or the filling may leak out when baking, then score the edges to secure the seal by gently tapping all around the cut sides using the back of a knife held horizontally.

4 Crimp the edges using your fingers. Reroll the pastry trimmings thinly and cut out 10–12 strips in 2 or 3 different sizes, varying from ½in (1cm) to 1in (2.5cm) wide and long enough to go over the domed part of the croûte. Trim to fit. Brush the croûte all over with beaten egg, then lay the strips over in a criss-cross pattern (you may not need all the pastry trimmings). Brush the strips with egg.

Bake the croûte to perfection

1 Transfer the pastry-wrapped salmon to a large baking sheet with the help of 2 fish slices to keep it stable. Retain the parchment paper underneath, as this will prevent the pastry from sticking to the sheet and make it easier to move once baked.

2 Baking the croûte at a high oven temperature will make the pastry light and crisp, especially on the base, and ensure that the salmon is cooked through. However, as the temperature is high, check after 20 minutes—if the pastry is already turning brown, lay a piece of foil loosely over the top to protect it from becoming overdone while the salmon finishes cooking.

Make a bright green sauce

1 Watercress can quickly discolor if heated for too long, so to keep the sauce a good green color, stir in the watercress off the heat: the heat of the sauce and pan will be sufficient to wilt the watercress while maintaining its color. The peas will also help to boost the color.

2 After puréeing the sauce, pour it back into the pan. Before serving, place it over low heat and stir in the crème fraîche, mint, and salt and pepper. Heat through for as short a time as possible. As with the watercress, you want to retain the fresh green color of the mint.

MARY'S TOP TIPS

Use fresh herbs

Fresh herbs taste so much better than dried. They're widely available nowadays and are also easy to grow—you don't even need a garden. Simply sow or plant them in pots on the windowsill or outside the kitchen door.

SERVES 4

*4 pieces skinned
salmon fillet, each
about 6 oz (175 g)*

ground white pepper

sunflower oil, for greasing

½ cucumber

For the marinade

*1 lemongrass stalk, tough
outer layer removed*

3 tbsp fish sauce (nam pla)

3 tbsp lime juice

*1½ tsp finely chopped
fresh ginger*

*2 garlic cloves,
finely chopped*

*1 fresh Thai or mild
red chilli, seeded and
finely chopped*

2½ tsp granulated sugar

GRILLED SALMON WITH THAI FLAVORS

This is my take on the popular pairing of salmon and cucumber.
Fish sauce ("nam pla") brings a special saltiness to the dish and complements
the sweet and sour flavors. Serve with Thai rice.

1. Lay the salmon in a shallow, nonmetallic dish in a single layer and season with pepper. Make the marinade: smash the lemongrass stalk with a rolling pin, slice it into thirds, and put the pieces in the dish with the salmon. Mix all the remaining marinade ingredients in a small bowl with 1 teaspoon of water. Set aside 2 tablespoons of the marinade and pour the rest over the salmon. Cover and chill for at least 2 hours (or overnight), turning the fish once.

2. Preheat the broiler for 5 minutes on its highest setting. Meanwhile, line a baking tray or broiler pan with foil and brush it with a little oil. Remove and discard the lemongrass from the marinade. Transfer the salmon from the marinade to the baking tray or broiler pan, placing it skinned-side down. Spoon the marinade over the salmon and broil for about 10 minutes (see below: *Succulent, flaky salmon*). Do not turn the salmon, or it may break.

3. While the salmon is broiling, partially peel the cucumber (if the skin is tough, remove it all using a vegetable peeler). Cut the cucumber into wafer-thin slices, put the slices in a wide, shallow dish, and pour over the reserved marinade. (See below: *Crunchy, decorative cucumber*.)

4. Serve the salmon fillet with the cucumber slices alongside. Spoon the marinade from the cucumber over both the fish and the cucumber.

KEYS TO PERFECTION

Succulent, flaky salmon

To test if the salmon is done, pull back a small piece of flesh with a fork. It should flake easily and no longer look opaque inside. If it does, cook a minute or so longer, but be careful not to overcook the fish, as it will dry out.

Crunchy, decorative cucumber

1 Using a vegetable peeler or small, sharp knife, peel off 3 or 4 slices of skin down the cucumber, with a gap between each. This will give a pattern of dark and light stripes. If sliced very thinly, the cucumber will curl slightly.

2 Marinate the cucumber for about 10 minutes only. If it's left in the marinade for too long, it will lose its crunchy texture and bright color. You want it to retain its vibrancy and bite.

2 fresh, medium-hot green chilies

2 tbsp sunflower oil

1 onion, halved lengthwise and thinly sliced

3 garlic cloves, finely chopped

2 tsp finely chopped fresh ginger

1½ tsp garam masala

1 tsp ground cilantro

1 tsp ground cumin

¼ tsp turmeric

1 tsp black mustard seeds

2 tsp plain flour

14 oz (400ml) can coconut milk

⅔ cup (150ml) vegetable stock

2 tsp mango chutney

2 tbsp lime juice

salt and freshly ground black pepper

14 oz (400g) monkfish

10 oz (300g) skinned cod loin

4 oz (115g) thin green beans, stem ends trimmed

2 tbsp roughly chopped fresh cilantro, to garnish

FISH CURRY WITH COCONUT MILK

*I've used a mixture of fish for this easy-to-cook, fragrant curry.
Monkfish keeps its shape well and complements the slightly softer texture
of cod loin. Serve with basmati rice and poppadums.*

1. Seed and finely shred the chilies (see p78: *Make a spicy, smooth coconut sauce*, step 1). Heat the oil in a large, deep-sided, nonstick frying pan or sauté pan. Add the onion and fry over medium–high heat for 5–6 minutes or until it starts to brown, reducing the heat if it browns too quickly.

2. Add the garlic, ginger, and half the shredded chilies to the pan and fry for another 2 minutes. Reduce the heat slightly and sprinkle in the garam masala, ground cilantro, cumin, turmeric, and mustard seeds. Fry for 1 minute, then stir in the flour and cook for another minute. (See p78: *Make a spicy, smooth coconut sauce*, steps 2 and 3.)

3. Pour in the coconut milk and then the stock. Increase the heat and bring to a boil, stirring. Let the liquid bubble for a couple of minutes while you continue to stir, to thicken the sauce slightly. Reduce the heat and stir in the mango chutney and lime juice. Season with salt and pepper. (See p78: *Make a spicy, smooth coconut sauce*, step 4.)

4. Remove the membrane from the monkfish and chop the monkfish and cod into chunky cubes, about 2in (5cm). (See p79: *Gently cook the fish*, steps 1 and 2.) Drop the beans into a pan of salted, boiling water and simmer for 4–5 minutes or until tender. Drain well, refresh in cold water for a few seconds, to keep the color, and drain again.

5. Add the monkfish and cod to the curry sauce. Cover the pan and simmer gently for 4–5 minutes or until the fish is just cooked. Gently stir the beans into the curry and remove the pan from the heat. (See p79: *Gently cook the fish*, steps 3 and 4.) Before serving, top with the chopped cilantro and remaining shredded chilies.

KEYS TO PERFECTION
See pp79–79

KEYS TO PERFECTION

Make a spicy, smooth coconut sauce

1 For the flavor of chili without too much heat, remove the seeds. Slice the chili in half lengthwise with a small, sharp knife. Using the tip of the knife, scrape out the seeds and membrane and discard. To shred, flatten each chili half and slice it lengthwise into thin strips. When working with chilies, keep your hands away from your eyes, which the chili will burn, and wash your hands well afterward; you may want to wear latex or rubber gloves to be on the safe side.

2 Frying the spices briefly before adding the liquid prevents them from tasting raw and draws out their flavors, adding depth to the finished dish. However, you need to be careful not to let them burn. Reduce the heat to medium before adding the dry spices to the pan, and stir continuously as they fry.

3 I stir a little flour into the sauce before the coconut milk goes in. It's not traditional, but I find it helps to stabilize the sauce and stop it from separating. You don't want the sauce to be too thick, so only a little flour is required.

4 Slowly pour in the coconut milk and then the stock, stirring all the time to make a smooth sauce and prevent any lumps from forming. After the sauce has thickened slightly, add the mango chutney, lime juice, and salt and pepper.

Gently cook the fish

1 Before cooking the fish, remove the purple-gray membrane that covers the monkfish tail. If left on it will shrink around the fish during cooking and make it tough. Use the tip of a long, thin, sharp knife to nick the membrane so you can get the knife between it and the flesh, then very carefully pull the membrane away, being careful not to damage the flesh. You'll probably have to do this in several stages.

2 Pat the fish dry with paper towels, then cut it into cubes. It's best to have fairly large cubes, as they hold their shape better during cooking and stay more tender and succulent. If the fish (especially the cod) is cut too small, it can disintegrate and disappear into the sauce. Both cod and monkfish are firm white fish, and when cut into equal-sized cubes they take the same length of time to cook.

3 Lay the fish in the sauce so it's well covered. Don't stir, just let it sink into the sauce, then cover the pan. Time the cooking carefully so the fish will stay tender and in good-sized pieces.

4 After adding the green beans, remove the pan from the heat, so the fish doesn't overcook, and don't stir the curry any more than necessary, otherwise the cod may start to break up.

¼ cup sunflower oil

2 tsp Chinese rice vinegar

1 garlic clove, crushed

4 tuna steaks, each about 5½ oz (150 g) and ¾ in (2 cm) thick

salt and freshly ground black pepper

1 red pepper, halved, cored, and seeded

8 scallions, trimmed

7 oz (200 g) snow peas

5½ oz (150 g) sugar snap peas

7 oz (200 g) bean sprouts

2 tbsp dark soy sauce

¼ tsp five-spice powder

PAN-FRIED TUNA AND MIXED PEA STIR-FRY

Tuna steaks make an extra-special quick supper, and they can be marinating while you prepare the vegetables for the stir-fry. Make sure you buy sustainable tuna from a reputable supplier.

1. Mix 2 tablespoons of the oil with the rice vinegar and garlic in a shallow, nonmetallic dish. Lay the tuna steaks in the marinade, season with pepper, and set aside for about 20 minutes while you prepare the vegetables. (See below: *Tender, moist tuna*, step 1.)

2. Slice the red pepper into long, thin strips. Cut the scallions into long, thin, diagonal slices. Slice the snow peas and sugar snap peas in half lengthwise. Rinse the bean sprouts in a colander and let drain.

3. Heat a large, nonstick, deep-sided frying pan, sauté pan, or wok. Remove the tuna steaks from the marinade, lay them in the hot, dry pan, and fry for 3 minutes over high heat. Turn and fry the other side for 2–3 minutes

(see below: *Tender, moist tuna*, step 2). Transfer to a warm plate, season with a little salt, cover with foil, and set aside while you fry the vegetables.

4. Heat another tablespoon of the oil in the pan, and with the heat on high, toss in the pepper and scallions. Stir-fry for 1–2 minutes or until tinged brown. Pour in the remaining tablespoon of oil, add the snow peas and sugar snap peas, and stir-fry for 2–3 minutes. They will turn a brighter green and be tender-crisp. Reduce the heat, then add the bean sprouts, soy sauce, five-spice powder, and 2 tablespoons of water, and stir-fry for 1 minute. (See below: *Super-quick vegetables*.) Serve immediately with the tuna.

KEYS TO PERFECTION

Tender, moist tuna

1 Tuna is a lean, meaty fish, so it can dry out easily when cooked. Marinating will introduce moisture as well as add flavor. Place the steaks in the dish in a single layer and turn them over so they're well coated in the marinade.

2 The pan must be really hot before putting in the steaks. As soon as they are browned underneath, turn and cook the other side. Do not overcook, or the steaks will be tough. You want the centers to be slightly pink

Super-quick vegetables

Have all the vegetables sliced and close at hand, and set the pan over high heat. When the oil is really hot, add the vegetables in the right sequence and fry quickly, stirring and tossing so they cook evenly.

SERVES 4

3½ oz (100 g) frozen peas

8 single lemon sole fillets, each about 3–3½ oz (85–100 g), or 4 double fillets, each about 6–7 oz (175–200 g) (see p84: Slice and skin the fillets, step 1)

¼ cup (30 g) plain flour

salt and freshly ground black pepper

6 tbsp (85 g) butter

1 tbsp lemon juice

3 oz (85 g) cooked and peeled rock shrimp (see p85, box)

1 tbsp chopped fresh flat-leaf parsley

lemon wedges, to serve

PAN-FRIED SOLE WITH ROCK SHRIMP

Serving little rock shrimp with lemon sole is my way of spoiling my supper guests. When the shrimp aren't available loose on their own, I buy the ones in cartons that are preserved in butter.

1. Add the peas to a small pan of boiling salted water, bring back to a boil, and simmer for 2 minutes. Remove, drain, and set aside.

2. If the sole fillets have their skin on, remove it. If you have bought double fillets, cut them in half lengthwise first. (See p84: *Slice and skin the fillets.*) Rinse the fillets if necessary and pat dry with paper towels.

3. Season the flour with salt and pepper. Dip the fillets into the seasoned flour to coat, and shake off any excess. Melt 2 tablespoons (30 g) of the butter in a large, nonstick frying pan. Lay 4 fillets in the pan and fry gently over medium–high heat for 2 minutes on each side. (See p84: *Gently fry the fillets.*) Remove the fish and keep warm. Fry the remaining 4 fillets.

4. Wipe the pan with paper towels, then add the remaining butter and melt over medium–high heat until it starts to turn golden brown. Reduce the heat and stir in the lemon juice, shrimp, and reserved peas; warm through very briefly. (See p85: *Make the shrimp sauce flavorsome.*)

5. Season with pepper to taste and add more lemon juice if you wish, then mix in the parsley. Spoon the shrimp and peas over the sole and serve with a drizzle of the buttery juices and lemon wedges.

KEYS TO PERFECTION
See pp84–85

KEYS TO PERFECTION

Slice and skin the fillets

1 When buying sole or tilapia, you may find what looks like one large fillet. This is the top or bottom half of the fish with the central bone removed, and consists of 2 smaller fillets, one on either side of where the bone would have been. It's best to divide these "double" fillets in half lengthwise. Alternatively, you may find "single" fillets, which are already divided, so there is no need to cut them.

2 To skin the fish, lay each fillet skin-side down on a board. Put a little salt on your fingers so you can get a good grip on the skin (it can be slippery). Starting at the tail end, make an incision between the skin and flesh using a sharp, thin, long-bladed knife. Holding the knife at an angle, slide it along the skin, wiggling the skin as you go in order to separate it from the flesh.

Gently fry the fillets

1 Before frying the fish, sprinkle the flour onto a plate and season with salt and pepper. Place each fillet in the seasoned flour and drag it through the flour to coat. Gently shake off any excess flour to give a light coating that will protect the fish as it cooks.

2 When the butter starts to foam, and before it changes color, lay 4 fillets in the pan with the unskinned side down. Never overcrowd the pan by frying too many fish at once. Turn after 2 minutes and press down with a fish slice if the fillets start to curl. You want them to sizzle and brown slightly, but not overcook, so adjust heat as needed. When done, the fish will look opaque and flake easily.

Make the shrimp sauce flavorsome

1 Browning the butter for a quick sauce gives it a nutty flavor. Once the butter starts to change color and release a nutty aroma (this will take about 2 minutes), swirl it around in the pan so that the butter can brown evenly.

2 As soon as the butter is a pale golden brown color, reduce the heat, pour in the lemon juice, and stir in the shrimp and peas. The heat should be quite low, just enough to warm them through. Don't leave the pan on the heat for any longer than 1 minute, or the peas will start to discolor and the shrimp become less juicy.

3 Season with pepper and taste the sauce to see if you need to add any more lemon juice. Mix in the parsley just before serving. If it is added too early, it will lose its color.

BUYING AND USING ROCK SHRIMP

Tiny, succulent, and packed with flavor, rock shrimp are translucent when raw, but turn amber-brown on cooking. They can be difficult to peel, but you can buy them in some supermarkets and fishmongers already cooked and peeled. If you can't find rock shrimp, use the tiniest shrimp you can find and cut them into small pieces.

SERVES 4

2 x 6 oz cans white crab meat (preferably in large chunks)

2 scallions, trimmed and finely chopped

1 small fresh red chili, seeded and finely chopped

½ cup (30 g) fresh white breadcrumbs

2 tbsp chopped fresh cilantro

finely grated zest of ½ lime

1 egg, beaten

salt and freshly ground black pepper

plain flour, for dusting

2–3 tbsp sunflower oil

hot chili sauce, to serve

lime wedges, to serve

SPICY CRAB CAKES

*The ingredients in this recipe combine the fresh, spicy flavors of
Thai crab cakes with the chunkier texture of American ones. Serve with
stir-fried bok choi and long-grain rice or Chinese noodles.*

1. Drain the crab meat thoroughly, then pat it dry with paper towels to remove any excess liquid, so the mixture will not be too moist.

2. Put the scallions, chili, breadcrumbs, cilantro, and lime zest in a medium bowl. Mix together and gently stir in the crab meat, without breaking up the chunks too much.

3. Stir in some of the egg, until the mixture is the right consistency, and season with salt and pepper. Divide the mixture into 8 equal-sized portions and shape into crab cakes. Chill for about 20 minutes. Lightly dust each crab cake with a little flour. (See below: *Create a good texture.*)

4. Heat 2 tablespoons of the oil in a frying pan. Fry the crab cakes on medium–high heat for 2–3 minutes on each side or until they are golden brown and heated through, adding more oil if needed. Serve 2 crab cakes per person, with hot chili sauce and lime wedges on the side.

KEYS TO PERFECTION

Create a good texture

1 Add the egg to the mixture a little at a time (you probably won't need it all). Use just enough to bind the mixture—it should hold together but not be too wet. Do not overmix, or the crab will break up.

2 On a lightly floured surface, shape the mixture into flat cakes, 2½in (6cm) across, gently patting with your fingers; do not overhandle. Make all the cakes a similar size and shape for even cooking. Chill the cakes.

3 Sprinkle a little flour onto a plate, lay each crab cake in the flour, and turn to coat (the flour seals in moisture when frying and stops the cakes from sticking to the pan). Gently shake off excess flour; it should be a light coating.

2 tbsp olive oil

1 onion, coarsely chopped

2 garlic cloves, chopped

⅔ cup (150ml) vegetable stock

14 oz can chopped plum tomatoes

1 tbsp sun-dried tomato paste

½ tsp hot smoked paprika (pimentón picante) (see below, box)

14 oz can green Puy lentils, rinsed and drained

salt and freshly ground black pepper

4 pieces skinned haddock (or halibut) fillet, each about 4½ oz (125 g)

chopped fresh flat-leaf parsley, to garnish

QUICK HADDOCK WITH TOMATO AND PUY LENTILS

When looking for ideas for simple midweek suppers,
there's nothing better than a dish like this one, which is cooked in one pan.
If you want something to go with it, a green salad is ideal.

1. Heat the oil in a large, nonstick sauté pan or deep-sided frying pan with a lid. Add the onion and garlic and fry over medium–high heat for 6–8 minutes or until browned, turning up the heat a little if necessary. Pour in the stock and stir to mix. (See below: *Well-browned onions*.)

2. Let the stock bubble briefly, then add the tomatoes. Stir in the sun-dried tomato paste, paprika, and lentils. Simmer for 8–10 minutes. Season to taste with salt and pepper.

3. Pat the fish dry with paper towels and season with salt and pepper. Lay the fillets on top of the tomatoes and lentils, pressing them lightly into the sauce but

not submerging them fully, then cover the pan (see below: *Moist, tender fish*). Simmer over low heat for 8–10 minutes or until the fish is just cooked and no longer opaque. The consistency of the sauce should be like a thick, spoonable soup. If you need to loosen it, simply pour in a little more hot water or stock at the end.

4. Transfer the fish and sauce to a warmed serving dish and serve immediately, garnished with chopped parsley.

KEYS TO PERFECTION

Well-browned onions

You want to create depth of flavor and color, so make sure the onion is softened and well browned before you add the liquid. While adding the stock, stir in the sticky bits at the bottom of the pan for extra flavor.

Moist, tender fish

Lay the fish on the lentils and press lightly to partly submerge it. Keep the fillets whole, so they stay moist while cooking. Covering the pan ensures the fish steams. Simmer very gently, so the fish doesn't overcook.

USING SMOKED PAPRIKA

Smoked paprika brings a unique taste to the dish. There are 2 types: hot smoked paprika, as used for this recipe, and sweet smoked paprika. As a little can go a long way, add cautiously at first. The amount I have suggested gives a subtle background flavor to the fish that doesn't overpower, but if you like it smokier, check and adjust to your taste at the end of step 2.

SERVES 4

Special equipment
Ridged cast-iron grill pan

4 sea bass fillets, each about 3½ oz (100 g)

olive oil, for brushing

salt and freshly ground black pepper

For the Sauce

4 tbsp (50 g) butter

⅔ cup (150 ml) light cream

juice and finely grated zest of ½ lemon

1 egg yolk

1 tsp plain flour

ground white pepper

2 tsp finely snipped fresh chives

SEA BASS WITH CREAMY LEMON SAUCE

*The sauce has a silky-smooth texture that goes beautifully
with the crispy-skinned sea bass. Thin green beans and new potatoes
tossed with butter make the ideal accompaniments.*

1. Make the sauce: melt the butter in a small pan. Remove it from the heat, then whisk in the cream, lemon juice, egg yolk, and flour until well mixed (see below: *Smooth, creamy sauce*). Stir in the lemon zest. Return the pan to low heat and stir continuously until the mixture thickens enough to coat the back of a wooden spoon. Season with salt and white pepper. Set aside.

2. Preheat the grill pan over high heat for about 5–10 minutes. Meanwhile, pat the fillets dry with paper towels and score the skin (see below: *Crispy golden skin*, step 1). Brush both sides of the fillets with olive oil and season with salt and black pepper.

3. Reduce the heat to medium–high and lay the fillets in the hot pan, skin-side down (see below: *Crispy golden skin*, step 2). Cook for 3–4 minutes until the skin is lightly charred and crisp. Carefully turn the fillets over using a fish slice, then grill for another 1–2 minutes on the other side. You will probably need to cook the fish in batches.

4. Warm the sauce through briefly over very low heat. Remove from the heat and stir in the chives. To serve, lay the fish on warmed plates, with the skin-side facing up, and spoon some of the sauce over the top. Pour the rest of the sauce into a jug and serve separately.

KEYS TO PERFECTION

Smooth, creamy sauce

Sprinkle the flour into the sauce and whisk vigorously with a wire whisk as it goes in, so no lumps can form. Heat the sauce very gently, because the egg yolk and cream will curdle if they're overheated.

Crispy golden skin

1 Using a sharp knife, score the fish skin by making 4 or 5 cuts to the point where you can see the flesh. Scoring the fillets helps to keep them flat in the pan, ensuring they don't curl up as they cook.

2 The pan must be very hot when you add the fillets, so that they can sear properly. Don't move the fish as it cooks, as it may break up and you'll lose the attractive charred pattern from the pan's ridges.

POULTRY AND GAME

SERVES 4

8 bone-in chicken thighs

salt and freshly ground
black pepper

2 tbsp olive oil

1 tbsp (15 g) butter

1 onion, coarsely chopped

1 stalk of celery, thinly
sliced

3 garlic cloves, finely
chopped

2 medium carrots, halved
lengthwise and cut into
chunks just under ½in
(1cm) thick

2 medium parsnips,
quartered and cut into
chunks just under ½in
(1cm) thick

1 large potato, about 10 oz
(300g), peeled and cut into
1–1¼in (2.5–3cm) cubes

¾ cup (200ml) white wine

1 tbsp Dijon mustard

2 tsp tomato paste

8 oz (230g) can chopped
plum tomatoes

1 cup (250ml) chicken stock

1 tbsp coarsely chopped
fresh flat-leaf parsley

COUNTRY CHICKEN CASSEROLE

Although this warming casserole is packed with vegetables, I like to serve it with mashed potatoes to soak up the sauce. An added bonus is that it's cooked in one pan, keeping cleanup to a minimum!

1. Remove the skin and fat from the chicken thighs and season the meat. Heat 1 tablespoon of the oil and the butter in a Dutch oven until hot. Fry the chicken (skinned-side down first) in 2 batches over medium–high heat until golden brown all over. Transfer to a large plate using a slotted spoon and set aside. (See p110: *Succulent, golden brown chicken*.)

2. Pour in the remaining tablespoon of oil. Add in the onion and celery and fry for 2–3 minutes or until the onion starts to soften. Stir in the garlic followed by the carrots, parsnips, and potato. Reduce the heat to medium and fry for 4–5 minutes, stirring often, until the onion starts to brown. Preheat the oven to 325°F (160°C).

3. Increase the heat and add the wine. Stir and let it bubble for about 2 minutes (see below: *Enhance the flavor*). Stir in the mustard and tomato paste, then the tomatoes and stock.

4. Return the chicken and its juices to the casserole (see below: *Partially immerse the chicken*). Bring to a boil, then reduce the heat, cover, and simmer for 10 minutes. Season with salt and pepper, cover the casserole, and transfer to the oven. Cook for 50 minutes to 1 hour or until the chicken and vegetables are tender. Serve sprinkled with the parsley.

KEYS TO PERFECTION

Enhance the flavor

Let the wine bubble rapidly over high heat, with the lid off, until it has reduced by about half. This cooks off some of the alcohol and concentrates the flavor for the sauce. It will create a thick, syrupy liquid.

Partially immerse the chicken

Sit the chicken thighs on top of the vegetables and gently press them down so that they're about three-quarters immersed in the liquid; this will keep them tender and succulent, while retaining their golden brown color.

SERVES 4

4 tbsp (60 g) butter (room temperature), plus extra for greasing and the legs

2 garlic cloves, crushed

1 tbsp chopped fresh tarragon, plus 3 extra sprigs

salt and freshly ground black pepper

4 lb (1.8 kg) whole chicken

1 lemon, halved

1 small red onion, halved and sliced into about 20 small wedges

For the roast potatoes

2¼ lb (1 kg) fluffy potatoes, such as russet, peeled and cut into equal-sized pieces, about 2in (5cm)

3 fresh bay leaves, plus extra to garnish

For the gravy

1 tbsp all-purpose flour

1¼ cups (300 ml) chicken stock

3 tbsp red wine

1 tbsp red currant jelly

ROAST CHICKEN WITH TARRAGON BUTTER AND ROAST POTATOES

I do like this way of roasting a chicken: spreading herb butter under the skin makes the meat extra moist and flavorful. While the roasted bird rests, turn up the oven for really crisp potatoes.

1. Preheat the oven to 400°F (200°C). Lightly grease a large roasting pan with butter. Make the tarragon butter: put the butter in a small bowl with the garlic and chopped tarragon and beat together with a small wooden spoon. Season with salt and pepper.

2. Sit the chicken, breast-side up, on a board and remove any string. Gently pull back the skin over the breasts and spread the tarragon butter under the skin over the flesh. Rub a little plain butter over the legs. Season the outside of the chicken with salt and pepper. Insert the lemon halves and tarragon sprigs in the cavity. Scatter the onion wedges in the center of the roasting pan and sit the bird, breast-side up, on top. Roast for 50 minutes. (See p98: *Prepare the chicken for roasting.*)

3. While the chicken is in the oven, put the potatoes in a large pan. Cover with cold water and bring to a boil. Add salt and simmer for 5 minutes, then drain well. Return the potatoes to the pan and gently shake it over a very low heat. (See p99: *Make crispy roast potatoes,* step 1.) Set aside.

4. After 50 minutes' roasting, remove the pan, baste the chicken, and put the potatoes around the bird (see p98: *Baste the chicken,* and p99: *Make crispy roast potatoes,* step 2). Tuck the 3 bay leaves among the potatoes.

Return the pan to the oven to roast for another 50 minutes, turning the potatoes halfway through. When the chicken is done, transfer it to a large, warmed serving platter and cover with foil (see p98: *Test for doneness*).

5. Increase the oven temperature to 425°F (220°C). Transfer the potatoes to a small roasting pan and pour all but 1 tablespoon of the top layer of fat from the large roasting tin over the potatoes, leaving all the juices and the onion behind in the large pan. Baste the potatoes with the fat, so they are coated all over, then return them to the oven to roast for about 10 minutes to get really crisp. (See p99: *Make crispy roast potatoes,* step 3.)

6. Meanwhile, make the gravy: sit the large roasting pan on a stovetop burner set at medium heat. Sprinkle in the flour and whisk. Gradually blend in the stock with the whisk and bring to a boil. Simmer for 2 minutes, then stir in the wine and red currant jelly. Stir until thickened. Season and strain into a jug or gravy boat. (See p99: *Make smooth, tasty gravy.*) Remove the potatoes and sprinkle with salt. Garnish the chicken with bay leaves and serve with the potatoes and gravy.

KEYS TO PERFECTION
See pp98–99

KEYS TO PERFECTION

Prepare the chicken for roasting

1 Spreading tarragon butter under the skin makes the chicken moist and flavorful. Starting at the open-cavity end, loosen the skin over the breasts. Do each breast separately, and use your fingers to carefully free the skin from the flesh, easing your way as far down the "pockets" as possible without tearing the skin. Spread the butter evenly over the flesh. Bring the skin back over to cover the butter.

2 Rub plain butter over the legs, season the outside of the chicken, and put the lemon halves and tarragon sprigs in the cavity. Place the chicken on a little pile of onion wedges in the middle of the roasting pan. This will prevent the bird from sitting directly on the pan, helping it to roast better and not stick, and giving extra flavor to the chicken and later to the gravy.

Baste the chicken

Halfway through cooking, baste the chicken all over with the buttery cooking juices to make it more succulent. If the breast skin is already golden brown at this point, cover the bird loosely with foil so that it doesn't burn later. After basting, add the parboiled potatoes.

Test for doneness

Insert a small, sharp knife into the thickest part of the thigh; if the juices run clear, the chicken is cooked. If they are still pink, roast for a bit longer. Once done, let the bird rest for about 10 minutes, covered with foil to keep it warm, which will make the meat more succulent.

Make crispy roast potatoes

1 Roast potatoes will be crisper and fluff up more easily if they're parboiled before roasting. Once the water comes to a boil, time them to simmer for just 5 minutes, or they will overcook and lose their shape. They should still be firm in the middle. Immediately tip the potatoes into a colander to drain, then return them to the pan and gently shake over a very low heat for about 1 minute. This will dry them off and create rough edges that will later get crispy.

2 After the chicken has roasted for 50 minutes and been basted, add the potatoes to the pan. Make sure they're in a single layer, so they cook on all sides, and toss them in the juices for maximum flavor and so they can turn crispy. If you're covering the chicken with foil, don't cover the potatoes, as they won't brown properly.

3 Once the chicken is cooked, transfer the potatoes to a smaller roasting pan using a slotted spoon, keeping them in a single layer so all sides can get crisp. Pour off most of the top layer of fat (but not the juices) from the large pan into the small pan. Baste with the fat. Increase the oven temperature to finish the crisping. If necessary, shake the pan after 5 minutes to prevent sticking.

Make smooth, tasty gravy

Making the gravy in the pan with the chicken juices gives the best flavor. Whisk in the flour to prevent lumps, and cook for 1–2 minutes to get rid of the raw taste. Add the stock a little at a time, whisking constantly for a smooth consistency. Simmer, then add the wine and red currant jelly. Stir to thicken. After the jelly has dissolved, taste for seasoning. You may not need salt if the stock is salty. Strain.

SERVES 4

4 boneless, skinless
chicken breasts

olive oil, for greasing
and drizzling

3 tbsp mango chutney

3 tbsp ketchup

3 tbsp dark soy sauce

1 tbsp grainy mustard

pat of butter

lime wedges, to serve

For the salsa

½ cucumber, halved
lengthwise, seeded,
and chopped

4 scallions, trimmed
and finely chopped

1 fresh, mild green chili,
seeded and finely chopped

½ oz (15 g) fresh cilantro
leaves with stalks, finely
chopped

2 tsp capers
(see box, opposite)

3 tbsp olive oil

juice of 1 lime

1 tsp granulated sugar

freshly ground black
pepper

GLAZED CHICKEN WITH CUCUMBER SALSA

This is one of those very quick and easy suppers that is ideal for making when you get home from work. If you have any chicken left over, it's also good cold. Serve with long-grain rice or wild rice.

1. Preheat the oven to 425°F (220°C). Make deep cuts in the top of the chicken breasts (see below: *Deeply flavored, succulent chicken*, step 1). Grease a small roasting pan, just large enough to accommodate the chicken breasts side by side, and put in the chicken.

2. Combine the chutney, ketchup, soy sauce, and mustard in a bowl and brush over the chicken (see below: *Deeply flavored, succulent chicken*, step 2). Drizzle with oil and roast for 25 minutes, basting several times.

3. While the chicken is cooking, make the salsa: put all the ingredients into a bowl, add pepper to taste, and mix well (you shouldn't need salt, as the capers are salty).

4. When the chicken is cooked, remove it from the oven and pour the pan juices into a small pan. Set the chicken aside for 10 minutes. Keep warm.

5. Add the butter to the pan juices and simmer over medium–high heat for a few minutes or until the juices reduce and just cover the bottom of the pan. Keep an eye on the glaze and stir frequently, so that it doesn't burn. Spoon the glaze over the chicken and serve hot, with the salsa and lime wedges on the side.

KEYS TO PERFECTION

Deeply flavored, succulent chicken

1 Make 4 diagonal slashes across the top of each chicken breast, cutting about one-third of the way down. The cuts will allow the mango chutney mixture to flavor the flesh and the oven heat to penetrate.

2 Put the chicken in the pan, slashed-side up. Brush the chutney mixture liberally all over the chicken, working it deep into the cuts. During roasting, spoon the cooking juices over the chicken to help make the meat succulent.

BUYING AND USING CAPERS

Capers are sold in small jars, pickled in brine or packed in salt. The ones in brine tend to be the largest and are quite vinegary. For this recipe, I prefer the salted, tiny "nonpareil" capers, because their saltiness contrasts well with the sweetness of the chicken. You can rinse off the salt if you like, but I leave it on when I'm using a small quantity, as here.

SERVES 6

Special equipment
*1½–2 quart (1.7–2 liter)
baking dish, about
12 x 9in (30 x 23cm)
and 2in (5cm) deep*

*1 lb 10 oz (750g)
fresh spinach*

*¼ tsp freshly
grated nutmeg*

*salt and freshly ground
black pepper*

*1 lb 9 oz (725g)
chicken breast fillets
(chicken breast tenders)*

2 tbsp olive oil

2 tbsp (25g) butter

*7 oz (200g) button
mushrooms, halved or
quartered according to size*

1 garlic clove, crushed

*7 oz (200ml) full-fat
crème fraîche*

*2½ oz (75g) Gruyère
cheese, grated*

SWISS CHICKEN, SPINACH, AND MUSHROOM BAKE

*For this quick-to-make, comforting supper dish, chicken breast
fillets are baked with spinach and a creamy mushroom sauce
and topped with Swiss Gruyère cheese.*

1. Pick over the spinach leaves and trim off any thick, coarse stalks. Wash the spinach, place it in a large pan with some water still clinging to the leaves, cover, and cook for 5 minutes or until tender. Drain the spinach thoroughly in a colander, chop it coarsely, and return it to the pan. Add the nutmeg and plenty of salt and pepper, and toss the spinach briefly over high heat, until dry. Transfer to the baking dish and spread the spinach over the bottom of the dish. (See pp104–105: *Non-soggy spinach layer.*)

2. Preheat the oven to 425°F (220°C). Season the chicken fillets with salt and pepper. Heat the oil until hot in a large, nonstick frying pan, add half of the chicken fillets, and fry over medium–high heat for 2 minutes, turning halfway. (See p105: *Tender, golden chicken.*) Transfer to the baking dish using a slotted spoon, arranging the fillets over the spinach in a single, even layer. Repeat with the remaining chicken.

3. Melt the butter in the frying pan, add the mushrooms, garlic, and some salt and pepper, and fry over medium–high heat for 5 minutes, stirring frequently. Add the crème fraîche, a few spoonfuls at a time, and stir for 1–2 minutes over medium heat to make a creamy sauce.

4. Pour the mushroom sauce over the chicken, then shake the dish and separate the fillets with a fork so that the sauce runs down between them. Sprinkle the cheese evenly over the top. Bake for 30 minutes. Remove from the oven and let it rest for 5 minutes before serving.

KEYS TO PERFECTION
See pp104–105

KEYS TO PERFECTION

Non-soggy spinach layer

1 Wash the leaves in a large bowl or sink full of cold water to get rid of dirt, then lift the leaves out a handful at a time, give them a good shake, and place them in a large pan. Push the leaves down with your hands until all of them are in. Don't worry if the pan seems rather full—the spinach will shrink as soon as it starts to cook.

2 Cover the pan with the lid and cook the spinach for 5 minutes over high heat with only the water that is clinging to the leaves after rinsing and draining. Don't add any more water, as this will make the spinach soggy. Stir a few times during cooking, moving the uncooked leaves from the top to the bottom of the pan.

3 You may be surprised at the relatively small amount of spinach you have left at the end of cooking, but the flavor is intense so you don't need a lot. Tip the contents of the pan into a colander held over the sink, and press and pound hard on the spinach using the edge of a wooden spatula to extract as much water as possible.

4 Place half the spinach onto a board and chop coarsely with a large chef's knife, using a fork in your other hand to steady the leaves on the board. Return the chopped spinach to the pan, then chop the remaining half in the same way.

5 Add the nutmeg and plenty of seasoning to the spinach, then toss over high heat for 1–2 minutes to remove any excess water. The spinach needs to be completely dry at this stage, or it will be too sloppy in the finished dish.

6 Transfer the spinach to the baking dish and spread it out as smoothly and evenly as possible using a spoon or spatula. The spinach should cover the entire bottom of the baking dish, right to the edges and into the corners.

Tender, golden chicken

1 Chicken breast fillets are long, tender strips of meat available in most supermarkets, usually with 7 or 8 fillets per pack. Before cooking, remove the white tendon, which will be tough to eat. Use a small, sharp knife to tease one end of the tendon away from the flesh, then grip this end with your fingers and slide the blade along the length of the tendon to release it cleanly from the flesh.

2 Fry the chicken fillets for only 1 minute on each side. This is just long enough to give them a light golden color on the outside, leaving them uncooked in the center. It's important not to overcook the chicken at this stage, because it has yet to be baked with the spinach and sauce for 30 minutes, and you don't want the meat to become tough.

MARY'S TOP TIPS

Get organized

*Before you start to cook,
clear any clutter from the worktop,
gather the equipment you'll
need, bring food to room
temperature if required, and
prepare the ingredients. You
don't want any last-minute panics!*

SERVES 4

*8 bone-in chicken thighs
(see p111, box)*

*salt and freshly ground
black pepper*

2 tbsp olive oil

*1 large onion, coarsely
chopped*

*¾ oz (20 g) fresh ginger,
finely chopped*

2 tsp ground cilantro

2 tsp ground cumin

1 tsp ground cinnamon

*3 large ripe tomatoes,
roughly chopped*

*2 large garlic cloves,
crushed*

1½ tsp harissa paste

1 tbsp honey

*2 cups (450 ml) chicken
stock*

2½ oz (75 g) dried apricots

2½ oz (75 g) pitted prunes

*1 preserved lemon
(see p111, box)*

*¼ cup coarsely chopped
fresh cilantro*

CHICKEN TAGINE

Since this special dish tastes even better when cooked a day ahead and reheated, it's very handy to make when entertaining. Serve with couscous to continue the Moroccan theme.

1. Skin, trim, and season the chicken. Heat the oil in a Dutch oven over medium–high heat until hot and fry the chicken in 2 batches until golden brown on all sides. (See p110: *Succulent, golden brown chicken.*) Remove using a slotted spoon, transfer to a large plate, and set aside.

2. Add the onion and ginger to the oil in the pan and soften over low heat for 5 minutes, stirring frequently and scraping the bottom of the pan to release any sticky bits left from the chicken. Add the ground spices and fry for 2–3 minutes, stirring constantly.

3. Stir in the tomatoes and increase the heat to medium. Add the garlic, harissa paste, and honey, and stir well again. Pour in the stock and bring to a boil, stirring often. Return the reserved chicken to the pan, together with the juices that have collected on the plate.

4. Quarter the apricots, prunes, and preserved lemon, and remove the seeds from the lemon (see p111: *Soft, velvety fruit*). Add the fruits to the pan. Press down the chicken and fruits to submerge them in the sauce.

5. Cover and simmer gently over medium–low heat for 1 hour or until the chicken is tender and cooked through. Lift the lid and check occasionally during this time, turning the chicken over to ensure even cooking. Let cool, cover, and refrigerate overnight. (See p111: *Rich, mellow flavors.*)

6. The following day, slowly reheat the tagine for about 10 minutes or until the chicken is hot and the sauce is gently bubbling. Stir in about half the chopped cilantro and taste the sauce for seasoning. Serve hot, sprinkled with the remaining cilantro.

KEYS TO PERFECTION
See pp110–111

KEYS TO PERFECTION

Succulent, golden brown chicken

1 If you're simmering chicken thighs in liquid, as in this recipe, it's best to remove the skin before cooking. This results in a less greasy sauce and helps keep the fat and calorie content down. To remove the skin, grip one end with your fingers and pull it away from the flesh—it should come off easily. Trim off any large pieces of white fat that may be clinging to the chicken flesh. Discard the fat.

2 Place the skinned chicken pieces on a large plate and season them well all over with salt and pepper. Do this just before cooking, or the salt will draw out the juices from the meat and make it dry.

3 Pick up each thigh, holding it firmly in shape, and add it to the hot oil with the smooth, skinned-side down. Fry 4 chicken thighs at a time. If you overcrowd the pan, the chicken will stew rather than fry and won't turn brown.

4 When the thighs are golden brown underneath, use tongs to turn them over. Don't use a fork, as this will pierce the meat and cause the juices to run out, making the chicken dry. Continue frying until the chicken is brown on all sides. Don't rush the browning stage—it can take as long as 12 minutes or so. Remove the chicken using a slotted spoon and set aside on a plate while you fry the second batch.

BUYING AND USING PRESERVED LEMONS

Preserved lemons can be found in jars at most supermarkets. They come whole, packed in brine, and look tiny compared with fresh lemons, but their tangy, sour-salty flavor packs a very big punch. Preserved lemons are traditional in Moroccan tagines and can be left in or out before serving, as you prefer. I find it's a nice surprise to come across the occasional piece of lemon in the sauce.

Soft, velvety fruit

Using a pair of sharp kitchen scissors, snip the apricots and prunes into quarters, so that during the cooking time they will soften and almost melt into the sauce to give it a velvety consistency. Cut the lemon into quarters lengthwise and flick out the tiny seeds with the tip of a small, sharp knife. Discard the seeds.

THE BENEFITS OF CHICKEN THIGHS

Chicken thighs are richer in flavor and less expensive than chicken breasts. They also remain moist longer, which is why they're the best choice for a slow-cooked dish such as this tagine. They are available bone-in or boneless, but I prefer to cook them on the bone, as it gives a better flavor and helps to keep the meat in shape. You can either leave the skin on, or remove it—which is best for this recipe.

Rich, mellow flavors

As with most spicy dishes, the resting and chilling time allows the flavors to mellow and mature. When the chicken is cooked, remove from the heat. Let the tagine cool to room temperature, then cover it with a lid and refrigerate overnight. The following day, bring the dish to room temperature and then reheat it slowly.

SERVES 4

¼ cup sunflower oil

2 skinless, boneless chicken breasts, about 9½ oz (280 g) in total, cut into 1½ in (3.5cm) chunks

1 lb 2 oz–1¼ lb (500–550 g) skinless, boneless chicken thighs, cut into 1½ in (3.5cm) chunks

1 onion, halved and thinly sliced

6 cardamom pods, slit down one side

½ cinnamon stick, about 2½ in (6cm) long

3 garlic cloves, crushed

2 tsp finely grated fresh ginger

1 tsp ground cilantro

1½ tsp garam masala

¼ tsp turmeric

½ tsp mild chili powder

5½ oz (150 g) plain, full-fat yogurt (room temperature)

1 tbsp ground almonds

4–5 tbsp heavy cream

¼ tsp freshly ground black pepper

salt

chopped fresh cilantro, to garnish

CHICKEN KORMA

This is a light, fragrant, creamy curry, ideal for those who like their curries mild, and it doesn't take long to make. Basmati rice goes well with it, as does some warm naan bread on the side.

1. Heat 2 tablespoons of the oil in a large, nonstick sauté pan. Add the chopped chicken breasts and thighs and fry over medium–high heat for 6–8 minutes until starting to color, stirring occasionally. Transfer to a large plate using a slotted spoon and set aside.

2. Pour the remaining 2 tablespoons of oil in the pan and add the onion, cardamom pods, cinnamon, garlic, and ginger. Fry for about 5 minutes or until the onion starts to brown.

3. Stir in the ground cilantro, garam masala, turmeric, and chili powder, and fry for 1 minute. Return the chicken to the pan together with any juices and cook, stirring, for 2 more minutes.

4. Reduce the heat to medium–low and add the yogurt gradually. Pour in ¾ cup (200 ml) of water, cover, and simmer over low heat for 15–20 minutes or until the chicken is tender. (See below: *Smooth, creamy sauce*.)

5. Stir in the ground almonds and 3 tablespoons of the cream. Season with the pepper and some salt and remove the cinnamon stick. Drizzle the remaining cream over the top and scatter a little cilantro over each serving.

KEYS TO PERFECTION

Smooth, creamy sauce

1 To prevent the yogurt from curdling, bring it to room temperature before using and stir it in just a tablespoonful at a time over medium-low heat, rather than adding it in all at once. Stir well between each spoonful.

2 As the chicken simmers, check the sauce's consistency. Add a drop more water if needed, but not too much, as the sauce should coat the chicken. When added, the almonds will thicken the sauce slightly and the cream will enrich it.

SERVES 4

Special equipment
1½–2 quart (1.7–2 liter) baking dish, about 10 x 7in (25 x 18cm) and 3in (7.5cm) deep

4 oz (115 g) dry Spanish chorizo, cut into ½in (1cm) thick slices and then small cubes

3 tbsp olive oil

1 onion, halved lengthwise and thinly sliced

2 garlic cloves, finely chopped

4 skinless, boneless chicken breasts, about 5 oz (140 g) each

salt and freshly ground black pepper

9 oz (250 g) crimini mushrooms, cut into ½in (1cm) thick slices

2 tsp paprika

1 tsp cornstarch

⅔ cup (150 ml) chicken stock

8 oz (170 ml) full-fat sour cream

12 pitted plump green olives

1 tbsp chopped fresh flat-leaf parsley, to garnish

SPANISH-STYLE CHICKEN PAPRIKA

I like this dish for casual entertaining: you can make it ahead and finish it in the oven before serving. If it's been in the fridge, allow a bit longer to heat up. Serve with a mix of long-grain and wild rice.

1. Heat a large, nonstick frying pan or sauté pan. Add the chorizo and fry until crispy. Remove using a slotted spoon, drain on paper towels, and set aside. Keep 1 tablespoon of the chorizo oil in the pan and drain off any excess. Add 1 tablespoon of the olive oil. (See below: *Use the chorizo oil for frying.*) When hot, add the onion and garlic and fry for 6–8 minutes over medium heat, stirring occasionally, until the onion starts to brown. Spread the onion over the bottom of the baking dish.

2. Preheat the oven to 400°F (200°C). Pour another tablespoon of the oil into the pan. Season the chicken and brown over medium heat for 10 minutes, turning once. Place on top of the onion.

3. Add the final tablespoon of oil to the pan, add in the mushrooms, and season with pepper. Fry for about 3 minutes over medium–high heat, stirring occasionally, until the mushrooms start to brown. Stir in the paprika and cornstarch. Pour in the stock, stirring to deglaze the bottom of the pan, and simmer for 1 minute. Stir in the sour cream and heat until just starting to bubble.

4. Pour the mushroom sauce over the chicken in the dish. Scatter the chorizo and olives over the top. Cover with foil and bake for 15–20 minutes or until bubbling around the edges. Serve sprinkled with the parsley.

KEYS TO PERFECTION

Use the chorizo oil for frying

1 Fry the chorizo in a hot, dry pan over medium heat for about 1 minute until the fat starts to run, then increase the heat for 2 minutes until crispy. Stir frequently so it doesn't burn. Remove using a slotted spoon.

2 Use 1 tablespoon of the spicy red oil released by the chorizo for frying the onion and garlic: its smoky paprika flavor adds depth to the dish. Don't use any more, as it can overpower; instead, add olive oil, if needed.

SERVES 2

2 oranges

3 tbsp dark soy sauce

2 duck breasts, each about 6 oz (175 g)

¾ tsp five-spice powder

freshly ground black pepper

1 red bell pepper, seeded

2in (5cm) piece of fresh ginger, peeled

6 scallions, trimmed

1 fresh red chili, seeded

8 oz (225 g) broccolini (see p118, box)

8 oz (225 g) can water chestnuts, drained

2 tbsp sunflower oil

1 tbsp honey

sesame oil, for sprinkling

STIR-FRIED DUCK

Stir-frying is all about speed, movement, high heat, and using only a little oil, making this recipe fresh, quick, and healthy. Serve with cooked egg noodles, plain boiled or tossed into the wok at the end.

1. Squeeze the juice from 1 of the oranges, pour it into a bowl, and add the soy sauce. Peel and segment the other orange, holding it over the bowl to catch the juice (see p118: *Prepare the ingredients for stir-frying*, step 1). Set the juice mixture and segments aside, keeping them separate.

2. Remove the skin and fat layer from the duck and discard. Slice the meat into strips, about 2in (5cm) long and no more than ¼in (5mm) thick, then cut each strip lengthwise in half (see p118: *Prepare the ingredients for stir-frying*, step 2). Put the strips into a bowl, sprinkle with the five-spice powder and a good grinding of pepper, and mix well. Set aside.

3. Slice the red bell pepper, ginger, scallions, and chili into strips about the same size as the duck. Cut the florets off the broccolini stems and set the florets aside. Cut the broccolini stems into thin strips. (See p118: *Prepare the ingredients for stir-frying*, step 3.) Finely slice the water chestnuts.

4. Heat a wok or large, deep-sided, nonstick frying pan or sauté pan over high heat until very hot. Pour in the sunflower oil and heat until it just begins to smoke. Add the duck and honey and stir-fry for a few minutes or until brown, then remove to a plate and set aside. Add the ginger, spring onions, and chili to the hot oil and stir-fry for a few minutes until softened, then add the red bell pepper and broccolini stems and stir-fry for a few minutes more until softened. (See p119: *Stir-fry to finish*.)

5. Pour the reserved orange juice mixture into the wok, then add the broccolini florets and water chestnuts. Stir-fry for a few minutes more before tossing in the reserved cooked duck and orange segments to heat through. Sprinkle with sesame oil, to taste, and more soy sauce if you like. Serve immediately.

KEYS TO PERFECTION
See pp118–119

KEYS TO PERFECTION

Prepare the ingredients for stir-frying

1 After removing the peel and pith from the orange using a sharp knife, cut down both sides of each membrane to free the segments from the core. Use a small, sharp knife and hold the orange over the bowl containing the orange juice and soy sauce, so the juice from the fruit falls into the bowl.

2 For fast, even cooking, all the ingredients need to be a similar size. Start with the duck, slicing it across the grain into thin strips about 2in (5cm) long and maximum ¼in (5mm) thick, then cut each strip lengthwise in half. Slicing it this way means that long fibers are cut through, giving tender meat; it also exposes a greater cut surface to the heat, so the duck cooks more quickly while retaining its shape.

3 Now slice the red bell pepper, peeled ginger, trimmed scallions, seeded chili, and broccolini stems into strips approximately the same length and thickness as the duck. Slicing the vegetables finely like this means that they can cook quickly yet remain al dente, and enables them to absorb the flavors of the oil and spices while frying.

USING BROCCOLINI FOR STIR-FRIES

Broccolini is thin and delicate and therefore good for stir-fries, because both the stems and florets cook in super-quick time. You can also use ordinary broccoli for this recipe, provided you discard the thick, woody stalks and cut off the stems just below the florets, slicing them very finely. Separate the florets into tiny sprigs, otherwise they won't cook quickly enough.

Stir-fry to finish

1 The great thing about a stir-fry is that it cooks in next to no time, but you need to get everything ready beforehand because once you start cooking you shouldn't stop. Put all the prepared ingredients into bowls, grouping them according to their cooking time, and line them up, ready to toss into the pan one after the other.

2 When you're ready to cook, get the wok as hot as possible over a high heat. Hold your hand over the pan—you should feel the heat rising. Add a drop of oil to test; it will sizzle when the wok is ready. Add the remaining oil and swirl it around the wok until it just begins to smoke very slightly.

3 Throughout the cooking process, keep the heat under the wok as high as possible. Add the ingredients to the hot oil, in the correct sequence, and then keep them constantly on the move around the bottom and sides of the wok by shaking the pan and tossing the contents together with a wok shovel, spatula, or two wooden spoons.

STIR-FRYING WITH AND WITHOUT A WOK

A wok isn't essential for stir-frying, but it does have several benefits—the main one being that the rounded shape and large size allow the food to be tossed around easily. If you don't have a wok, it's fine to use a large, deep-sided, nonstick sauté pan or frying pan instead. When stir-frying, you want to ensure you don't have the pan more than one-third full, so there's plenty of space for moving the ingredients around quickly and easily.

SERVES 4

4 boneless pheasant breasts, skinned

2 tbsp all-purpose flour

salt and freshly ground black pepper

1 tbsp olive oil

2 tbsp (25 g) butter

5½ oz (150 g) bacon, cut into ½ in (1 cm) pieces

1 crisp apple, such as Braeburn or Cox, peeled, cored, and cut into 1 cm (½ in) cubes

4 shallots, thinly sliced

1¼ cups (300 ml) hard cider

⅔ cup (150 ml) pheasant or chicken stock

1 tbsp red currant jelly

4 fl oz (120 ml) full-fat crème fraîche

1½ tsp finely chopped fresh sage

1½ tsp finely chopped fresh thyme

PHEASANT BREASTS WITH APPLE AND CIDER

*Supper always feels special when I cook pheasant.
Here, I've teamed it with apples and cider, as they go so well
with the richness of the meat. Serve with curly kale.*

1. Place the pheasant breasts on a board and cover with plastic wrap. Pound with the base of a saucepan to flatten very slightly. Put the flour on a plate, season, and coat the pheasant in the flour. Heat the oil and butter in a large, deep-sided, nonstick frying pan or sauté pan over medium–high heat. As soon as the butter is foaming, add the meat, skinned-side down. Fry for 2 minutes on each side until golden brown, pressing it flat with a spatula. Transfer the meat to a dish and set aside.

2. Put the bacon in the pan and cook for 5 minutes over medium–low heat, stirring often. Add the apple and shallots and fry for 5 minutes over medium heat, stirring frequently or until softened and lightly colored. Add the cider, stock, red currant jelly, and some salt and pepper.

Bring to a boil, stirring constantly until the jelly has melted. Reduce the heat and return the pheasant and its juices to the pan. Simmer gently for 2 minutes, turning the breasts halfway and basting frequently. Remove the pheasant to a board, cover loosely with foil, and let rest for 10 minutes.

3. Meanwhile, increase the heat to high and stir the crème fraîche into the sauce. Add 1 teaspoon each of sage and thyme and simmer gently until thickened. Season. Slice the pheasant and arrange on warmed plates (see below: *Tender, thinly sliced pheasant*). Spoon the sauce over and around the meat. Serve immediately, sprinkled with the remaining sage and thyme.

KEYS TO PERFECTION

Tender, thinly sliced pheasant

1 After the pheasant has rested, slice the breasts thinly on the diagonal with a sharp chef's knife or carving knife. Ideally, slice no more than ¼in (5mm) thick.

2 If you keep the slices close together as you carve the pheasant breasts, you can easily transfer each breast to a dinner plate with a spatula.

BUYING AND USING PHEASANT BREASTS

Sometimes it can be difficult to buy pheasant breasts on their own, but whole birds are inexpensive so you can buy 2 pheasants and remove the breasts, or ask your butcher to remove the breasts for you. If you buy whole birds, you can use the carcass, wings, and legs to make a flavorful stock. Some of this stock can be used in this recipe and the rest can be frozen. Pheasant breasts are lean and should not be overcooked, or they will be dry. Cook for the time stated and no longer.

SERVES 6

Special equipment
1½–2 quart (1.7–2 liter) baking dish, about 12 x 9in (30 x 23cm) and 2in (5cm) deep

2 lb (900g) stewing venison (see p125, box), cut into bite-sized cubes

2½ cups (600ml) red wine

finely grated zest and juice of 1 orange

finely grated zest of 1 lemon

1 heaping tsp allspice berries, crushed

salt and freshly ground black pepper

3 tbsp (30g) all-purpose flour

2–3 tbsp sunflower oil

1 piece bacon, about 7 oz (200g), cut into ½in (1cm) cubes

1 large onion, coarsely chopped

9 oz (250g) crimini mushrooms, quartered

2 bay leaves

2 tbsp red currant jelly

For the topping

1¾ lb (800g) carrots, cut into ½in (1cm) thick slices

1¾ lb (800g) smooth potatoes, such as Yukon gold, peeled and quartered

4 tbsp (50g) butter (room temperature)

VENISON COTTAGE PIE

Roughly mashed carrots and potatoes make the perfect rustic topping for this wintry pie, as the taste and texture hold their own against the robust flavor of the venison.

1. Put the venison in a large, nonmetallic bowl. Pour in the wine and add the orange zest and juice, lemon zest, allspice, and black pepper. Stir well, submerging the meat. Cover with plastic wrap and marinate in the fridge for a minimum of 12 hours, preferably up to 2 days. Remove the meat using a slotted spoon, drain, and pat dry with paper towels, then transfer it to another large bowl. (See p124: *Marinate and dry the meat.*) Reserve the marinade.

2. Preheat the oven to 325°F (160°C). Spread out the flour on a large plate or tray and season. Coat one-third of the meat in the flour. Heat 2 tablespoons of the oil in a large, nonstick frying pan until hot. Fry the floured meat over medium–high heat until browned all over; this should take about 6 minutes. Remove the meat from the pan using a slotted spoon and transfer to a bowl or large plate. Set aside. Divide the remaining meat into 2 batches and repeat the flouring and browning, adding more oil if needed.

3. Pour the oil and juices from the frying pan into a Dutch oven. Add the bacon and fry over medium heat until the fat begins to run, then add the onion and fry for about 5 minutes, stirring occasionally, until the bacon and onion are lightly colored. Stir in the mushrooms and fry for a few minutes until the juices run.

4. Add the venison and its juices and pour over the reserved marinade. Stir, then add up to ⅔ cup (150 ml) cold water, just enough so the liquid barely covers the meat. Stir again, increase the heat, and bring to a simmer. Add the bay leaves, red currant jelly, and season with salt. Cover, transfer to the oven, and cook for 2 hours or until the venison is tender.

5. Meanwhile, make the topping: cook the carrots and potatoes together in a large pan of salted boiling water for 15–20 minutes or until tender. Drain in a colander, return to the pan with half the butter, and mash roughly with a potato masher. (See p124: *Make a stable mashed topping.*) Season.

6. Remove the pot from the oven and increase the oven temperature to 400°F (200°C). Transfer just the meat and vegetables to the baking dish and spread them out in an even layer. Discard the bay leaves. Measure ¾ cup (200 ml) of the gravy and pour this over the meat and vegetables. Spread over the mashed potatoes and carrots and mark it in a crisscross pattern with a fork. Grind black pepper over the top and dot with the remaining butter. (See p125: *Assemble the pie carefully.*) Bake for 30–40 minutes until golden. Reheat the remaining gravy in a pan, pour it into a jug, and serve separately.

KEYS TO PERFECTION
See pp124–125

KEYS TO PERFECTION

Marinate and dry the meat

1 Stir the marinating venison every now and then, pressing the chunks of meat under the liquid with the back of a spoon. You can marinate the meat for as little as 12 hours, but 2 days is ideal (stirring about 3 times during this period). Keep the bowl covered between stirrings, to prevent evaporation.

2 After marinating, make sure the meat is as dry as possible before coating it in flour, otherwise it won't brown. Drain the pieces well when you lift them out of the liquid using a slotted spoon, then tip each spoonful onto a double sheet of paper towels and pat the meat thoroughly dry with more paper. Reserve the marinade.

Make a stable mash topping

1 The mash should be quite stiff, so that it holds its own above the meat and gravy. Carrots are more watery than potatoes, so take care to drain them well with the potatoes. Shake the colander to get rid of as much water as possible, then return the vegetables to the pan and toss them over low heat for a few minutes until they're very dry.

2 Remove the pan from the heat and mash the carrots and potatoes with half the butter, simply breaking them up roughly with a potato masher, just enough to mix them together. When combining carrots in a mash like this, it's best not to over-mash and make the mixture too smooth or it will get sloppy.

Assemble the pie carefully

1 For a perfect cottage pie, it's all about ratio and consistency—juicy meat and gravy at the bottom and a good, thick layer of mash on top. Transfer the meat and vegetables from the casserole to the dish using a slotted spoon, leaving behind as much of the gravy as possible. This is the way to control the amount of liquid that goes in the dish.

2 Now you should add just enough gravy to moisten the meat without making the pie too runny. If there's too much gravy, it will bubble up into the mash during baking and make it sloppy. Pour the measured gravy slowly over the venison, shaking the dish so that the liquid flows between the pieces of meat.

3 Spoon the mash on top of the meat mixture, then spread it out using a palette knife to make as even a layer as possible. Take care to go right to the edge of the dish, to seal in the gravy and prevent it from seeping up the sides. Finally, make crisscross markings with a fork, grate pepper liberally over the top, and dot with pats of butter.

USING STEWING VENISON

Butchers often sell ready-cubed "stewing venison" without identifying the cut. Generally, it's either shoulder or shin, both of which are suitable for this pie. Venison is a lean, low-fat meat that benefits from marinating before cooking to help make it juicy and tender. Steeping the cubes of meat in a marinade softens the tough fibers of the meat and gives it more flavor.

MEAT

SERVES 6

*1 center-cut piece of beef
filet, 2¾ lb (1.25 kg) (room
temperature)*

1 tbsp olive oil

2 tbsp Dijon mustard

*6 tbsp black peppercorns,
coarsely crushed*

For the gravy

2 tbsp (30 g) butter

1 tbsp all-purpose flour

⅔ cup (150 ml) red wine

1 cup (250 ml) beef stock

2 tsp red currant jelly

1 tsp Dijon mustard

salt

PEPPERED FILET OF BEEF

This is an easy roast, with guaranteed "wow factor" and no waste at all. Mustard and peppercorns protect the meat from the intense heat of the oven, while giving a zingy crust around each slice.

1. Rub the beef all over with the oil. Heat a large, nonstick frying pan (or roasting pan if the filet is too large) and brown the beef on all sides, except the ends (see below: *Sear the beef*). Remove the beef from the pan and let it cool to room temperature. Preheat the oven to 425°F (220°C).

2. Spread the mustard over the seared beef, except the ends, then roll the mustard-covered sides in the crushed peppercorns (see below: *Make a peppery crust*). You can sear and coat the filet up to 12 hours ahead (if you do so, keep the filet in the fridge and bring to room temperature 1–2 hours before roasting). Place the beef on a rack in a roasting pan and roast for 25 minutes. Transfer the beef to a carving board and let it rest for 10 minutes.

3. Meanwhile, make the gravy: put the butter in the roasting pan and place the pan on a stovetop burner set to medium–low heat. Stir until the butter has melted, scraping up bits on the bottom of the pan, then sprinkle in the flour and cook for 1–2 minutes, whisking constantly with a wire whisk.

4. Slowly whisk in the wine and stock and bring to a boil, then add the red currant jelly and mustard. Simmer for a few minutes, whisking all the time, until the jelly has melted and the gravy thickens. Add salt to taste. Carve the beef into thick slices and serve with the gravy in a jug or gravy boat.

KEYS TO PERFECTION

Sear the beef

Once the frying pan is very hot, sear the filet for 1 minute on all sides (except the ends) until the outside is brown. This releases juices that caramelize and give depth of flavor.

Make a peppery crust

After spreading mustard over the sides of the cooled beef, put the crushed peppercorns on a sheet of wax paper and roll the beef in them until evenly coated.

BUYING AND COOKING FILET OF BEEF

The thickest part of the filet—called the center or middle cut—is essential for even cooking, as it will be the same thickness along its length. Don't doubt the roasting time in this recipe—25 minutes in the oven guarantees perfect rare beef every time. If you prefer your beef medium rare, roast it for 30 minutes.

SERVES 6

Special equipment
*1 quart (1.2 liter) pie dish,
about 10½ x 8in (27 x 20cm)
and 2in (5cm) deep*

2 lb (900 g) braising steak,
cut into bite-sized cubes

3 tbsp (30 g) all-purpose
flour

1 tsp mustard powder

salt and freshly ground
black pepper

2–3 tbsp sunflower oil

1 large onion, coarsely
chopped

3 stalks of celery, cut
diagonally into slices
1in (2.5cm) thick

2 large carrots, cut into
rings ½in (1cm) thick,
then quartered

2 cups (500 ml) Guinness

¾ cup (200 ml) beef stock

2 tbsp red currant jelly

2 bay leaves

1 lb 2 oz (500 g) store-
bought puff pastry
(preferably all-butter)

2 tbsp chopped fresh
parsley

2 tsp chopped fresh thyme

1 egg, beaten

STEAK AND GUINNESS PIE

This is a classic, hearty pie. To make it ahead, cook the meat to the end of step 3, then leave it in the fridge overnight before finishing off the pie. Serve with mashed potatoes and seasonal green vegetables.

1. Preheat the oven to 325°F (160°C). Pat the meat dry with paper towels. Put the flour on a large plate or tray and season with the mustard, ½ teaspoon salt, and a few grindings of pepper. Coat one-third of the meat in the flour. Heat 2 tablespoons of the oil in a large, nonstick frying pan until hot and fry the floured meat over medium–high heat. (See p132: *Brown the meat well.*) Remove the meat from the pan using a slotted spoon and transfer to a Dutch oven. Divide the remaining meat into 2 batches and repeat the flouring and browning, adding more oil if needed.

2. Add the onion to the frying pan, with a little more oil if necessary, and fry for 3 minutes or until golden brown, stirring frequently. Add the celery and carrots and stir to mix, then fry for 2 minutes before spreading the vegetables on top of the meat in the Dutch oven.

3. Pour the Guinness and stock into the pot and add the red currant jelly. Mix well and bring to a boil, stirring. Add the bay leaves and season with salt and pepper. Place the lid on the pot, transfer it to the oven, and cook for 2½ hours or until the meat is tender. Remove from the oven, taste the gravy for seasoning, and let cool completely.

4. Make the pastry lid: preheat the oven to 425°F (220°C). Roll out the pastry and cut out a lid and a strip for the lip of the pie dish. Remove the bay leaves from the casserole and stir in the parsley and thyme, then transfer the meat and vegetables to the pie dish using a large spoon, together with enough of the gravy to come just below the lip of the dish. Reserve any remaining gravy. Brush water around the lip of the dish; cut the pastry strip into smaller pieces and place the strips on the moistened lip. Moisten the strips, cover with the lid, and press to seal. (See pp132–33: *Make a well-fitting, decorative pie lid*, steps 1–3.)

5. Trim, tap a knife into the edge of the pastry, and scallop the edge, then brush the pastry lid with beaten egg to glaze. Use the trimmings to make decorations and reglaze with as much of the remaining egg as needed. Cut a small slit in the center of the lid. (See p133: *Make a well-fitting, decorative pie lid*, steps 4–6.)

6. Bake the pie for 30–35 minutes or until the pastry is risen and golden brown. If you have any gravy left over, reheat until bubbling, pour it into a jug, and serve alongside the pie.

KEYS TO PERFECTION
See pp132–133

KEYS TO PERFECTION

Brown the meat well

1 Flour will thicken the gravy during the long time in the oven, but it needs to be cooked at the initial frying stage, otherwise it will taste raw in the finished dish. Before frying the batches of meat, toss the chunks in the seasoned flour until lightly coated on all sides.

2 Make sure the oil is really hot before browning. This is vital to sear the meat and give it a good color and flavor. Place the floured beef chunks in the oil, spacing the pieces well apart, and fry over medium–high heat until browned on all sides (this takes 6 minutes or so). Remove the meat using a slotted spoon, so that the fat and juices remain in the pan.

Make a well-fitting, decorative pie lid

1 Roll out the pastry on a lightly floured, cool surface until it is about ¼in (5mm) thick. Place your pie dish upside down in the center of the pastry and press it down firmly. With a small, sharp knife, cut out a lid that is about ¾in (2cm) larger all around than the outside edge of the dish.

2 Lift off the dish and set aside the excess pastry. Using the pie dish indentation as a guide, cut off the strip from around the outside of the pastry lid. Spoon the cold pie filling into the dish, mounding it up slightly in the center and adding enough gravy to come just below the lip of the dish. Brush the lip with water and attach the pastry strip to it, cutting it into smaller pieces and joining them together as needed.

Make a well-fitting, decorative pie lid (continued)

3 Check the size of the pastry lid over the pie dish and roll it out a little larger if necessary. You don't want to have to stretch the pastry to fit it over the dish, as this would cause shrinkage when baking. Brush the pastry strip with water, then roll the pastry lid loosely around the rolling pin, lift it over the dish, and gently unroll it. Press all around the edge to seal the lid to the strip.

4 Trim off any surplus pastry with the knife if necessary, cutting downward against the edge of the dish. "Knock up" the edge of the pastry by holding the back of the knife horizontally against the edge and tapping all the way around. This will help the pastry rise evenly.

5 For an attractive finish, scallop all around the edge of the pie by making indentations with the back of the knife and your forefinger, alternating the knife marks and finger indentations. Brush all over the pastry with beaten egg, using a pastry brush. Coat the surface lightly; too much egg will prevent the pastry from puffing up.

6 Roll out some pastry trimmings and cut out leaf shapes. Make patterns using the back of the knife. Place the pastry leaves on top of the pie and brush all over the lid again with more egg. Cut a small slit, about ¾in (2cm) long, in the middle of the lid, to allow steam to escape during baking. This prevents the pastry from becoming soggy.

SERVES 2

Special equipment
*Ridged cast-iron
grill pan*

2 tbsp (30 g) butter

3 echalion (banana) shallots
(see below, box), halved
lengthwise

2 tbsp (30 g) granulated
sugar

¾ cup (200 ml) hot beef
stock

2 ribeye steaks, about
7 oz (200 g) each
(room temperature)

2 tbsp sunflower oil

salt and freshly ground
black pepper

⅓ cup (90 ml) red wine

1 fresh red chili, seeded
and finely chopped

1 garlic clove,
finely chopped

½ tsp Dijon mustard

2 tbsp chopped fresh flat-
leaf parsley

1 tbsp full-fat crème fraîche

RIBEYE STEAK WITH CARAMELIZED SHALLOTS

For the most tender steaks that are full of flavor, ask your butcher to cut them from the sirloin end of the rib. Spinach and rösti (see pp216–217) make the perfect accompaniments.

1. Melt the butter in a nonstick frying pan over medium heat. When the butter bubbles, add the shallots and fry for 3–4 minutes until golden brown on each side, turning once. Sprinkle in the sugar, stir, and allow to color and caramelize for a few minutes, then stir in half the stock. Bring to a boil, cover the pan, and reduce the heat to low. Simmer for 10 minutes, turning and basting once (see below: *Soft, caramelized shallots*).

2. Preheat the grill pan over high heat for 5–10 minutes or until piping hot. Meanwhile, wipe the steaks dry with paper towels, brush them on both sides with oil, and season with pepper. Place the steaks in the pan and grill for 2–3 minutes on each side for rare to medium rare (see below: *Juicy, grilled steaks*). Lift the steaks out of the pan, season with salt and more pepper if required, and let them rest.

3. Pour the wine and remaining stock into the grill pan and scrape to release the sticky bits. Add the chili and garlic. Simmer until reduced by about half. Take off the heat and stir in the mustard and parsley.

4. To serve, reheat the shallots and stir in the crème fraîche. Arrange 3 shallot halves on each plate and spoon the sauce over the top. Place the steaks alongside or on top, and drizzle with the wine and stock mixture.

KEYS TO PERFECTION

Soft, caramelized shallots

To ensure even cooking, turn and baste the shallots with the stock halfway through. At the end, they should feel soft when pierced with a fork, yet still retain their shape.

Juicy, grilled steaks

As the steaks grill, press them with a spatula but don't move them around. This way they will look good with charred lines and will cook perfectly in the time given.

ECHALION (BANANA) SHALLOTS

Echalions, also known as banana shallots, are best for this recipe. Not only is their long oval shape appealing, but being a cross between an onion and a shallot they are easier to peel than ordinary shallots and stay in shape when cut in half. If you can't find echalions in the store, ordinary shallots will do.

MARY'S TOP TIPS

Stock up on staples

Keep a well-stocked cupboard and have back-up in the freezer of bread, milk, and stock. It's always reassuring to know you have the basics on hand so you can rustle up an impromptu meal.

SERVES 4

1¾ cup (150 g) stale
white bread slices,
at least 1 day old

1 tsp black peppercorns,
coarsely crushed

½ tsp smoked paprika

½ tsp salt

¼ tsp crushed dried chilies

4 thinly cut boneless pork
chops, about 1 lb (450 g) in
total, trimmed of fat

2 tbsp all-purpose flour

1 egg, beaten

3–5 tbsp sunflower oil

lemon wedges, to serve

**For the lemon and garlic
mayonnaise**

4 heaping tbsp mayonnaise

4 tbsp finely chopped fresh
flat-leaf parsley

1 garlic clove, crushed

finely grated zest of
1 lemon

squeeze of lemon juice

SPICY SCHNITZELS WITH LEMON AND GARLIC MAYONNAISE

This is a classic Wiener schnitzel, except I've used pork instead of veal, as it's less expensive and more available, but just as tender. I like to serve it with a simply dressed tomato and red onion salad.

1. Preheat the oven to 325°F (160°C). Spread the bread on a baking sheet and bake for 20 minutes or until crisp and dry, turning halfway through cooking. Remove from the oven and let cool a little, then break the slices (with their crusts) into pieces and drop them into a food processor fitted with a metal blade. Add the peppercorns, paprika, salt, and chilies and process to fine crumbs.

2. Beat out the pork chops and coat first in the flour, then in the egg, and finally in the breadcrumbs (see below: *Prepare the chops for frying*). In a small bowl, combine all the ingredients for the lemon and garlic mayonnaise.

Cover and chill the mayonnaise in the fridge until serving time.

3. Heat 3 tablespoons of the oil in a large, nonstick frying pan over medium heat. Add 2 of the breaded chops (schnitzels) and fry for 1–2 minutes on each side or until golden brown and crisp. As they fry, press down hard with a spatula to ensure they make contact with the pan. Drain and keep warm while frying the rest. If you need more oil, be sure it is hot before adding the meat. Serve immediately, with the mayonnaise and lemon wedges.

KEYS TO PERFECTION

Prepare the chops for frying

1 Cover a chop with plastic wrap and pound to flatten using a heavy-based pan (a pan is better than a rolling pin because it's flat, so it doesn't leave ridge marks). Beat the meat as thinly as possible without tearing it.

2 Coat the chops in the spicy breadcrumb mixture. You want an even coating of flour (shake off the excess), then egg (let excess drain back into the dish), then breadcrumbs (pat them firmly into the egg so they stick).

PREPARE THE DISH A DAY AHEAD

You can prepare the garlic and lemon mayonnaise and get the schnitzels ready for frying up to 24 hours ahead. If not frying the schnitzels right away, arrange them in a single layer on a large plate and put them in the fridge uncovered, or the coating will get soggy.

SERVES 6 GENEROUSLY

Special equipment
Utility knife (or ask your butcher to make the incisions)

1 boneless loin of pork, 3 lb 10 oz (1.65 kg)

4 tsp olive oil

2 tsp coarse sea salt

salt and freshly ground black pepper

¾ oz (20 g) fresh rosemary sprigs

For the stuffing

2 tbsp (30 g) butter

1 onion, finely chopped

1½ cups (125 g) fresh white breadcrumbs

1 large egg, beaten

3 tbsp coarsely chopped fresh sage

1 tbsp finely chopped fresh rosemary

1 heaping tbsp capers, chopped

2 tsp anchovy paste

finely grated zest of 1 orange

For the gravy

2 tbsp (20 g) butter

2 tbsp (20 g) all-purpose flour

½ cup (100 ml) dry white wine

1¼ cups (300 ml) chicken stock

juice of 1 orange (5–6 tbsp)

2 tsp red currant jelly

2 tsp Dijon or grainy mustard

1 tsp very finely chopped fresh sage

ROAST LOIN OF PORK

Crispy crackling is hard to resist, but it's not always easy to get right if you keep the skin on the pork. If you cook the skin separately, as shown here, you'll have success every time.

1. Make the stuffing: melt the butter in a small, nonstick frying pan, add the onion, and fry for 8–10 minutes over medium–low heat until softened but not browned, stirring occasionally. Put the remaining stuffing ingredients into a bowl. Add the softened onion and the butter and mix well.

2. Remove the skin from the pork and make small incisions all over the skin using the utility knife (see p142: *Make crispy crackling*). Alternatively, ask the butcher to do this. Rub the skin with 2 teaspoons of the oil, then the coarse sea salt. Place the skin, salted-side up, on a rack in a roasting pan.

3. Preheat the oven to 425°F (220°C). Place the pork loin, skinned-side down, on a board and open out the meat to make room for the stuffing. Place the stuffing on the pork, then fold over and roll the meat to enclose it. Turn the meat over so that the seam is underneath. Tie the loin with string. Brush with the remaining 2 teaspoons of oil, sprinkle with salt and pepper, and tuck rosemary sprigs under the string. Put the pork in a roasting pan. (See pp142–143: *Stuff, roll, and tie the loin*.)

4. Place the pork on a low rack in the oven, with the pan of crackling on the shelf above. Roast for 30 minutes, then reduce the oven temperature to 350°F (180°C) and

roast for another 1½ hours. (If you have a meat thermometer, the internal temperature should reach 165°F/ 75°C.) Check after 30–45 minutes to see if the crackling is crisp enough. If it is, remove it from the oven and keep it warm. Transfer the pork to a board, cover loosely with a tent of foil, and set aside to rest for 20 minutes.

5. Make the gravy: put the butter in the roasting pan and place the pan on a stovetop burner set to medium–low heat. Stir until the butter has melted, scraping up any sediment from the bottom of the pan, then sprinkle in the flour and cook for 1–2 minutes, whisking constantly.

6. Pour in the wine and whisk vigorously to combine, then slowly whisk in the stock and orange juice and bring to a boil. Add the red currant jelly, mustard, and sage. Simmer over medium–high heat for about 5 minutes, whisking all the time, until the jelly has melted and the gravy thickens. Season with salt and pepper. Keep on a very gentle simmer until serving time, whisking occasionally.

7. Cut the crackling into strips with scissors or a sharp knife, or snap it with your fingers. Remove the string from the pork, carve, and serve with the crackling and piping-hot gravy in a jug or gravy boat.

KEYS TO PERFECTION
See pp142–143

KEYS TO PERFECTION

Make crispy crackling

1 Remove the skin from the loin. Using a very sharp chef's knife in a sawing action, cut horizontally between the meat and the skin, taking most of the fat away with the skin.

2 Using a utility knife, make parallel cuts in the skin, about ½in (1cm) apart, working from the center out, then from the center out to the opposite side. Cut right through the skin into the fat beneath. Massage olive oil into the skin, then rub coarse sea salt all over the surface, working it into the cuts with your fingers. Place the skin on a rack in a roasting pan with the salted side facing up.

Stuff, roll, and tie the loin

1 To open out, or "butterfly" the loin, place the loin flat on a board, skinned-side down. Using a very sharp chef's knife and starting at the fattier side of the loin, make a horizontal cut through the center of the thick, meaty part of the loin, stopping short of the opposite edge. Work slowly, using a sawing action with the knife.

2 Lift up the flap of meat and fold it back like the page of a book, so that the loin lies flat on the board.

Stuff, roll, and tie the loin (continued)

3 Place the caper and herb stuffing along the central groove created by opening out the loin, and squash it into a long sausage shape using your hands.

4 Cover the stuffing with the flap of meat, folding it over and tucking it in. Now roll the pork over and keep rolling firmly. The seam should end up underneath.

5 Take a piece of string that is 6 times longer than the length of the loin and run it lengthwise around the bottom and top of the loin. Cross the string at one end of the loin and run it lengthwise again, this time around the sides of the loin. Tie at one end. Cut 4 pieces of string about 8in (20cm) longer than the circumference of the loin and tie them at regular intervals around the meat.

6 Oil and season the loin all over, and tuck sprigs of rosemary under the string on top of the loin. Put the pork in a roasting pan.

SERVES 4

2 red bell peppers, halved, cored, and seeded

olive oil, for brushing

4 boneless, lean pork chops, about 6 oz (175 g) each and ideally 1in (2.5cm) thick

salt and freshly ground black pepper

For the sauce

2 tbsp olive oil

1 onion, finely chopped

2 garlic cloves, finely chopped

14 oz (400 g) can chopped tomatoes

1 tsp sugar

¼ tsp dried crushed chilies

PORK CHOPS ARRABBIATA

*Arrabbiata is a tomato sauce made spicy with crushed chilies,
and it really livens up grilled pork chops for a no-fuss supper.
Serve with spaghetti tossed in olive oil and shredded basil.*

1. Preheat the broiler to its highest setting for 5 minutes. Place the pepper halves, cut-side down, on a lightly oiled baking sheet and broil about 4in (10cm) from the heat for 15–20 minutes or until well blistered and charred. Transfer the peppers to a plastic food bag, seal, and let cool completely.

2. While the peppers are broiling, make the sauce: heat the oil in a medium pan, add the onion and garlic, and fry over medium–high heat for 5–6 minutes or until softened and starting to brown. Stir in the tomatoes, sugar, and chilies. Simmer for 12–15 minutes, stirring occasionally. When the peppers are cool, remove them from the bag and peel off the skins. Chop two of the pepper halves into small pieces and stir into the sauce. (See below: *Thick, piquant sauce*.) Season. Set aside with the remaining pepper halves.

3. Lightly trim the chops, brush both sides with oil, and season with pepper. Broil the chops about 4in (10cm) from the heat for about 8 minutes on each side or until the juices run clear. Remove to a warmed serving dish, season with salt, and keep warm. (See below: *Moist, tender pork*.)

4. Broil the remaining pepper halves for about 1 minute to heat through, then cut into long, thin strips. Reheat the sauce and serve with the broiled chops and sliced peppers.

KEYS TO PERFECTION

Thick, piquant sauce

Simmer the sauce until it's fairly thick but still moist, then add the chopped red pepper. It should be chopped fairly small so it blends in well. As well as enlivening the flavor, the peppers will add good texture.

Moist, tender pork

1 Remove and discard a little of the fat, but not too much, as a thin layer of fat keeps the meat moist as it broils and also improves the flavor. Oil and season with pepper but not salt at this stage, as salt draws out the juices.

2 Time the broiling carefully, because if the pork is overcooked it will be dry. It's important to have the broiler very hot, and watch the chops as they cook, turning only once with tongs. Add salt after cooking.

SERVES 10

1 bone-in, smoked, butt portion, wet-cured, skinned ham, about 6¼ lb (2.4 kg) (see p148, box)

3 (12 oz) bottles hard cider

2 cups (500 ml) orange juice

6in (15cm) cinnamon stick, snapped in half

5 star anise

For the relish

2 oranges

½ cup mango chutney

5 heaping tbsp cranberry sauce

½ tsp five-spice powder

salt and freshly ground black pepper

For the decoration

¼ cup mango chutney

about 30 whole cloves

GLAZED HAM WITH SPICED CRANBERRY RELISH

I like to decorate this glazed ham the traditional way – in a diamond pattern, studded with cloves. The subtly spiced, fruity flavorings and cranberry relish make it that little bit special.

1. Make the relish: finely grate the zest of the oranges into a small bowl. Peel and segment the oranges, holding them over the bowl to catch the juice. Roughly chop the segments and place in a medium pan with the orange zest and juice, mango chutney, cranberry sauce, and five-spice powder.

2. Bring to a boil and simmer over medium–high heat for about 5 minutes or until thickened, stirring often. Remove from the heat, add a good pinch of salt and a few grindings of pepper, and pour into a small heatproof bowl. Let cool, cover, and chill in the fridge until serving time.

3. Preheat the oven to 325°F (160°C). Place the ham, cut-side down, in a large, lidded, ovenproof pan or Dutch oven. Pour in the cider and orange juice and add enough cold water so the liquid covers the ham (you will need about 4 cups/750 ml of water). Add the cinnamon and star anise, cover the pan, and bring the liquid to a boil on the stove, then allow it to simmer for a few minutes. Transfer to the oven and cook for 2 to 2½ hours. Remove the pan from the oven and turn the ham over in the liquid. Set aside until lukewarm, turning over once or twice during this time, then lift the meat out of the liquid and place it on a large board. Save 2 cups of the cooking liquid and discard the rest. (See p148: *Cook the ham in liquid.*)

4. To decorate, score the fat of the ham in a diamond pattern. Brush the scored fat with mango chutney all over, then stud with cloves. Wrap aluminum foil around the sides of the meat, so only the glazed fat is showing— this prevents the meat from drying out. (See p149: *Decorate and glaze the ham before roasting.*)

5. Preheat the oven to 425°F (220°C). Place the ham on a rack in the roasting pan and pour the reserved liquid into the bottom of the pan. Roast for 25–30 minutes or until bubbling and glazed to a dark golden color.

6. Transfer the ham to a cutting board, cover loosely with aluminum foil to keep warm, and let it rest for 15–20 minutes before carving into thick or thin slices, as you wish. This resting time lets the juices be distributed more evenly through the meat so that the fibers relax, making the meat easy to carve into neat slices. Serve hot or cold, with the chilled relish on the side.

KEYS TO PERFECTION
See pp148–149

KEYS TO PERFECTION

Cook the ham in liquid

1 It's important that the ham fits snugly in the pan, skin-side up, and is totally covered by liquid. For this size of roast, use a 10in (25cm) lidded ovenproof pan or a Dutch oven with a capacity of 5 quarts.

2 With the lid on the pan, bring the liquid to a boil over high heat. This may take longer than you think, about 10 minutes, but it's essential for the cooking time in the oven to be accurate. Once the liquid is bubbling, let it simmer for a few minutes to get the cooking started before transferring the pan to the oven.

3 At the end of cooking, you can check the internal temperature of the ham if you have a meat thermometer—it should be around 175°F (80°C). Let the ham cool down in the liquid for at least 2–3 hours. During this time, the meat will continue cooking in the residual heat, which will help redistribute the juices evenly through the meat and make it easier to slice.

BUYING THE RIGHT HAM

Most hams available in grocery stores are bone-in and fully cooked. These types of hams are cured and smoked. Even though they can be eaten as-is, they are even more delicious baked with a sweet glaze on top. For the best flavor, avoid hams that have been injected with a saltwater or liquid smoke solution. They typically will have labels that read "ham, water added" or "ham and water product."

Decorate and glaze the ham before roasting

1 Cut the string off the ham, then using a sharp knife, strip the skin away from the fat. Start at one end of the joint and cut slowly using a horizontal sawing action, holding the skin in one hand while you cut with the knife in the other.

2 With the tip of the same knife, score parallel diagonal lines in the fat to make a diamond pattern. For this size of ham roast, cutting 8 lines in one direction and 9 lines in the other will make an attractive pattern, but you could do more or fewer, as you prefer and according to the size of your roast.

3 Brush the mango chutney evenly all over the top of the ham, working it into the cuts in the fat, then press cloves into the intersections of the diamond shapes. The chutney glaze gives the fat a deliciously sweet finish and the cloves give a decorative effect.

PREPARING THE HAM AND RELISH AHEAD

The ham can be prepared up to the end of step 3 of the method several hours in advance. Once roasted, you can keep the ham in the fridge for up to 5 days and slice it as and when you need it. When the ham is sliced right from the fridge, you'll be able to get thinner slices and up to double the number of servings. The cranberry relish can be made several days ahead and kept in a rigid container in the fridge. It's best served chilled.

Special equipment
*12 wooden skewers,
about 8in (20cm) long*

*1 lb 2 oz (500 g) minced
lamb*

*1 small onion, very finely
chopped*

*¾ oz (20 g) piece of fresh
ginger, peeled and very
finely chopped*

*1 garlic clove, very finely
chopped*

1 tsp harissa paste

*1 heaping tbsp instant
oatmeal*

1 large egg, beaten

*½ oz (15 g) fresh cilantro
leaves and stalks, very finely
chopped, plus 1–2 tbsp
chopped leaves, to garnish*

*salt and freshly ground
black pepper*

For the tzatziki

2 tbsp chopped fresh mint

1 garlic clove, crushed

2 tsp mint sauce

½ tsp granulated sugar

*8 oz (200 g) tub Greek-style
yogurt*

*¼ cucumber, about 2½ oz
(75 g), peeled and diced*

*extra virgin olive oil,
to drizzle*

LAMB KOFTA KEBABS WITH TZATZIKI

Instant oatmeal may seem an unlikely ingredient for these hot, spicy kebabs, but I got the idea from an Indian friend, who said there's nothing better for binding the mixture and giving a good texture.

1. Put the lamb into a large bowl with the onion, ginger, garlic, harissa paste, oats, and egg. Add the cilantro leaves and stalks and season well. Mix everything together with your hands until well combined (see below: *Mold well for firm kebabs*, step 1). Cover and chill in the fridge for 1–48 hours.

2. Make the tzatziki: put the mint, garlic, mint sauce, sugar, and some salt into a bowl. Stir with a fork, then whisk in the yogurt. Add the cucumber. Cover and chill until serving time. Soak the skewers (see below, box).

3. Drain the skewers and preheat the grill to its highest setting. Divide the lamb mixture into 12 equal-sized portions, roll each into a ball, and mold to shape

around the skewers (see below: *Mold well for firm kebabs*, step 2).

4. Arrange the skewers on the broiler rack over a broiler pan. Broil for 8–10 minutes or until the kebabs are sizzling and turning brown. Turn them once and do not overcook—they should be juicy.

5. Transfer the tzatziki to a serving bowl and drizzle with the oil. Serve the kebabs, on or off the skewers, drizzled with the pan juices and sprinkled with the cilantro leaves. Pass around the bowl of tzatziki separately.

KEYS TO PERFECTION

Mold well for firm kebabs

1 Use your hands to combine all the kebab ingredients, pressing and squeezing the meat for several minutes until it looks almost like a paste. Chill the mixture.

2 Form the chilled mixture into 12 balls and push a skewer through the center of each. With wet hands, squish the meat around the skewer into a long torpedo shape.

SOAK THE SKEWERS BEFORE USE

Wooden skewers are best for these kebabs, because the meat sticks to them better than it does to metal skewers. To prevent the wood from burning under the broiler, soak the skewers in a dish of cold water for 6 hours before using.

SERVES 6

1 whole shoulder of lamb, about 5 lb (2.25 kg), blade bone removed and tied, and excess fat removed

1 tbsp olive oil, plus extra for greasing

4 tsp chopped fresh rosemary

4 tsp chopped fresh thyme

2 garlic cloves, crushed

salt and freshly ground black pepper

1 tbsp red currant jelly

For the vegetable layer

2¼ lb (1 kg) fluffy potatoes, such as russet

1 lb 10 oz (750 g) parsnips

1 large onion

6 garlic cloves

a few fresh thyme sprigs

a few fresh rosemary sprigs

1¾ cups (425 ml) dry white wine

1¾ cups (425 ml) chicken stock

SLOW-ROAST LAMB LYONNAISE

*Cooking the lamb slowly, on a bed of potatoes and parsnips,
ensures everything becomes very tender with lots of flavor.
It's a meal in itself, but I like to serve a green vegetable, too.*

1. Make incisions in the top of the lamb with a small, sharp knife. Put the oil into a small bowl with 2 teaspoons each of the chopped rosemary and thyme, the garlic, ½ teaspoon salt, and a good grinding of pepper. Mix to a paste and rub all over the skin of the lamb, working it into the incisions with your fingers. (See p154: *Add flavor to the meat*.)

2. Preheat the oven to 425°F (220°C). Prepare the vegetable layer: peel all the vegetables (including the garlic), then cut the potatoes into slices about ¼in (5mm) thick, the parsnips into slices about ½in (1cm) thick, and the onion into thin rings. Brush the inside of a large roasting pan with oil. Put the vegetables into the pan with some salt and pepper and add the garlic cloves and sprigs of thyme and rosemary. Combine the wine and stock and pour over the vegetables. (See p154: *Prepare the vegetables for even cooking*.)

3. Place the lamb on top of the vegetables, put the roasting pan in the oven, and roast for 40 minutes until the lamb is golden brown. Reduce the oven temperature to 325°F (160°C) and roast for another 4 hours.

4. Transfer the lamb to a cutting board, cover loosely with aluminum foil, and let rest for 15–20 minutes. Meanwhile, lift the vegetables out of the cooking liquid with a slotted spoon and transfer them to a baking dish. Place the dish in the oven while you make the gravy.

5. Pour the cooking liquid into a liquid measuring cup and let it stand for about 5 minutes or until the fat has risen to the top. Scoop off the fat with a spoon, then pour the remaining juices into a pan and add the red currant jelly. Bring to a boil, whisking all the time, then reduce the heat. Add the remaining 2 teaspoons each of chopped rosemary and thyme, and taste for seasoning. Let simmer gently on the stove while the lamb rests, whisking occasionally, until you are ready to serve. (See p155: *Make a flavorful red currant gravy*.)

6. To serve, remove the string from the lamb and carve the meat into thick slices. Serve with the dish of potatoes, parsnips, and onion, and the gravy in a jug or gravy boat.

KEYS TO PERFECTION
See pp154–155

KEYS TO PERFECTION

Add flavor to the meat

1 To inject flavor into the meat and ensure crispy skin, make about 12 deep slits in the lamb with a sharp knife. Space these incisions at regular intervals all over the top part of the lamb (the side with the skin), cutting through the skin deep into the meat to make little "pockets" about ¾in (2cm) long.

2 Use a teaspoon to mix the oil, herbs, garlic, and seasoning to a paste in a small bowl, then tip the paste on top of the lamb and spread it out with your fingers. Rub the paste all over the skin, pressing it into the incisions in the meat.

Prepare the vegetables for even cooking

1 The vegetables are all sliced into different thicknesses according to how long they take to cook. Cut the parsnips on the diagonal, and don't worry if the cores seem a little tough. The parsnips are cooked for so long that any toughness will disappear. Don't be tempted to slice the potatoes ahead of time and keep them in water, as this will wash away some of the starch that's needed to hold them together.

2 When the potato, parsnip, and onion slices are in the roasting pan with the seasoning, toss the vegetables with your hands to mix everything together, then spread them out in an even layer so that they all take the same time to cook. Push the whole garlic cloves and sprigs of thyme and rosemary in among the vegetables and drench them with the white wine and chicken stock.

Make a flavorful red currant gravy

1 Shoulder of lamb is fairly fatty compared with the leg and loin. During long, slow roasting, the fat melts into the meat and vegetables to make them very tender and flavorful, but the gravy is better without it. After removing the vegetables from the liquid using a slotted spoon, pour the juices from the pan into a liquid measuring cup and set aside. The fat will rise to the top and float on the surface.

2 Using a metal spoon, skim the fat off the surface and discard. Do this slowly and carefully, a spoonful at a time, trying not to disturb the juices underneath. You won't manage to remove all of the fat, but it doesn't matter at this stage.

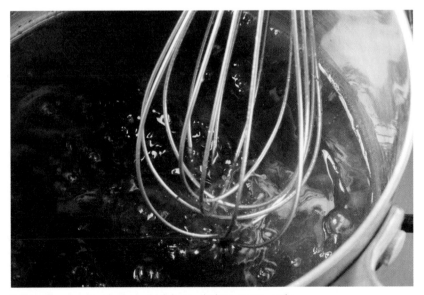

3 Bring the gravy to a boil over high heat, whisking continuously, then reduce the heat and let it simmer, whisking occasionally. Any remaining fat will disperse throughout the gravy and the red currant jelly will absorb any greasiness.

BUYING AND CARVING SHOULDER OF LAMB

Shoulder of lamb is one of the best cuts to slow-roast for succulent and juicy meat, but it has an odd shape that can be difficult to carve. For ease of carving, ask your butcher to remove the blade bone and then tie the meat with string to hold it together. Remove the string before carving.

SERVES 6

6 lamb neck filets, about
1¾–2 lb (800–900 g) in total

2–3 tbsp olive oil

1 large onion,
finely chopped

2 garlic cloves, crushed

½ tsp ground cinnamon

½ tsp ground allspice

14 oz (400 g) can chopped
tomatoes

2 tbsp tomato paste

1¼ cup (300 ml) dry
white wine

2 tbsp lemon juice

2 tsp sugar

1 chicken bouillon cube

1 tbsp chopped
fresh thyme

salt and freshly ground
black pepper

9 oz (250 g) orzo
(see below, box)

To serve

3 oz (85 g) feta cheese

1 tbsp chopped
fresh thyme

1 tbsp chopped fresh mint

finely grated zest of
1 lemon (optional)

GREEK LAMB PILAF WITH ORZO

This one-pot meal needs only a green salad to accompany it.
You can make it a day ahead up to the end of step 3. To serve,
heat it until bubbling, add the orzo, and continue with the recipe.

1. Preheat the oven to 325°F (160°C). Cut each neck filet in half lengthwise, without trimming away any fat, then cut each halved filet crosswise into 6–8 bite-sized pieces (see below: *Use the right lamb*). Heat 2 tablespoons of the oil in a large, nonstick frying pan until hot, and sear the lamb in 4 batches over medium–high heat until browned on all sides. You may need to add another tablespoon of oil. As each batch is seared, transfer the lamb to a large Dutch oven using a slotted spoon.

2. Reduce the heat and add the onion to the frying pan. Fry, stirring often, for 3 minutes until golden brown. Add the garlic, cinnamon, and allspice and fry for 1–2 minutes, then add the onion mix to the casserole.

3. Pour the canned tomatoes over the meat and onion. Fill the tomato can twice with water and add to the casserole. Stir, then add the tomato paste, wine, lemon juice, and sugar. Crumble in the stock cube and add the thyme, ½ teaspoon salt, and pepper to taste. Bring to a boil, stirring, then cover the pan and transfer to the oven. Cook for 2 hours, stirring halfway.

4. Stir in the orzo, cover the pan again, and return to the oven. Cook for another 20 minutes or until the orzo is plump and tender, stirring halfway (see below: *Time the orzo*). To serve, gently stir the meat and orzo, crumble the feta over the top, and sprinkle with the herbs and lemon zest, if using.

KEYS TO PERFECTION

Use the right lamb
Neck filets are ideal for this dish: marbled with fat, the meat becomes juicy and tender when slow-cooked. Don't confuse them with the leaner loin filets, which would become dry.

Time the orzo
Orzo swells quickly to several times its size, so don't use too much and be careful not to overcook it. Stir after 10 minutes' cooking, or it can clump together and stick to the pan.

BUYING AND USING ORZO

Orzo looks like large grains of rice, but it is in fact a small pasta shape made from durum wheat. Mostly used in soups and stews, it is readily available in the pasta section at supermarkets and Italian delicatessens. I like it in this Greek stew, because it swells to just the right size if cooked properly and complements the lamb.

PASTA AND RICE

SERVES 4

1 lb 2 oz (500g) baby
squid, either whole or
pre-prepared baby squid
pouches (see p162, box)

1¼ cups (300ml) dry
white wine

2 garlic cloves, crushed

salt and freshly ground
black pepper

1¼ cups (300ml)
heavy cream

finely grated zest of
1 lemon

juice of ½ lemon

14 oz (400g) linguine

pat of butter

½ tsp anchovy paste

5½ oz (150g) cooked,
peeled jumbo shrimp

2 tbsp (25g) fresh
flat-leaf parsley, chopped

CREAMY SEAFOOD LINGUINE

*This creamy pasta dish reminds me of summer's warmth
and relaxing vacations. However, it's delicious any time of year,
bringing you a taste of the sea wherever you are.*

1. If using whole squid, prepare it as follows: pull the tentacles from the body pouch (the head and guts will be attached), then cut off the tentacles just below the eyes. Retain the tentacles and discard the head and guts. At the top of the tentacles you may find a small, hard black "beak;" squeeze it out and discard it. Feel inside the pouch and remove and discard the "quill" (a clear sliver of cartilage that feels like a plastic shard). Wash the inside of the pouch thoroughly and peel off the spotty purplish outer skin. Rinse the tentacles in cold water.

2. Slice the pouches into rings, about ¼in (5mm) wide. Put the rings and prepared tentacles (if using whole squid) into a Dutch oven with the wine and garlic. Grind in plenty of black pepper. Bring to a simmer over medium heat, cover the pan, and simmer gently for 10 minutes. Transfer the squid to a bowl and set aside. (See p162: *Well-prepared, tender squid.*)

3. Add the cream, lemon zest and juice to the liquid in the pan. Let it bubble over high heat for 5–7 minutes, occasionally stirring it in from the edge of the pan with a wooden spoon. Simmer the sauce until thickened and reduced by about half.

4. Cook the linguine in a large pan of salted boiling water for 10–15 minutes, or according to package instructions. Drain, reserving a cupful of the pasta cooking water. (See p163: *Cook pasta the foolproof way.*)

5. Add the butter and anchovy paste to the cream sauce, stirring until they are melted. Taste for seasoning, adding salt if needed. Stir in the reserved squid, the shrimp, and half the parsley. Leave the sauce over a low heat to gently warm through the squid and shrimp. Don't let them overcook, or they will become rubbery.

6. Add the cooked linguine to the sauce and toss to mix, adding a splash or two of the reserved pasta cooking water to get the consistency you like (you may not need it all). Transfer to a serving bowl, sprinkle with the remaining parsley, and serve immediately.

KEYS TO PERFECTION
See pp162–163

KEYS TO PERFECTION

Well-prepared, tender squid

1 Lay the squid on a board. If using whole squid, hold the body pouch with one hand and pull the tentacles with the other. The tentacles should come away easily, together with the head and guts. Using a sharp knife, cut off the tentacles just below the eyes and discard the head and guts. Remove the "beak" from the tentacles, if necessary, and discard. Take out the "quill" from inside the pouch and discard. Repeat for all the squid.

2 Thoroughly rinse the inside of the pouch and peel away the dark outer skin, so you're left with white meat. Rinse the tentacles under cold running water. Whether you're using whole squid or pre-prepared pouches, slice the pouches across into equal-sized rings.

3 Cook the squid rings and tentacles, if using, in a covered casserole with the wine and garlic until tender. The squid will turn opaque and will shrink in size. Using a slotted spoon, lift the cooked squid out of the wine a few pieces at a time and transfer to a bowl. Hold the spoon against the side of the pan and let the liquid drain through. The wine in the pan, now flavored by the squid, will be used as the base for a delicious creamy sauce.

BUYING AND USING SQUID

You can buy squid rings, but sometimes these can be quite large and chewy. I prefer to buy whole baby squid, as shown here, then prepare and slice it into rings myself. Alternatively, pre-prepared baby squid pouches are available, which reduce the preparation time, but they won't have the decorative tentacles attached.

Cook pasta the foolproof way

1 Three-quarters fill a 5-quart (5-liter) pan with cold water. With the lid on the pan, bring the water to a boil over high heat. Add 1 tablespoon of salt (the water will bubble furiously), then add the linguine. Lower the strands into the water and bend and coil them around as they soften until they're submerged.

2 Bring the water back to a rolling boil and cook the linguine over high heat with the pan uncovered. Stir from time to time to keep the strands separate and prevent them from sticking together.

3 After 10 minutes, lift out a strand or two with tongs and bite into the pasta. The usual cooking time is 10 minutes for al dente (tender but firm to the bite) or 12–15 minutes if you like your pasta a little softer. Scoop out a cupful of the cooking water and reserve. This will be used when you coat the linguine in the sauce—the starch in the water helps the sauce cling to the pasta.

4 Tip the contents of the pan into a large colander placed over the sink and shake the colander to let the water drain through. This prevents the pasta from becoming waterlogged and soggy.

SERVES 4

1 oz (30 g) pine nuts

4 tbsp olive oil

1 onion, finely chopped

3 garlic cloves, crushed

14 oz (400 g) cherry vine tomatoes, halved

½ tsp granulated sugar

salt and freshly ground black pepper

12 oz (350 g) penne

9 oz (250 g) Broccolini, ends trimmed and halved lengthwise

1 tbsp chopped fresh flat-leaf parsley

3 tbsp shredded fresh basil

1¾ oz (50 g) pecorino cheese, grated or shaved into strips

PENNE WITH CHERRY TOMATO SAUCE

*There is so much flavor in this simple, colorful pasta dish,
it doesn't need any meat or fish added. It's the perfect vegetarian supper,
topped with pecorino cheese to finish it off.*

1. Heat a large, nonstick frying pan until hot. Add the pine nuts and dry-fry over medium–low heat for a few minutes, tossing them in the pan, until golden brown. Transfer them to a small bowl and set aside.

2. Heat 2 tablespoons of the oil in the same frying pan. Add the onion and garlic and fry for 6–8 minutes or until softened and just starting to brown. Add another tablespoon of oil and heat, then stir in the tomatoes and sugar. Fry for 2–3 minutes or until the tomatoes have softened and released their juices but have not lost their shape. Season and set aside.

3. Plunge the penne into a large pan of salted boiling water and cook for 10–12 minutes. About 3 minutes before the end of the cooking time, add the broccolini.

Reserve some of the cooking water (see below: *Use the pasta cooking water*, step 1). Drain the pasta and broccolini.

4. Heat the tomatoes through and stir in about 4 tablespoons of the pasta cooking water (see below: *Use the pasta cooking water*, step 2). Add the pasta and broccolini to the tomatoes and toss gently with a couple more tablespoons of the cooking water, if needed. Stir in the parsley and basil. To serve, scatter the pine nuts on top, drizzle with the remaining tablespoon of oil, sprinkle the pecorino, and add an extra grinding of pepper.

KEYS TO PERFECTION

Use the pasta cooking water

1 After the pasta is cooked, scoop out and reserve a couple of ladlefuls of the cooking water for the sauce. The starch in the water helps the sauce cling to the pasta, and it also extends the sauce.

2 Spoon some of the reserved pasta water into the tomato juices—about 4 tablespoons to start with. You're aiming for a light sauce, just enough to coat the pasta. You don't want to drown it and can add more if you need to.

SERVES 6

Special equipment
*2 quart (2.2–2.5 liter)
baking dish, about
14 x 10in (35 x 25cm)
and 2in (5cm) deep*

3 tbsp olive oil

*1 onion, very finely
chopped, plus ¼ onion*

*1 carrot, very finely
chopped*

*2 stalks of celery, very
finely chopped*

10 oz (300 g) minced beef

10 oz (300 g) minced pork

1 large garlic clove, crushed

3 tbsp tomato paste

½ cup (75 ml) red wine

*1½ tbsp chopped fresh
thyme*

*salt and freshly ground
black pepper*

*2½ cups (600 ml) full-fat or
semi-skim milk*

1 bay leaf

a few black peppercorns

2 tbsp (40 g) butter

*2 tbsp (40 g) all-purpose
flour*

a few gratings of nutmeg

*24 oz (680 g) jar tomato
sauce*

18 cannelloni tubes

*2½ oz (75 g) aged Cheddar
cheese, coarsely grated*

*1¼ oz (40 g) Parmesan
cheese, coarsely grated*

CANNELLONI WITH DOUBLE CHEESE SAUCE

I've used both a tomato and a béchamel sauce for this luxurious version of the classic cannelloni. Using a combination of beef and pork is traditional in northern Italy and gives great flavor.

1. Make the filling: heat the oil in a large, deep, nonstick frying pan over medium heat. Add the chopped onion, carrot, and celery and fry gently for about 10 minutes or until softened but not browned, stirring often. Add the beef, pork, and garlic and fry for about 5 minutes or until the meat loses its redness, stirring frequently and breaking up lumps with a wooden spoon.

2. Stir in the tomato paste, wine, 1 tablespoon of the thyme, and some salt and pepper. Cook for about 10 minutes, stirring often, until the mixture is very dry. Remove from the heat and set aside.

3. Make the béchamel sauce: pour the milk into a small pan, add the bay leaf, peppercorns, and onion quarter and bring just to a boil. Cover the pan, remove from the heat, and leave to infuse for 30 minutes, then strain into a measuring cup. Melt the butter in a pan over medium heat, add the flour, and cook for 1–2 minutes. Remove the pan from the heat and gradually add the strained milk, whisking all the time. Return to the heat and whisk until the sauce thickens. Season with the nutmeg and salt and pepper. Set aside. (See p168: *Make a classic, smooth béchamel sauce.*)

4. Heat the tomato sauce in a pan with ¾ cup (200 ml) water, the remaining ½ tablespoon of thyme, and some salt and pepper. Cover the bottom of the baking dish with about half the sauce mixture.

5. Stir 6 tablespoons of the béchamel sauce into the meat, pressing with a fork to mash the mixture together. Fill the cannelloni tubes with the meat mixture and arrange side by side in the dish. (See p169: *Fill and arrange the tubes with care.*) If you have any leftover meat mixture, tuck it in between the tubes. Cover with the remaining sauce mixture, and wiggle the tubes apart so that the sauce runs between them.

6. Pour the remaining béchamel sauce over the cannelloni and shake the dish so that it settles evenly around the tubes. Sprinkle the Cheddar and Parmesan over the top, then let stand for at least 2 hours (see p169, box).

7. When you are ready to bake, preheat the oven to 375°F (190°C). Bake the cannelloni for 45 minutes or until bubbling and golden brown. Check that the tubes are soft by piercing them with a skewer, and cook a little longer if necessary.

KEYS TO PERFECTION
See pp168–169

KEYS TO PERFECTION

Make a classic, smooth béchamel sauce

1 First, infuse the milk with the flavorings: "scald" the milk in a pan over medium–high heat (that is, bring it to just below the boiling point). Watch carefully, and turn off the heat as soon as you see tiny bubbles appear around the edge, as the milk can quickly boil over or scorch on the bottom of the pan. Cover the pan and remove from the heat. Leave to infuse for about 30 minutes, then strain the milk into a measuring cup to remove the flavorings.

2 Melt the butter over medium heat until it foams, then sprinkle in the flour and mix it immediately with the butter using a small balloon whisk. Keep whisking for 1–2 minutes. The butter and flour mixture ("roux") must cook properly, or you'll taste raw flour in the sauce. When the mixture changes color from white to pale golden, remove the pan from the heat. Don't let this "blond roux" turn brown, as the color and flavor of the sauce will be impaired.

3 With the pan off the heat, pour in the strained milk a little at a time, whisking constantly and vigorously to work it into the roux and keep the sauce smooth. Not all recipes for béchamel sauce use hot or warm milk, but I find the roux absorbs it better than cold milk, and it also helps to prevent lumps from forming.

4 Once you've added all the milk, return the pan to medium heat and cook for a few minutes more until the sauce thickens, still whisking continuously. The finished sauce should have a medium–thick consistency. If it coats the back of a wooden spoon without running off, it is ready to use.

Fill and arrange the tubes with care

1 Filling the tubes can be a messy job, but it's not difficult once you get the hang of it. First, make the meat mixture as smooth and dry as possible; a lumpy, sloppy mixture will be harder to work with. As you cook the meat, break up any lumps with a wooden spoon, then once the sauce is cooked, mash the béchamel into the meat mixture with a fork to make the filling even smoother. The béchamel will help to bind the meat together.

2 Hold a cannelloni tube upright in the palm of your hand so that the bottom end is sealed off. Take a teaspoonful of the meat mixture and push it into the tube right down to the bottom, using the handle of the spoon if you find this helps. Repeat with more filling until the tube is full along its entire length.

3 Lay the tubes in a single layer in the baking dish, which should measure about 14 x 10in (35 x 25cm) and 2in (5cm) deep. The size doesn't have to be exact, because it depends on the cannelloni you're using, but you should be able to leave a small gap between each tube. This allows room for the sauces to run between the tubes and lets the oven heat penetrate.

PREPARE AHEAD FOR BEST RESULTS

I like to prepare and assemble cannelloni (and lasagne) several hours before baking, and leave it covered at room temperature, as it allows the sauces to get absorbed into the pasta, making it softer and more flavorful. You can do this the day before, which is ideal if you're entertaining and want to get ahead. If keeping it overnight, cover the dish and place it in the fridge. Allow the cannelloni to come to room temperature for about an hour before baking, or it won't cook through in the time.

12 oz (350 g) spaghetti

salt and freshly ground black pepper

5½ oz (150 g) bacon, cut across into thin strips

3 tbsp olive oil

5½ oz (150 g) small crimini mushrooms, quartered

2 garlic cloves, crushed

2 large eggs, beaten

3 oz (85 g) Parmesan cheese, grated

4 tbsp heavy cream

1 tbsp chopped fresh flat-leaf parsley

MY NEW SPAGHETTI CARBONARA

*By adding crimini mushrooms and some bacon, I've
made this a more special pasta dish. It's perfect for when you want
to have supper made and ready to eat in less than half an hour.*

1. Cook the spaghetti in a large pan of salted, boiling water for about 10 minutes (or according to package instructions) until just tender. Meanwhile, heat a large, deep, nonstick frying pan or sauté pan, add the bacon, and fry over low heat until the fat starts to run. Pour in 1 tablespoon of the oil, increase the heat, and fry for 3–5 minutes or until the bacon is crisp, stirring. Remove using a slotted spoon and transfer to paper towels to drain.

2. Pour the remaining 2 tablespoons of oil into the frying pan, add the mushrooms and garlic, and fry over medium–high heat for 3–4 minutes or until the mushrooms are golden. Set aside.

3. In a small bowl, combine the eggs and most of the Parmesan (reserve 2 tablespoons for sprinkling). Season with salt and pepper. When the pasta is almost done, return the frying pan to low heat. Scoop out a cup of the pasta cooking water and reserve. Drain the pasta in a colander or large sieve.

4. Add the spaghetti to the pan with the bacon and mushrooms. Remove the pan from the heat and mix in the eggs and cheese. Stir in the cream and ½ cup (120 ml) of the reserved pasta cooking water. (See below: *Creamy, smooth eggs and sauce*.) Place the spaghetti on 4 plates or in bowls (see box, left) and scatter the parsley, reserved Parmesan, and a grinding of pepper on top.

KEYS TO PERFECTION

Creamy, smooth eggs and sauce

1 Mix in the eggs and cheese quickly off the heat, so the warmth of the pan and the other ingredients cook the eggs enough to lightly set them and keep them smooth, without scrambling them. Use tongs to lift the pasta.

2 Pour in the heavy cream and enough pasta cooking water to make a sauce that will coat the spaghetti strands. The consistency should be creamy. The high fat content in the heavy cream will enhance this.

HOW TO SERVE SPAGHETTI

You can, of course, simply pile spaghetti onto plates or into bowls in an informal way. However, for a neater, more stylish presentation, twirl the pasta around a long-pronged fork and place the twirl in a pile in the center of a plate, helping it off with a small fork; then, using the same technique, lay another, smaller pasta twirl on top of the first.

MARY'S TOP TIPS

Attractive presentation

Try to present your meals beautifully, on serving dishes that set off the food well. Even the simplest garnish, such as shavings of Parmesan cheese or a scattering of fresh herbs, can make a dish look so much more appetizing.

2 tbsp sunflower oil

*3 onions (2 halved
and thinly sliced,
1 finely chopped)*

*salt and freshly ground
black pepper*

*12 oz (350 g) smoked
undyed haddock fillets*

*3½ oz (100 g)
smoked salmon*

9 oz (250 g) basmati rice

3 cardamom pods, split

*½ cinnamon stick, about
1¼ in (3 cm) long*

½ tsp turmeric

2 large eggs

2 tbsp (30 g) butter

*½ cup (100 ml)
light cream*

*2 tbsp finely chopped
fresh cilantro*

cayenne pepper, to taste

juice of ½ lemon

SMOKED SALMON AND HADDOCK KEDGEREE

Gently spiced and slightly creamy, this is one of my suppertime favorites. The crispy onion topping isn't traditional, but it provides a wonderful contrast of color, flavor, and texture.

1. Heat 1 tablespoon of the oil and fry the sliced onions (see below: *Make the topping crispy*). Season with salt and pepper, drain on paper towels, and set aside in a warm place. Put the haddock, skin-side down, in a large frying pan and pour over enough water to just cover. Simmer, covered, over low heat for 5–8 minutes until opaque and cooked through. Remove from the heat. Lay the smoked salmon in the liquid, cover, and let stand for 2 minutes. Drain the fish and discard any skin and bones. Set aside.

2. Prepare the rice (see below: *Rinse the rice*). Heat the remaining tablespoon of oil in a large, nonstick, deep-sided frying pan or sauté pan. Add the chopped onion, cardamom pods, and cinnamon and fry over medium–high heat until the onion is golden, about 5 minutes.

Stir the drained rice into the onion in the pan. Pour in 2 cups (450 ml) cold water and stir in the turmeric. Bring to a boil. Reduce the heat to low, stir, cover, and cook for 12–15 minutes or until the water is absorbed. Take the rice off the heat and let it stand, covered, for 5 minutes before fluffing up the grains with a fork. Boil, peel, and quarter the eggs (see below: *Lightly hard-boil the eggs*).

3. Flake the fish into large pieces. Remove the cinnamon stick from the rice and carefully stir in the butter, cream, cilantro, fish, and eggs. Season with salt and cayenne pepper, and add the lemon juice. Heat through over low heat, stirring gently only once or twice so you don't break up the fish. Serve the kedgeree with the warm crispy onion on top.

KEYS TO PERFECTION

Make the topping crispy

Fry the onions slowly in a large, nonstick frying pan over medium heat for 20–25 minutes, stirring occasionally. You're aiming for a crispy texture and deep golden color.

Rinse the rice

Put the rice in a sieve and hold under cold running water until the water runs clear. This removes the starch and prevents clumping, making the rice lighter and fluffier. Drain well.

Lightly hard-boil the eggs

Place the eggs in a small pan, cover with cold water, and bring to a boil. Simmer for 6 minutes, at which point the white should be set and firm but the yolks slightly soft.

SERVES 4

2 boneless, skinless
chicken breasts, cut
into bite-sized pieces

salt and freshly ground
black pepper

2 tbsp olive oil

5½ oz (150 g) pancetta,
finely diced

1 onion, finely chopped

1 garlic clove, crushed

10 oz (300 g) risotto rice
(see p179, box)

⅔ cup (150 ml) dry
white wine

5 cups (1.2 liters) hot
chicken stock

6 oz (175 g) frozen
peas, thawed

large pat of butter

finely grated zest
and juice of 1 lemon

1 tbsp chopped fresh
flat-leaf parsley

1 tbsp chopped fresh mint

a few fresh basil leaves,
finely shredded

LEMON CHICKEN RISOTTO

Enjoy the relaxing process of stirring a risotto as it cooks—
it's a very satisfying thing to make. Use a good stock, as the quality
of the stock is very important for the overall flavor of any risotto.

1. Season the chicken. Heat the oil in a large, deep, nonstick frying pan or wide-based, nonstick pan over medium heat until hot. Add the chicken and cook, stirring often, for 3–5 minutes or until golden on all sides and just tender. Remove with a slotted spoon, transfer to a plate, and set aside.

2. Put half the pancetta in the pan and fry, stirring, for 3–5 minutes or until crisp. Scoop out using a slotted spoon and let drain on paper towels.

3. Add the onion and garlic to the pan with the remaining pancetta. Reduce the heat to low and fry for 8–10 minutes or until the onion is softened but not browned, stirring occasionally. Increase the heat to medium and add the rice. Cook for a few minutes until the grains are coated and shiny, stirring almost the entire time. (See p178: *Heat the stock and rice*.)

4. Pour in the wine and simmer, stirring, until it has been absorbed. Now add the hot stock gradually, a ladleful at a time. Stir constantly and wait until each ladleful has been absorbed before adding more. After 10 minutes, just after adding a ladleful of stock, stir in the peas, then continue with the stirring and adding stock for another 8–10 minutes or until the stock is almost all used up. (See pp178–179: *Add the liquids gradually*.)

5. Add the chicken and the remaining stock, and stir gently until the chicken is heated through and the stock absorbed. At this stage, the rice should be plump, slightly sticky, and al dente.

6. Remove the pan from the heat and gently stir in the butter, lemon zest, parsley, and mint. Taste for seasoning, then sprinkle the lemon juice over the top and cover the pan. Let sit for 5 minutes (see p179: *Let the risotto rest*). Gently fluff the risotto with a fork and serve immediately, topped with the reserved crispy pancetta and the shredded basil.

KEYS TO PERFECTION
See pp178–179

KEYS TO PERFECTION

Heat the stock and rice

1 Both the stock and the rice must be hot before they're combined, so the rice can absorb the stock and release its starch slowly during cooking, to give a creamy texture. Bring the stock just to a boil and keep it simmering all the time while you're making the risotto.

2 Stir the rice into the onion, garlic, and pancetta and fry for several minutes so it reaches the required temperature before adding the liquid. The rice will become shiny and change color, but it shouldn't turn brown. Watch carefully, stir often, and listen—you'll know the rice is ready for the liquid when you hear a quiet "popping" sound.

Add the liquids gradually

1 For a silky-smooth consistency, it's vital that the liquids are added to the rice gradually. First, pour in the wine—it will splutter, hiss, and steam. Stir to combine with the rice mixture and then keep stirring until you can no longer see it.

2 Add the first ladleful of hot stock and stir until it disappears. This is the beginning of the gentle nurturing phase, when you need to stand by the stove and add the stock a ladleful at a time, waiting for it to be absorbed before adding more. The total cooking time should be about 20 minutes, but this can vary slightly depending on the type of rice and the exact degree of heat.

Add the liquids gradually (continued)

3 Keep patiently adding the stock and stirring until it's absorbed. The rice and liquid should be gently simmering throughout, so if needed adjust the heat under the pan. Add the peas about halfway through the cooking time, just after adding a ladleful of stock.

4 Toward the finish, when the stock is coming to an end and before you add the chicken, check the consistency of the risotto by drawing a line through the middle with a spatula or spoon—the two sides should stay apart. If it's too wet and soupy, cook a little longer without adding the last of the stock. If it seems too dry, add more stock. The rice should have a slightly "nutty" bite to each grain.

THE DIFFERENT TYPES OF RISOTTO RICE

You may find three types of risotto rice in the store—Arborio, Carnaroli, and Vialone Nano. Often, the package will be labeled simply "risotto rice," which is invariably Arborio. You can experiment with different types to see which one you like best. My favorite is Arborio. I find it has just the right amount of starchiness to get the creamy consistency I like.

Let the risotto rest

The all-important final stage of this recipe is the resting. Once removed from the stove, the rice will continue to cook in the residual heat of the risotto. Leave it covered and undisturbed to let the butter and lemon juice do their work.

SERVES 6

Special equipment
*9–9½in (23–24cm)
nonstick frying pan*

*1⅓ cups (250g) long-grain
rice, rinsed and drained
(see opposite, box)*

*salt and freshly ground
black pepper*

1¾oz (50g) frozen peas

2 large eggs

2 tbsp sunflower oil

*1 red bell pepper,
seeded and diced*

*8 scallions, trimmed
and thinly sliced*

*2 garlic cloves,
finely chopped*

1 tsp five-spice powder

2 tsp sesame oil

*2 tsp dark soy sauce
mixed with 1 tsp water,
plus extra soy sauce to
serve (optional)*

5 oz (140g) bean sprouts

*1 tbsp snipped fresh chives,
plus extra to garnish*

*1¾oz (50g) roasted
cashews, to serve*

MY SPECIAL EGG-FRIED RICE

*Fresh herbs and five-spice powder bring a new fragrance
to this rice dish. Instead of stir-frying the egg with the rice, as is usual,
I've made a very thin omelette to give the egg more structure.*

1. Put the rice in a medium pan, pour in 2 cups (450 ml) cold water, and add 1 teaspoon of salt. Bring the water to a boil. Stir, reduce the heat to low, and cover with a tight-fitting lid. Simmer gently for 12–15 minutes or until all the water has been absorbed. Take the pan off the heat and let it stand, covered, for 5 minutes. Fluff up the grains, separating them with a fork.

2. While the rice is cooking, cook the peas in a pan of salted boiling water for 2 minutes. Drain and set aside. Make the omelette: beat the eggs in a bowl and season. Heat 1 tablespoon of the sunflower oil in the frying pan over a medium heat. Pour in the egg and cook for 2 minutes. Slice the omelette finely. (See below: *Make a thin omelette.*)

3. Heat the remaining tablespoon of sunflower oil in a wok or a large, deep-sided, nonstick frying pan or sauté pan. Add in the red pepper and fry over high heat, stirring, for 2–3 minutes. Add the scallions, garlic, and five-spice powder, and stir-fry for 1 minute.

4. Reduce the heat to medium and stir in the sesame oil, the soy sauce mixed with water, the rice and peas, the omelette, and the bean sprouts. Gently stir-fry for 1–2 minutes or until heated through. Stir in the chives and serve sprinkled with extra chives, the cashews, and a splash of soy sauce, if you like.

KEYS TO PERFECTION

Make a thin omelette

1 As you pour the egg into the pan for the omelette, tilt the pan so the egg completely covers the bottom to an even thickness. It will look set and no longer runny when done. Do not turn the omelette.

2 When the omelette is cooked, slide it onto a board and let it cool slightly, so that it will be easier to handle. Roll it up tightly like a cigar, then use a sharp knife to slice it across into very thin ribbons.

PREPARE THE RICE FOR COOKING

To make really light, tender rice and to ensure it isn't mushy, it's essential to measure the grains and water accurately. Before cooking the rice, put it in a large sieve and rinse under cold running water until the water runs clear, then drain well.

SERVES 2

4 oz (115 g) dried Thai rice noodles (gueyteow)

1 tbsp palm sugar (namtarn peep) or light brown sugar

1 tsp tamarind paste (makham piek)

1 tsp shrimp paste (kapi)

juice of 1 lime

2 tbsp fish sauce (nam pla)

2 tbsp sunflower oil

1 small red onion, sliced into thin half-moons

1 small red chili, seeded and thinly shredded lengthwise

1 tbsp finely chopped fresh ginger

1 garlic clove, finely chopped

7 oz (200 g) raw, peeled large shrimp, deveined and halved crosswise

2 large eggs

2 tbsp chopped fresh cilantro

To serve

1 oz (30 g) peanuts, very finely chopped

1 oz (30 g) bean sprouts

2 scallions, trimmed and finely shredded lengthwise

2 lime wedges

CLASSIC PAD THAI

*Thai cooks wouldn't make more than one or two portions of this
dish at a time, as the ingredients would overcrowd the pan and not cook
as well. To guarantee perfection, I follow the same rules.*

1. Lay the noodles flat in a wide, shallow pan and pour
in 4¼ cups (1 liter) of cold water. Bring to a boil, then
simmer over medium heat for 10 minutes. Drain the
noodles and rinse under cold running water until cold.
Set aside. (See below: *Keep the noodles separate*.) Put
the palm sugar into a small bowl with the tamarind and
shrimp pastes. With a small spoon, mix in the lime juice
and fish sauce until evenly blended.

2. Heat a wok or large, deep-sided, nonstick frying pan
or sauté pan over high heat until hot. Spoon in the
oil and heat until hot, then add the onion, chili, ginger,
and garlic. Let the ingredients sizzle over medium–high
heat for 30–60 seconds or until just starting to brown,
then add the shrimp and stir vigorously for 30–60
seconds or until they begin to turn pink at the edges.

3. Pour in the lime juice mixture and stir-fry for about
1 minute or until the shrimp are pink all over. Add in the
noodles and stir constantly for 1½ minutes. Scoop the
stir-fry to one side and crack the eggs into the empty
part of the wok. Allow them to set around the edges for
about 1 minute before stirring for another minute until
softly scrambled.

4. Mix the eggs into the noodles with the cilantro
and keep stirring for a minute or so until the mixture
is dry. Serve immediately, topped with the peanuts,
bean sprouts, and scallions, and a lime wedge
on each plate.

KEYS TO PERFECTION

Keep the noodles separate

1 Rice noodles stick together if
not prepared properly. Use lots
of water for boiling, and swish
around with a spatula between
the strands as they cook to keep
them separate.

2 As you rinse and drain the
noodles, shake the colander
and lift and separate the strands
with your hands. If they start to
feel sticky before you stir-fry, rinse
and drain again.

VEGETABLES

AT-A-GLANCE GUIDE TO COOKING VEGETABLES

Most vegetables can be cooked in a number of different ways, as indicated in the chart below. The cooking times given here are guidelines only, as timings vary according to the size and quantities of vegetables and the temperature of the stove or oven. More detailed information on each cooking method is given later in this chapter.

VEGETABLE	BOILING *see pp194–195*	BRAISING *see pp194–195*	STEAMING *see pp194–195*
CABBAGES	Remove tough outer leaves and thick stalks; shred leaves. Cook 4 mins.	Remove tough outer leaves and thick stalks; shred leaves. Cook 40 mins.	Remove tough outer leaves and thick stalks; shred leaves. Cook 6 mins.
BRUSSELS SPROUTS	Remove tough or discolored outer leaves; trim stalks; halve lengthwise. Cook 3 mins.	Not suitable	Remove tough or discolored outer leaves; trim stalks; halve lengthwise. Cook 6 mins.
BROCCOLI	Trim stalk; cut into equal-sized florets. Cook 3 mins.	Not suitable	Trim stalk; cut into equal-sized florets. Cook 6 mins.
CAULIFLOWER	Remove tough central core; cut into equal-sized florets. Cook 5 mins.	Not suitable	Remove tough central core; cut into equal-sized florets. Cook 7 mins.
SPINACH & CHARD	Trim thick stalks; shred large leaves. Cook with just water that clings to the leaves for 3–5 mins.	Trim thick stalks. Cook 6 mins.	Trim thick stalks; shred large leaves. Cook 3–5 mins.
BOK CHOI	Cut lengthwise into quarters. Cook 2 mins.	Cut lengthwise in half or quarters. Cook 12 mins.	Cut lengthwise into quarters. Cook 3 mins.
TOMATOES	Not suitable	Remove stalk; halve crosswise. Cook cut-side down 5 mins.	Not suitable
ZUCCHINI	Trim ends; thickly slice. Cook 2 mins.	Not suitable	Trim ends; thickly slice. Cook 5 mins.
SQUASH & PUMPKIN	Peel; halve lengthwise; seed; cut into 1in (3cm) chunks. Cook 5 mins.	Not suitable	Peel; halve lengthwise; seed; cut into 1in (3cm) chunks. Cook 8 mins.
EGGPLANT	Trim ends; cut into 1in (3cm) chunks or ½in (1cm) thick slices. Cook 3 mins.	Trim ends; cut into 1in (3cm) chunks. Cook 15 mins.	Not suitable
PEPPERS	Not suitable	Not suitable	Not suitable
SWEET CORN/ BABY CORN	Cobs: remove husks and silk; cut stalk. Cook cobs 10 mins, loose kernels 2 mins, baby corn 4 mins.	Not suitable	Cobs: remove husks and silk; cut stalk. Cook cobs 12 mins, loose kernels 5 mins, baby corn 6 mins.
GLOBE ARTICHOKES	Trim stalk; discard dry outer leaves. Add 1 tsp lemon juice to the water. Cook 10–20 mins.	Not suitable	Trim stalk; discard dry outer leaves; sprinkle with lemon juice. Cook 20–30 mins.
FAVA BEANS	Shell the beans. Cook 3 mins. Rinse in cold water; slip off skins, if desired.	Not suitable	Shell the beans. Cook 5 mins. Rinse in cold water; slip off skins, if desired.
GREEN BEANS	Trim stem end. Cook 4 mins.	Not suitable	Trim stem end. Cook 6 mins.

ROASTING *see pp200–201*	GRILLING & BROILING *see pp206–207*	SAUTÉING *see pp212–213*	STIR-FRYING *see pp218–219*
Not suitable	Not suitable	Remove tough outer leaves and thick stalks; shred leaves. Cook 5 mins.	Remove tough outer leaves and thick stalks; shred leaves. Cook 4 mins.
Not suitable	Not suitable	Remove tough or discolored outer leaves; trim stalks; halve lengthwise. Parboil 2 mins, then sauté 4 mins.	Remove tough or discolored outer leaves; trim stalks; halve lengthwise. Parboil 2 mins, then stir-fry 2 mins.
Trim stalk; cut into equal-sized florets. Cook 20 mins.	Not suitable	Trim stalk; cut into equal-sized florets. Blanch 2 mins, then sauté 4 mins.	Trim stalk; cut into equal-sized florets. Blanch 2 mins, then stir-fry 2 mins.
Remove tough central core; cut into equal-sized florets. Cook 25 mins.	Not suitable	Remove central core; cut into equal-sized florets. Parboil 2 mins, then sauté 5 mins.	Remove central core; cut into equal-sized florets. Parboil 2 mins, then stir-fry 4 mins.
Not suitable	Not suitable	Trim thick stalks; shred large leaves. Cook 5–6 mins.	Trim thick stalks; shred large leaves. Cook 5–6 mins.
Not suitable	Grill only: cut lengthwise in half or quarters. Cook 2 mins each side.	Not suitable	Cut stems into wide strips; shred leaves. Cook stems 2 mins, leaves 30 seconds.
Remove stalk; halve crosswise. Cook cut-side up 15 mins.	Remove stalk; halve crosswise. Cook cut-side down 4 mins.	Not suitable	Not suitable
Trim ends; cut into 1in (3cm) chunks. Cook 20 mins.	Trim ends; cut into ½in (1cm) slices. Cook 2 mins each side.	Trim ends; thinly slice. Cook 4 mins.	Trim ends; thinly slice or dice. Cook 2–3 mins.
Peel; halve lengthwise; seed; cut into 2in (5cm) chunks. Cook 25 mins.	Grill squash only: peel; halve lengthwise; seed; cut into ¾in (2cm) thick slices. Cook 5 mins each side.	Squash only: peel; halve lengthwise; seed; cut into 1in (3cm) chunks. Cook 10 mins.	Not suitable
Trim ends; cut into 1½in (4cm) chunks. Cook 25 mins.	Trim ends; cut into ½in (1cm) thick slices. Cook 5 mins each side.	Trim ends; cut into 1in (3cm) chunks. Cook 10 mins.	Trim ends; cut into 1in (3cm) chunks. Cook 10 mins.
Halve lengthwise; core; seed. Cut into 1½in (4cm) chunks, if desired. Cook 25–30 mins.	Halve lengthwise; core; seed. Cook 8 mins each side.	Halve lengthwise; core; seed. Cut into ½in (1cm) thick slices. Cook 6 mins.	Halve lengthwise; core; seed. Cut into ½in (1cm) thick slices. Cook 4 mins.
Cobs: remove husks and silk; cut stalk. Parboil cobs 8 mins, roast 10 mins.	Baby corn: thread on skewers with other suitable vegetables. Cook 4 mins each side.	Not suitable	Baby corn: cut into ¾in (2cm) pieces or in half lengthwise. Cook 3 mins.
Not suitable	Not suitable	Not suitable	Not suitable
Not suitable	Not suitable	Not suitable	Not suitable
Not suitable	Not suitable	Not suitable	Trim stem end; cut in half crosswise. Cook 4 mins.

AT-A-GLANCE GUIDE TO COOKING VEGETABLES (CONTINUED)

VEGETABLE	BOILING *see pp194–195*	BRAISING *see pp194–195*	STEAMING *see pp194–195*
PEAS	Shell the peas. Cook 3 mins.	Shell the peas. Cook 7 mins.	Not suitable
SNOW PEAS & SUGARSNAPS	Trim stem end. Cook 2 mins.	Not suitable	Trim stem end. Cook 4 mins.
ONIONS	Trim ends; peel. Cook whole 25 mins.	Trim ends; peel; halve lengthwise. Cook cut-side down 35 mins.	Not suitable
SHALLOTS	Trim ends; peel. Cook whole 12 mins.	Trim ends; peel; halve lengthwise. Cook 20 mins.	Not suitable
LEEKS	Discard outer leaves; trim base; cut into 1in (3cm) slices. Cook 4 mins.	Discard outer leaves; trim base; cut into 1in (3cm) slices. Cook 15 mins.	Discard outer leaves; trim base; cut into 1in (3cm) slices. Cook 8 mins.
FENNEL	Trim roots and stem tips; quarter. Cook 8 mins.	Trim roots and stem tips; quarter. Cook 30 mins.	Trim roots and stem tips; quarter. Cook 15 mins.
CELERIAC	Peel; cut into 2in (5cm) chunks. Cook 15 mins.	Peel; cut into 1–2in (2.5–5cm) chunks. Cook 40 mins.	Peel; cut into 2in (5cm) chunks. Cook 25 mins.
CELERY	Trim; cut into 2¾in (7cm) long sticks. Cook 5 mins.	Trim; cut into 2¾in (7cm) long sticks. Cook 40 mins.	Not suitable
ASPARAGUS	Snap off woody ends; leave whole. Cook 3–4 mins.	Snap off woody ends; halve lengthwise. Cook 12 mins.	Snap off woody ends; leave whole. Cook 8 mins.
CARROTS	Peel; trim; slice into sticks or rounds. Cook 3–4 mins.	Peel; trim; slice into sticks or rounds. Cook 15 mins.	Peel; trim; slice into sticks or rounds. Cook 10 mins.
PARSNIPS	Peel; trim; cut into ¾in (2cm) slices. Cook 8 mins.	Peel; trim; slice into sticks or rounds. Cook 15 mins.	Peel; trim; cut into ¾in (2cm) slices. Cook 12 mins.
BEETS	Leave whole, do not trim. Cook 30 mins. Slip off skins when cooked.	Peel; trim; cut into quarters. Cook 40 mins.	Leave whole, do not trim. Cook 40 mins. Slip off skins when cooked.
RUTABAGAS & TURNIPS	Peel; trim; cut into 1½in (4cm) chunks. Cook 15 mins.	Peel; trim; cut into 1in (3cm) chunks. Cook 30 mins.	Peel; trim; cut into 1in (3cm) chunks. Cook 25 mins.
POTATOES	Main crop potatoes: peel; cut into 2½in (6cm) chunks. Cook 20 mins. New potatoes: scrub skins. Cook 12 mins.	Main crop potatoes: peel; cut into 2½in (6cm) chunks. Cook 35 mins. New potatoes: scrub skins; halve crosswise. Cook 20 mins.	Main crop potatoes: peel; cut into 2in (5cm) chunks. Cook 30 mins. New potatoes: scrub skins; halve crosswise. Cook 30 mins.
SWEET POTATOES	Peel; trim; cut into 2½in (6cm) chunks. Cook 20 mins.	Peel; trim; slice into sticks or rounds. Cook 15 mins.	Peel; trim; cut into 1in (3cm) chunks. Cook 30 mins.
JERUSALEM ARTICHOKES	Cook 20 mins. Peel, if desired.	Not suitable	Cook 30 mins. Peel, if desired.
MUSHROOMS	Not suitable	Not suitable	Not suitable

ROASTING *see pp200–201*	CHARGRILLING & GRILLING *see pp206–207*	SAUTÉING *see pp212–213*	STIR-FRYING *see pp218–219*
Not suitable	Not suitable	Not suitable	Not suitable
Not suitable	Not suitable	Trim stem end. Blanch 2 mins, then sauté 2 mins.	Trim stem end; halve lengthwise, if desired. Blanch 2 mins, then stir-fry 2 mins.
Trim ends; peel; cut into wedges. Cook 30 mins.	Not suitable	Trim ends; peel; slice or chop. Cook 4–6 mins.	Trim ends; peel; slice or chop. Cook 4 mins.
Trim ends; peel; halve lengthwise, if desired. Cook 20 mins.	Not suitable	Trim ends; peel; quarter or slice. Cook 6 mins.	Trim ends; peel; quarter or slice. Cook 5 mins.
Discard outer leaves; trim base; cut into 2in (5cm) lengths. Cook 20 mins.	Grill only: discard outer leaves; trim base; halve lengthwise; cut into 4in (10cm) pieces. Cook cut-side down 4 mins, turn and cook 2 mins.	Discard outer leaves; trim base; cut into 1in (3cm) slices. Cook 4 mins.	Discard outer leaves; trim base; cut into ¾in (2cm) slices. Cook 4 mins.
Trim roots and stem tips; quarter. Cook 30 mins.	Trim roots and stem tips; slice lengthwise into ½in (1cm) slices. Cook 5 mins each side (if broiling, parboil 3 mins first).	Trim roots and stem tips; quarter. Cook 10 mins.	Trim roots and stem tips; slice finely. Cook 3 mins.
Peel; cut into 1–2in (2.5–5cm) chunks. Cook 25 mins.	Not suitable	Not suitable	Not suitable
Trim; cut into 2¾in (7cm) long sticks. Cook 25 mins.	Not suitable	Trim; cut into ½in (1cm) slices. Cook 4 mins.	Trim; cut into ½in (1cm) slices. Cook 3 mins.
Snap off woody ends; leave whole. Cook 25 mins.	Snap off woody ends; leave whole. Cook 10 mins, turning occasionally.	Snap off woody ends; cut each stalk into thirds. Cook 8 mins.	Snap off woody ends; slice thinly. Cook 4 mins.
Peel; trim; slice into sticks. Cook 25 mins.	Not suitable	Peel; trim; slice into sticks or quartered rounds. Cook 10 mins.	Peel; trim; slice into matchsticks. Cook 5 mins.
Peel; trim; quarter lengthwise. Cook 35–40 mins.	Not suitable	Not suitable	Not suitable
Peel; trim; quarter; add 3 tbsp water; cover with foil. Cook 30 mins.	Not suitable	Peel; trim; quarter. Cook 25 mins.	Not suitable
Peel; trim; cut into 2in (5cm) chunks. Cook 40 mins.	Not suitable	Peel; trim; cut into 1in (3cm) chunks. Cook 20 mins.	Not suitable
Main crop potatoes: peel; cut into 2in (5cm) chunks. Parboil 5 mins; roast 60 mins. New potatoes: scrub skins; cut into ⅛in (3mm) slices. Cook 40 mins.	Not suitable	Main crop potatoes: Peel; cut into 1in (3cm) chunks. New potatoes: scrub skins; cut into ¾in (2cm) slices. Cook 25 mins.	Not suitable
Peel; trim; cut into 2½in (6cm) chunks. Cook 30 mins.	Not suitable	Peel; trim; cut into ¾in (2cm) slices. Cook 15 mins.	Not suitable
Not suitable	Not suitable	Not suitable	Not suitable
Wipe with damp paper towel. Cook whole 10–15 mins.	Wipe with damp paper towel. Cook whole 5 mins, turning once.	Wipe with damp paper towel; cut into ¼in (5mm) slices. Cook 5 mins.	Wipe with damp paper towel; cut into ¼in (5mm) slices. Cook 3 mins.

10 oz (300 g) fresh spinach

3 tbsp olive oil

1 red onion, halved and
thinly sliced

2 tbsp (30 g) butter

2 garlic cloves, crushed

1½ oz (45 g) pine nuts,
toasted

1 oz (30 g) raisins (preferably
crimson raisins)

salt and freshly ground
black pepper

STIR-FRIED SPINACH WITH RAISINS AND PINE NUTS

*Raisins bring a touch of sweetness to the spinach, which can be bitter,
while butter introduces a mellow flavor, giving a perfect balance.
The pine nuts add crunch. Serve with grilled meats.*

1. Wash and drain the spinach; trim off the tough stalks and coarsely shred the leaves (see below: *Prepare the spinach for stir-frying*).

2. Heat a large, deep-sided, nonstick frying pan or wok over high heat until very hot. Pour in the oil and heat until very hot. Add the onion, reduce the heat to medium, and stir-fry for a few minutes until softened and tinged a light golden brown.

3. Add the butter and garlic and stir to mix with the onion. When the butter has melted, throw a large handful of the spinach into the pan. Toss until the

spinach leaves wilt, then add the remaining spinach in handfuls and keep stir-frying until all the spinach is in the pan. This whole process should take about 5 minutes in total.

4. Reduce the heat and toss in the pine nuts and raisins, plus salt and pepper to taste. Stir-fry for another minute or so, just to heat through the nuts and raisins, then transfer the contents of the pan to a warmed serving dish and serve at once.

KEYS TO PERFECTION

Prepare the spinach for stir-frying

1 Plunge the spinach into cold water in a large bowl or sink and swish the water around to get rid of grit. Drain in a colander, but not too thoroughly, as the leaves should still have a little water clinging to them for stir-frying.

2 Pick over the leaves and discard any that are discolored. If the leaves are young, the stalks should be thin enough to stir-fry, but thick stalks should be removed as they will not soften down in the short cooking time.

3 Working a batch at a time, put a mound of spinach on a board. Using a chef's knife, slice across the leaves to coarsely shred them. The shreds should be ½–¾in (1–2cm) wide. Repeat for the remaining batches.

SERVES 6

Special equipment
*1½–2 quart (1.7–2 liter)
baking dish, about
12 x 9in (30 x 23cm)
and 2in (5cm) deep*

*1 butternut squash,
about 1 lb 10 oz (750 g)*

2 tbsp olive oil

*salt and freshly
ground black pepper*

*9 oz (250 g) leeks, trimmed
and thickly sliced*

*7 oz (200 g) savoy
cabbage, shredded*

4 tbsp (60 g) butter

¼ cup (60 g) plain flour

2½ cups (600 ml) hot milk

*3¼ oz (90 g) Red Leicester
or fontina cheese, coarsely
grated*

*3¼ oz (90 g) aged Cheddar
cheese, coarsely grated*

1 tsp Dijon mustard

VEGETABLE GRATIN

A gratin is great for preparing ahead—especially for a
Sunday lunch, when everything needs to come together at once.
Squash is irresistible combined with leeks, cabbage, and a cheese sauce.

1. Preheat the oven to 425°F (220°C). Peel and seed the squash and cut it into chunks (see below: *Prepare the squash for roasting*). Put the chunks into the baking dish. Pour in the olive oil, season, and stir to coat the squash in the oil. Roast for 20–25 minutes or until just tender.

2. While the squash is roasting, plunge the leeks into a large pan of salted boiling water over high heat and bring back to a boil. Reduce the heat slightly and simmer for 3 minutes. Add the cabbage and simmer for another minute. Drain the leeks and cabbage in a colander.

3. Melt the butter in a pan over medium heat, sprinkle in the flour, and whisk using a small balloon whisk for

1–2 minutes until pale golden. Remove from the heat and gradually add the milk, whisking constantly.

4. Return the pan to medium heat and continue whisking until the sauce bubbles and thickens. Remove from the heat. Combine both the cheeses; add half to the sauce with the mustard and whisk until smooth.

5. Remove the squash from the oven and reduce the temperature to 400°F (200°C). Add the leeks and cabbage and stir to mix. Pour the sauce over the vegetables, cover with the remaining grated cheese and a grinding of pepper, and bake for 30–35 minutes or until golden brown.

KEYS TO PERFECTION

Prepare the squash for roasting

1 Roasting the squash keeps it chunky and improves the flavor (boiling would make it soggy). First, use a sharp chef's knife to slice off both ends and discard, then divide the squash in half by cutting across its "waist."

2 Stand each piece on its trimmed end and shave off the peel from top to bottom, holding the squash firmly and sawing with the knife. It can be difficult, as some skins can be very tough. Cut each piece in half lengthwise.

3 With a teaspoon, scrape out the seeds and stringy fibers and discard. Cut each piece of squash lengthwise into quarters, then slice across into 2in (5cm) chunks. When roasted, the edges will become slightly caramelized.

HOW TO BOIL, STEAM, AND BRAISE VEGETABLES

There are several ways of cooking vegetables using water or stock. Boiling is quick and versatile, steaming preserves maximum nutrients, while braising enhances the flavor of vegetables.

How to boil vegetables

Most vegetables (greens and roots) can be boiled. Drop them into a large pan of boiling salted water and bring back to a boil as quickly as possible. Reduce the heat and simmer until the vegetables are just tender, then drain. Don't boil them for too long, or their flavor and texture will be impaired, and they will lose color and nutrients.

Blanch green vegetables

When stir-frying or sautéing green vegetables you may like to blanch them first, to speed up the cooking time. Put them into a pan of boiling salted water, leave for a few minutes so they start to cook, rinse under cold running water until cold, then drain. This will stop further cooking and set the green color.

How to steam vegetables

Steaming is a healthy way of cooking delicate vegetables, such as broccoli or asparagus. Put them in a single layer in a steamer placed above a pan of rapidly boiling water. Sprinkle with a little salt. Cover the steamer with a tight-fitting lid and steam until just tender. If you don't have a steamer, use a large saucepan with a steamer basket, or a wok with a lid and a bamboo steamer.

Beets are great boiled or steamed and used in salads.

MASHED VEGETABLES

Many vegetables (not just potatoes) can be boiled or steamed then mashed: celeriac, carrots, rutabagas, squash, and parsnips all mash well. They can be served on their own, or in combination with other vegetables, and also make a good topping for pies. If mashing several vegetables, you may need to boil them separately, as some take longer to cook than others.

Enlivening plain vegetables

Plain boiled or steamed vegetables are made more interesting if they're dressed, however simply. Toss them with butter or some good-quality olive oil, and add some fresh herbs just before serving.

How to braise vegetables

Cabbage, celery, carrots, and other root vegetables are ideal for braising. Put the vegetables into a heavy pan or Dutch oven, add a small amount of water or stock (1¼ cups/150–300 ml of liquid per 1 lb/450 g of prepared vegetables), and bring to a boil. Season with salt and pepper and add a pat of butter. Cover with a tight-fitting lid and cook gently until just tender. Remove the vegetables, reduce the juices by rapid boiling, then pour over the vegetables.

See also At-a-glance Guide to Cooking Vegetables, pp186–89

SERVES 4

*8 oz (225 g) broccolini,
ends trimmed*

7 oz (200 g) sugarsnap peas

3 oz (85 g) diced pancetta

3 tbsp olive oil

*7 oz (200 g) crimini
mushrooms, quartered*

2 garlic cloves, thinly sliced

*salt and freshly ground
black pepper*

BROCCOLINI, SUGARSNAP PEA, AND PANCETTA STIR-FRY

This is a great combination that goes particularly well with grilled or fried meats. I find it better to boil the broccolini and peas briefly before stir-frying, to ensure the vegetables are tender.

1. Put the broccolini and sugarsnap peas in a large pan of salted boiling water, bring back to a boil, and boil for 2 minutes. Drain thoroughly in a colander, rinse under cold running water, and drain well again. (See below: *Blanch the vegetables*.)

2. Heat a large, nonstick sauté pan, deep-sided frying pan, or wok over low heat. Add the pancetta and stir-fry until crisp, for 4–5 minutes, increasing the heat as necessary (see below: *Crispy pancetta*). Using a slotted spoon, transfer to paper towels to drain.

3. Leave 1 teaspoon of the pancetta fat in the pan (remove any excess), then add the olive oil and heat. Add in the mushrooms and garlic, and stir-fry over medium–high heat for 2–3 minutes. Add the drained broccolini and sugarsnap peas and stir-fry for about 2 minutes (see below: *Stir-fry briefly*).

4. Mix in the drained crispy pancetta, season with salt and pepper, and serve drizzled with the juices from the pan.

KEYS TO PERFECTION

Blanch the vegetables

Boiling these whole vegetables before stir-frying means they don't need to fry for as long, so they retain their color and nutrients. To prevent overcooking, quickly drain and cool them down under cold running water.

Crispy pancetta

For the pancetta to be crisp (not tough), fry the cubes over low heat at first until they release some fat, then increase the heat to medium–high; they will quickly turn crisp. Keep moving them around for even cooking.

Stir-fry briefly

When the mushrooms are tinged brown and the juices are just starting to run, add the broccolini and sugarsnap peas, and stir-fry just long enough to heat them through. You want them to be tender but crisp (al dente).

1 lb 5 oz (600 g)
butternut squash

12 oz (350 g) celeriac

3 medium parsnips

¼ cup olive oil

5 sprigs of fresh thyme

freshly ground
black pepper

2 tbsp honey

finely grated zest of
½ small orange

1 tbsp orange juice

sea salt flakes

HONEY-ROASTED WINTER VEGETABLES

A hearty mix of root vegetables goes well with most roast meats, poultry, and game. Here, the honey and orange mix that is added toward the end complements the flavors of the vegetables.

1. Preheat the oven to 425°F (220°C). Peel the vegetables. Cut the squash and celeriac into chunks, about 1in (2.5cm). Cut the parsnips into quarters lengthwise. (See below: *Equal-sized vegetables.*)

2. Put all the prepared vegetables in a large roasting pan, pour in the oil, and toss them together to coat well, spreading oil on the bottom of the pan too, so the vegetables won't stick. (See below: *Don't overcrowd the pan.*) Tuck in the thyme sprigs and season with pepper. Roast for about 30 minutes or until golden.

3. In a small bowl, mix together the honey and orange zest and juice. Remove the vegetables from the oven, pour the honey and orange mix over the top, and return to the oven for another 5–8 minutes or until the vegetables are more golden and crispy around the edges. (See below: *Flavor at the last minute.*)

4. Spoon over any juices left in the roasting pan and sprinkle with sea salt flakes before serving.

KEYS TO PERFECTION

Equal-sized vegetables

Trim then peel the celeriac, squash, and parsnips. When peeling the celeriac, you'll need to cut off any knobbly parts first. It's important to cut all the vegetables to a similar thickness so they roast evenly.

Don't overcrowd the pan

Choose a roasting pan that's large enough to accommodate the vegetables in a single layer so they're not overcrowded and can turn a lovely golden color all over. A good coating of oil also helps the vegetables brown.

Flavor at the last minute

Pour in the honey and orange mix only once the vegetables have browned and are almost done. If the mixture is left on for too long, it can burn and dry out, and there won't be any lovely sticky juices to spoon over.

HOW TO ROAST VEGETABLES

When vegetables are roasted in a hot oven, their natural sugars caramelize and their flavors intensify. The dry heat of the oven also gives the vegetables an attractive golden brown exterior.

Equipment for roasting

Use a large roasting pan with relatively shallow rather than deep sides, and space the food well apart in the pan: you want the vegetables to roast rather than steam. A metal roasting pan is best, as it conducts heat better than other materials.

Estimating quantities

Vegetables shrink considerably when roasted, so you need to take account of this. As a rule of thumb, 2 lb (900 g) of vegetables generally serves six, and for this quantity of vegetables you'll need about 1½ tablespoons of oil.

Prepare the vegetables

Wash and trim off the ends, peel if appropriate, and cut the vegetables into pieces all the same size. Before roasting potatoes, parboil them first. Make sure they're well drained, so they won't make the dish watery, and fluff them up by shaking the pan or colander before roasting.

Arrange, oil, and season the vegetables

Heat some fat in the roasting pan until it's piping hot, then add the vegetables in a single layer. If they're overcrowded, they will sweat rather than roast. Toss

Drizzle olive oil over the vegetables and toss to coat.

the vegetables really well in hot fat. Olive oil, goose fat, and duck fat are usually used for roasting. Season the vegetables with salt and freshly ground black pepper. You may also like to add herbs and spices or another flavoring, such as lemon or garlic.

Oven temperatures

When roasting vegetables, oven temperatures should be on the high side, about 400°F (200°C). Cooking timings vary depending on the vegetables and how they're cut, so sometimes you'll need to roast different vegetables separately, or add some to the pan later. About half- to two-thirds of the way through the cooking time, turn the vegetables. They are done when they are tender and starting to char around the edges.

STUFFED VEGETABLES

Several vegetables, including eggplants, peppers, mushrooms, zucchinis, tomatoes, and butternut squash, can be stuffed with a flavorful mixture and baked, sometimes with cheese or breadcrumbs on top. You can serve stuffed vegetables as a first course or light lunch or, if filled with rice, couscous, or meat, they can make a satisfying main meal.

See also At-a-glance Guide to Cooking Vegetables, pp186–89

SERVES 4

1 bunch of scallions, trimmed and thickly sliced on the diagonal

2 tsp mint jelly

1 bunch of spring greens, about 5½ oz (150 g)

10 oz (300 g) frozen peas

4 tbsp (50 g) butter

salt and freshly ground black pepper

2 tbsp chopped fresh mint, to garnish

BUTTERED PEAS WITH COLLARD GREENS AND MINT

*This is my take on the French recipe "petits pois à la française,"
in which lettuce is cooked with peas. As a change from lettuce, I like
to use collard greens. These peas go really well with roast lamb.*

1. Put the scallions into a large, wide pan or sauté pan. Add the mint jelly and pour in 1 cup (250 ml) cold water. Bring to a boil over high heat, stirring to break up the jelly, then cover and simmer over medium heat for 10 minutes or until the scallions are tender and the liquid begins to look slightly syrupy. Meanwhile, finely shred the leaves of the collard greens (see below: *Tender collard greens*).

2. Add the peas, half the butter, and ½ teaspoon salt to the pan. Increase the heat to high and stir until the liquid is bubbling, then cover the pan again. Reduce the heat to medium and sweat the peas for 3 minutes or until they are just tender. (See below: *Sweet-tasting peas*.)

3. Add in the shredded collard greens and stir to mix with the peas. Increase the heat to high to reduce the liquid, and cook, uncovered, for 2–3 minutes or until the greens are tender. To serve, sprinkle with the mint and a grinding of pepper, and top with the remaining butter.

KEYS TO PERFECTION

Tender collard greens

1 Separate the leaves by pulling them from the hard stalk at the base of the bunch. Cut away and discard the tough stalks and thick midribs. Retain the soft parts of the leaves only, as they will be tender and sweet.

2 Stack a few leaves on top of each other and roll them up like a cigar. Cut across the roll into very fine shreds; the collard green leaves need to be this thinly sliced in order to cook as quickly as possible with the peas.

Sweet-tasting peas

Cooking the peas gently with butter and a little liquid (rather than fast boiling in lots of water) retains their sweet flavor. Shake the pan occasionally, to distribute the butter and to help the peas cook evenly.

MARY'S TOP TIPS

Cook simple food well

Healthy, everyday meals can taste every bit as good as more elaborate dishes. It's important to use fresh ingredients whenever possible, prepare and cook them properly, and season them well to enhance their flavor.

HOW TO BROIL AND GRILL VEGETABLES

Many vegetables can be cooked under the broiler or in a ridged cast-iron grill pan. It's a quick, easy, and healthy way to cook, requiring little fat, and gives vegetables a lovely smoky flavor.

Suitable vegetables

The most suitable vegetables for broiling and grilling tend to be relatively robust and reasonably fast-cooking: peppers, eggplant, zucchini, onions, fennel, asparagus, tomatoes, and mushrooms are all ideal.

Prepare the vegetables

Halve the vegetables or cut the larger ones into slices. Brush or toss the vegetables with olive oil before cooking, otherwise they will dry out and burn. You need only a light coating—too much can result in flare-ups under the broiler. Skewers are useful for threading through small vegetables or vegetable chunks before grilling. If using wooden skewers, make sure you soak them in a dish of water for 6 hours to prevent burning.

Broiling and grilling temperatures

The grill pan or broiler must be piping hot, so preheat for 5–10 minutes before use. Do not oil the grill pan, or it will smoke. Set the heat to medium–high when you add the

Threading vegetables onto skewers makes grilling easier.

> ### MARINADES
>
> *For added flavor, soak vegetables in a marinade for at least 1 hour before broiling or grilling. Combine 1 cup (250 ml) of olive oil with 2 finely chopped garlic cloves, 1 tablespoon of chopped fresh herbs (such as rosemary, thyme, or oregano), and salt and pepper. Before cooking, shake off any excess marinade.*

vegetables, and turn them at least once for even cooking. You don't want the temperature to be too high, or they will burn on the outside without being cooked through.

Cooking times

The broiling and grilling times of different vegetables vary, so consider this if you're planning to serve several vegetables together. Onions and eggplant take the longest time, followed by peppers, zucchini, asparagus, and mushrooms.

Don't overcrowd the grill pan

You may need to cook the vegetables in batches so as not to overcrowd the grill pan. The vegetables should be in a single layer for even cooking, and to ensure they grill rather than steam in their juices.

Attractive ridged markings

When grilling, try to leave the vegetables in one place as much as possible before you turn them, rather than moving them around in the pan. You want to encourage charred stripes from the ridges, as they're attractive and boost the smoky flavor. If you move the food around, the lines will not be distinct.

See also At-a-glance Guide to Cooking Vegetables, pp186–89

1 lb (450 g) Brussels sprouts

1 large orange (preferably unwaxed)

3 tbsp (45 g) butter

2 oz (60 g) blanched hazelnuts, coarsely chopped

¼ cup snipped fresh chives

salt and freshly ground black pepper

BRUSSELS SPROUTS WITH HAZELNUTS

I always cut my Brussels sprouts in half, as I find they cook much more quickly and look more attractive, too. They're traditional for Christmas, but this recipe is good all through the winter.

1. Prepare the sprouts: cut off the tough ends of the stalks and peel away any dirty, dark green, or yellowed outer leaves. Wash the sprouts in a colander under cold running water, then cut them in half lengthwise through the stem. Finely grate the orange rind (see below: *Finely grate the orange rind*).

2. Melt the butter in a small, nonstick frying pan over medium heat until foaming. Add the hazelnuts and stir to coat in the butter, then continue cooking for 2 minutes, stirring constantly (see below: *Gently fry the hazelnuts*). Remove the pan from the heat and stir in the orange zest. The sauce will bubble furiously and then subside. Set aside and keep warm.

3. Plunge the sprouts into a large pan of salted boiling water. Bring the water back to a boil and simmer, uncovered, for 3 minutes or until the sprouts are just tender (see below: *Briefly cook the sprouts*).

4. Drain the sprouts well, shaking them in a colander to get rid of as much water as possible, then tip them into a warmed serving dish. Pour the hazelnut butter over the sprouts, add the chives and some salt and pepper, and toss quickly to combine. Serve immediately.

KEYS TO PERFECTION

Finely grate the orange rind

Ideally use an unwaxed orange (or wash and dry the fruit first). Rub it lightly over a fine microplane grater, making sure you grate the colored rind only, not the bitter-tasting white pith beneath. Brush the rind out of the holes.

Gently fry the hazelnuts

Stir the hazelnuts in the foaming butter for 2 minutes, without taking your eyes off the contents of the frying pan. The moment the butter turns golden brown and the nuts smell toasted, remove the pan from the heat.

Briefly cook the sprouts

It's vital to cook sprouts for the shortest possible time and serve them as soon as they're cooked, or they will smell and taste unpleasant. To test, pierce a sprout with a fork; if it's just tender, it's done.

3 small zucchini,
about 1 lb (450 g)
in total

4 oz (115 g) small shallots

2 tbsp olive oil

1 garlic clove, finely
chopped

salt and freshly ground
black pepper

½ tsp finely chopped fresh
rosemary

PAN-FRIED ZUCCHINI WITH CRISPY SHALLOTS

Fried shallots give great flavor to this dish. However, they can sometimes be difficult to peel. If you put them in boiling water for about 5 minutes, the skins will soften and peeling will be easy.

1. Trim the zucchini and halve them lengthwise. Scoop out and discard the central seeds (see below: *Seed the zucchini*). Slice the zucchini across into ½in (1cm) thick pieces.

2. Cut the shallots into small wedges. Heat 1 tablespoon of the oil in a large, nonstick frying pan or sauté pan. Add the shallots and fry over medium–high heat for

about 4 minutes, stirring occasionally. (See below: *Make crispy shallots.*)

3. Stir in the garlic with the remaining tablespoon of oil, then add in the zucchini and fry for 6–8 minutes or until golden all over and just tender, stirring occasionally. Remove the pan from the heat, season with salt and pepper, and sprinkle the rosemary over the top.

KEYS TO PERFECTION

Seed the zucchini

Run a teaspoon down the center of each zucchini half and scoop out the seeds, leaving the flesh intact. This prevents the zucchini from becoming watery and creates an interesting shape when sliced.

Make crispy shallots

1 Cut the shallots into small wedges, so that they will cook and brown evenly with the zucchini. Halve the shallots lengthwise, lay them cut-side down, and slice each half into about 3 wedges.

2 The shallots should be slightly brown when you add the garlic and zucchini. Reduce the heat if the shallots are browning too fast. At the end of the cooking time they should be crispy, but not burned.

HOW TO SAUTÉ VEGETABLES

*Vegetables that are sautéed, or pan-fried, are crisp and golden
on the outside, and soft and tender inside. Being partially caramelized,
they're full of flavor and look appetizing, too.*

Suitable vegetables

The best vegetables for sautéing are those that are tender, such as zucchini, onions, mushrooms, and eggplant. Other, harder vegetables (such as root vegetables) will have to be precooked, for instance parboiled (and then drained) before frying.

Equipment for sautéing

Use a large, wide-based, nonstick sauté pan or frying pan. The wide base and low sides allow steam to evaporate, so the vegetables will brown rather than steam in their juices and turn soggy. Sauté pans tend to be straight-sided, a little deeper than frying pans, and have a lid, making them more versatile.

Prepare the vegetables

Cut the vegetables into thin slices or small pieces, so they cook quickly without needing a lot of oil. Don't use vegetables straight from the fridge; if cold, vegetables won't cook as well or brown properly. They must also be completely dry before sautéing.

Types of fat for sautéing

Use a good-quality oil or a mixture of oil with butter. Butter gives good flavor, but if it gets too hot it will

Slice onions thinly for sautéing, so they cook quickly.

burn. Don't use much fat; as long as the pan is hot enough, it won't be necessary.

Sauté in batches

Make sure the pan is big enough to take the vegetables easily, without overcrowding; if the pan is too full, the vegetables won't brown. Sauté in batches if the pan isn't large enough.

Heat and movement

To begin with, sauté the vegetables over high heat, stirring and turning constantly, until they start to brown. Reduce the heat and continue cooking, stirring occasionally, until tender. Keep the vegetables moving to be sure that they cook evenly. Use a wooden spoon or spatula to move them around, or shake the pan.

PAN-FRIED POTATO CAKES

Potato cakes make a great accompaniment to grilled meats, especially steak. Use leftover mashed potatoes, or cook potatoes in a pan of salted boiling water for 15–20 minutes until soft, then drain and mash. Mix with chopped fresh herbs, for instance parsley or chives, and chopped scallion or shredded parboiled savoy cabbage, then add an egg yolk and salt and pepper. Shape into round cakes, chill for about an hour, then fry for 2–3 minutes on each side until golden.

See also At-a-glance Guide to Cooking Vegetables, pp186–89

SERVES 4

Special equipment
*Roasting pan, about
14 x 11in (35 x 28cm) and
1½in (3.5cm) deep*

1¾ lb (800g) new potatoes,
such as baby Yukon gold,
scrubbed

¼ cup olive oil

3 garlic cloves, thinly sliced

5 sprigs of fresh rosemary

freshly ground black
pepper and sea salt flakes

ROAST NEW POTATOES WITH GARLIC AND ROSEMARY

I like to roast new potatoes in slices, combining them with garlic and fresh herbs. Make sure you use a large enough roasting pan, so the potatoes can spread out and their tops become brown and crisp.

1. Preheat the oven to 400°F (200°C). Slice the potatoes lengthwise to a thickness of about ⅛in (3mm). There is no need to peel them first. Pat the slices dry with paper towels. (See below: *Crisp, tender potatoes*, steps 1 and 2.)

2. Spoon 1 tablespoon of the oil into the roasting pan and brush it all over the bottom of the pan using a pastry brush.

3. Scatter the potato and garlic slices into the pan, pour in the remaining 3 tablespoons of oil, and toss everything together so the slices are all thoroughly coated with the oil. Spread the potatoes out evenly in the pan and tuck in the rosemary sprigs, rubbing a little of the oil from the potatoes over them so they don't burn, then season with pepper. (See below: *Crisp, tender potatoes*, step 3.)

4. Roast for 35–40 minutes or until the potatoes are tender and golden. Put them in a serving dish and scatter the sea salt flakes over the top.

KEYS TO PERFECTION

Crisp, tender potatoes

1 Slice the potatoes thinly and evenly along their length using a sharp knife. This ensures that they roast evenly and become crisp once they're cooked.

2 Pat the sliced potatoes dry with paper towels to remove excess moisture from the cut surfaces. Again, this will help them to become crisp in the oven.

3 When the potatoes and garlic are in the roasting pan, drizzle the rest of the oil over them and use your hands to mix so they're well coated. Spread them out for even cooking.

SERVES 8

Special equipment
10½in (26cm) nonstick frying pan

¼ cup olive oil

2 medium onions, halved lengthwise and thinly sliced lengthwise

3 lb (1.35 kg) smooth potatoes, such as Yukon gold, peeled

salt and freshly ground black pepper

2 tbsp (25 g) butter, plus a pat, about 1 tbsp (15 g)

RÖSTI WITH ONIONS

I've added caramelized onions to bring extra flavor to a classic Swiss rösti. Serve it as a potato side dish, or put a fried egg and some crisp bacon on top for an indulgent, informal supper.

1. Heat 2 tablespoons of the oil in the frying pan. Add the onions and fry over medium heat for 15–20 minutes, stirring only occasionally, until golden, softened, and reduced down. Set aside.

2. Coarsely grate the potatoes. Put half of them in a clean kitchen towel and squeeze out the excess water (see below: *Crispy outside, soft center*, steps 1 and 2). Place in a large bowl. Repeat with the remaining potatoes. Stir in the onion, forking it through to combine. Season with salt and pepper.

3. Heat another tablespoon of oil in the same pan with the 2 tbsp (25 g) of butter. Once the butter has melted, add in the potatoes and onions. Spread them

out and flatten with a spatula. Dot pats of the remaining 1 tbsp (15 g) of butter over the top. Fry over medium heat for 18–20 minutes or until the base is golden and crisp. (See below: *Crispy outside, soft center*, step 3.)

4. Put a large plate over the top of the pan and carefully invert the rösti onto it. Pour the last tablespoon of oil into the pan and when hot slide the rösti back into the pan. Tuck the edges under using a small, round-bladed knife, then cook for 10 minutes until the other side is golden and the potatoes are cooked.

5. Remove the rösti from the heat and let rest for 2 minutes, then slide it onto a large board or plate and cut into 8 wedges.

KEYS TO PERFECTION

Crispy outside, soft center

1 After peeling the potatoes, grate them on the coarse side of a box grater. If you use one of the finer sides of the grater, too much starch will be released from the potatoes, which will spoil their flavor.

2 Put half the grated potatoes in a clean kitchen towel, tighten it up like a pouch, and squeeze well to get as much excess moisture out as you can. This will ensure the potatoes are not wet and the rösti will not be soggy.

3 When frying, reduce the heat slightly if you think the potatoes are browning too quickly. You don't want them to burn before they're cooked through. The total frying time for the rösti is about 30 minutes.

HOW TO STIR-FRY VEGETABLES

*Stir-frying is one of the fastest and healthiest ways of cooking.
It involves very fast cooking over an intense heat, which ensures
the texture, flavor, and nutrients of the vegetables are retained.*

Prepare the vegetables

Prepare all the vegetables before you start cooking, because once you start stir-frying, speed is essential for success. Chop the vegetables into thin, equal-sized strips, dice, or shreds, so they cook quickly and evenly. Scallions are best sliced on the diagonal. Remove any tough stems.

Equipment for stir-frying

A wok is ideal for stir-frying, as it's made of thin metal and has a rounded shape. However, a large, deep-sided, nonstick frying pan or sauté pan is fine, too. Buy the largest wok you can, as you want the food to fit in with plenty of room for tossing. The wok should never be more than one-third full, and the food should have room to touch the hot sides of the pan. You will also need a wok shovel, or a wooden spoon or spatula (or two if you find it easier), for tossing the food.

Slice carrots into thin matchsticks for stir-frying.

ORDER OF WORK

With stir-frying, the order of work is crucial. The aromatics are added to the wok or pan first (these include fresh ginger, chilies, and scallions), then the vegetables in order of their cooking times, with those that require the longest times first—for instance, carrots require longer cooking so should go in the pan first, followed by broccoli and peppers, then mushrooms, then finally green leafy vegetables such as spinach. Any liquid for a sauce is added at the end of cooking.

Temperature and timing

The wok or pan must be really hot before you add the oil, then the oil must be really hot before you add the vegetables. To test the temperature, add a drop of oil; it will sizzle when the wok is ready. Add the vegetables in sequence according to their cooking times (see below, box). Retain a high heat throughout; it's vital to cook the vegetables quickly. They should take just a few minutes, until they are tender but still crisp, and should not require long cooking.

Toss the food

As you stir-fry the vegetables, keep tossing and stirring them around in the wok or pan using the shovel, wooden spoon, or spatula—the food must always be on the move.

Fry in batches

If you're using a frying pan or sauté pan instead of a wok, you may need to stir-fry the vegetables in two batches to ensure the pan isn't overcrowded.

See also At-a-glance Guide to Cooking Vegetables, pp186–89

Special equipment
1–1½ quart (1.4–1.5 liter) baking dish, about 10 x 8in (25 x 20cm) and 2in (5cm) deep

7 tbsp olive oil, plus extra for greasing

2 eggplants, halved widthwise and cut lengthwise into slices just under 1½in (1cm) thick

1 zucchini, halved widthwise and cut lengthwise into slices about ⅛in (3mm) thick

1 onion, coarsely chopped

2 garlic cloves, crushed

14 oz (400g) can chopped tomatoes

1 tbsp tomato paste

1 tbsp chopped fresh basil, plus 12 whole basil leaves and a few extra small ones for garnish

salt and freshly ground black pepper

1¾ oz (50g) coarsely grated Parmesan cheese for the layers, plus 1 oz (30g) for the topping

6 oz (175g) firm goat's cheese (from a log), sliced into rounds about ¼in (5mm) thick

¾ cup (60g) fresh white breadcrumbs

EGGPLANT AND GOAT'S CHEESE CRUMBLE

This is a substantial and delicious vegetarian main course, consisting of layers of grilled vegetables, tomato sauce, fresh basil, Parmesan, and goat's cheese finished with a crispy topping.

1. Preheat the broiler to its highest setting. Put 5 tablespoons of the oil in a small bowl. Brush a little of it onto a large, nonstick baking sheet, place as many of the eggplant and zucchini slices as will fit in a single layer, and brush the tops generously with some of the oil. Broil for 7–8 minutes, then turn, brush with more oil, and broil for 4–5 minutes (see below: *Tender vegetables*). Set aside and repeat for the remaining vegetables, grilling in batches. Preheat the oven to 400°F (200°C).

2. Grease the baking dish. Make the sauce: heat 1 tablespoon of the remaining oil in a pan. Add the onion and garlic and fry over medium heat for 5–6 minutes. Stir in the tomatoes, tomato paste, and chopped basil. Season. Simmer for about 15 minutes, stirring occasionally, until very thick.

3. Spread 3 tablespoons of the sauce in the dish. Lay the zucchini on top, then sprinkle over one-third of the Parmesan. Put half the eggplants on top, then another third of Parmesan, and half the remaining sauce, seasoning each layer as you go. Finish with the remaining eggplants, Parmesan, and sauce. Scatter the 12 basil leaves on top and cover with the goat's cheese. Mix the breadcrumbs with the final tablespoon of oil, rub together, stir in the 1oz (30g) of Parmesan, and sprinkle over the goat's cheese. (See below: *Neat layers*.) Bake for 25 minutes or until golden. Garnish with basil leaves.

KEYS TO PERFECTION

Tender vegetables

Grill the vegetables until golden and tender, oiling and turning once they soften and start to brown. Watch carefully, and remove any before they become too brown and crisp.

Neat layers

1 Spread a little sauce in the dish to stop the zucchini from sticking and keep them moist, then add the Parmesan and eggplant in neat layers so they bake evenly.

2 Add more Parmesan, then a layer of sauce and seasoning. Repeat the layers, then lay the goat's cheese rounds on top of the sauce and basil leaves. Cover with the topping.

**SERVES 4
(MAIN COURSE)
OR 6 (SIDE DISH)**

*1 small cauliflower,
about 14 oz (400 g)
trimmed weight*

2 tbsp sunflower oil

*1 onion, halved lengthways
and thinly sliced lengthways*

2 garlic cloves, crushed

*1 tsp finely grated
fresh ginger*

½ tsp black mustard seeds

½ tsp cumin seeds

*1 fresh, mild red chili,
seeded and chopped*

*2 tomatoes, roughly
chopped*

*1 sweet potato, about 9 oz
(250 g), peeled and cut into
1½ in (3.5 cm) chunks*

*4 oz (115 g) thin green
beans, stem ends trimmed
and cut across into 3 pieces*

1½ tsp garam masala

¼ tsp turmeric

4 oz (115 g) frozen peas

salt

*3 tbsp chopped fresh
cilantro*

2 oz (60 g) roasted cashews

*plain, full-fat yogurt,
to serve*

CAULIFLOWER AND
SWEET POTATO CURRY

*Cauliflower and potatoes are a classic curry combination, and
sweet potatoes work well in curries, too. This dish can accompany
a meat curry or make a vegetarian main meal with rice or naan.*

1. Cut the cauliflower into small florets (see below:
Tender vegetables, step 1). Heat 1 tablespoon of the oil
in a large pan. Add the onion, garlic, ginger, mustard
seeds, and cumin seeds and fry over medium–high heat
for 6–8 minutes or until the onion is golden brown,
stirring often and adjusting the heat as necessary.

2. Stir in the chili and tomatoes and fry for 1 minute or
until the tomatoes start to soften. Add the remaining
tablespoon of oil, then when hot add the cauliflower
florets and fry for 3 minutes. Stir in the sweet potato,
green beans, garam masala, and turmeric, stirring to

deglaze the bottom of the pan. Pour in 1 cup (250 ml)
water and bring to a boil.

3. Reduce the heat, cover the pan, and simmer for
15–20 minutes, stirring occasionally, until tender
(see below: *Tender vegetables*, step 2). Add 1–2 more
tablespoons water, if necessary, just to keep things moist
and to give a little more sauce.

4. Add in the peas and simmer for another 3 minutes.
Season with salt. Just before serving, stir in the cilantro
and cashews. Serve with plain yogurt.

KEYS TO PERFECTION

Tender vegetables

1 Slice the cauliflower in half
lengthwise, then cut out the hard,
tough central core in a V-shape. This,
combined with cutting the florets into
smaller, same-sized pieces, ensures
the cauliflower will cook evenly.

2 Toward the end of the cooking time,
insert the tip of a sharp knife into
the vegetables. If it goes in easily, the
vegetables are done. You don't want
them to overcook, or they will lose
their shape, texture, and flavor.

SERVES 6

Special equipment
*1½–2 quart (1.7–2 liter)
baking dish, about
10 x 7in (25 x 18cm)
and 3in (7.5cm) deep*

3 tbsp olive oil

2 onions, coarsely chopped

2 garlic cloves, finely
chopped

2 carrots, chopped into
about ½in (1cm) cubes

7 oz (200g) piece of
rutabaga, chopped into
about ½in (1cm) cubes

4½oz (125g) dried
red lentils

14 oz (400g) can plum
tomatoes

1 tbsp sun-dried
tomato paste

1½ cups (350ml)
vegetable stock

salt and freshly
ground black pepper

3 oz (85g) fresh spinach,
chopped

2 lb (900g) smooth
potatoes, such as Yukon
gold, peeled and cut
into large chunks,
about 2in (5cm)

2 tbsp (30g) butter

5 tbsp whole or
low-fat milk

5 oz (140g) aged cheddar
cheese, coarsely grated

VEGETABLE AND LENTIL COTTAGE PIE

This vegetarian pie is just as satisfying as the meaty version.
You can make the filling ahead and chill it in its dish, which will give
a really stable base for the mashed potatoes; bake it for 5–10 minutes longer.

1. Heat 2 tablespoons of the oil in a large, nonstick sauté pan. Add the onions and garlic and fry for 8–10 minutes over medium–high heat or until they start to turn golden, stirring occasionally. Pour the remaining tablespoon of oil into the pan, add in the carrots and rutabaga, and fry for 3 minutes.

2. Reduce the heat to medium. Stir in the lentils, tomatoes, sun-dried tomato paste, and stock. Season and simmer, covered, for 35–40 minutes over low heat, until the carrots and rutabaga are tender and the lentils have softened.

3. Remove from the heat, stir in the spinach, and let it wilt. Check the sauce's consistency (see below: *Moist,*

juicy filling). Pour the mixture into the baking dish. Let cool. Preheat the oven to 400°F (200°C).

4. Put the potatoes into a large pan and cover with cold water. Bring to a boil, add salt, and simmer for 15–20 minutes or until tender. Drain well. Put the butter and milk in the pan and warm through over low heat. Remove from the heat, return the potatoes to the pan, and mash with the milk and butter, then whisk until smooth (see below: *Smooth, creamy potatoes*). Season, then stir in the cheese.

5. Spread the potatoes over the filling (see below: *Decorative topping*). Bake for 30–40 minutes until golden and bubbling.

KEYS TO PERFECTION

Moist, juicy filling

The filling should be moist with plenty of sauce, but not sloppy. Add 2–3 tablespoons of water if it's too dry. Let the filling cool before adding the topping, as it will support the potatoes better.

Smooth, creamy potatoes

The potatoes are ready for mashing when a knife goes in easily. If undercooked, the mash will be lumpy; if overcooked, it will be sloppy. Mash the potatoes with hot milk and butter off the heat, then whisk with a balloon whisk.

Decorative topping

Spoon the cheesy, seasoned potatoes over the cooled vegetable and lentil layer. Spread it evenly over the surface, making patterns like furrows with a round-bladed knife to create an attractive, textured effect.

SALADS

SERVES 4

Special equipment
Mandoline

*1 fennel bulb, about
8 oz (225 g), trimmed*

1 stalk of celery

*4 medium tomatoes
on the vine*

6 oz (175 g) cherry tomatoes

2 tbsp extra virgin olive oil

2 tsp lemon juice

*sea salt flakes and freshly
ground black pepper*

balsamic glaze, to drizzle

VINE TOMATO AND SHAVED FENNEL SALAD WITH BALSAMIC GLAZE

The combination of tomatoes and fennel is lovely for a summer buffet. Balsamic glaze—balsamic vinegar that has been reduced and sweetened—is perfect for drizzling and adds a tangy flavor.

1. Slice the fennel very thinly on the mandoline. Cut the celery stalk in half widthwise and slice that thinly on the mandoline, too. Slice the vine tomatoes and halve the cherry tomatoes using a sharp knife. (See below: *Create contrasting shapes and textures*.)

2. In a small bowl, mix together the oil and lemon juice. Lay the tomato slices and halves on a serving plate or platter. Sit the fennel and celery on top in a loose, casual pile. Season with salt and pepper.

3. Drizzle the oil and lemon juice over the top, then a little balsamic glaze to finish (see below: *Drizzle the glaze*). Serve immediately.

KEYS TO PERFECTION

Create contrasting shapes and textures

1 Use a mandoline on its finest setting to give you ultra-thin shavings. By slicing the vegetables very finely, you're sure to get the flavor of the dressing into them. The blade is very sharp, so be careful of your fingers.

2 Slice the vine tomatoes relatively thickly using a sharp knife (ideally serrated), so they and the halved cherry tomatoes will provide a striking contrast in shape, as well as texture, to the crunchy fennel and celery shavings.

Drizzle the glaze

Drizzle just enough of the balsamic glaze to add visual interest and flavor contrast, but be careful not to use too much, as it's quite strong. You can use balsamic vinegar if you can't find glaze.

SERVES 6

15 oz (400 g) can kidney
beans

15 oz (400 g) can cannellini
beans

15 oz (400 g) can brown
lentils

½ small red onion

1 fresh, mild red chili

3½ oz (100 g) piece
cucumber

For the dressing

1 tbsp harissa paste

¼ cup extra virgin olive oil

2 tbsp lime juice

salt and freshly ground
black pepper

LENTIL AND CHILI BEAN SALAD

Harissa paste, made with chili peppers and a lively blend of spices, brings a special heat and flavor to this salad, which goes well with cold cuts. I've used three different beans for variety.

1. Make the dressing: put the harissa paste in a small bowl, then stir in the oil and lime juice. Season with salt and pepper and set aside.

2. Drain and rinse each of the cans of beans and the lentils separately. Allow to drain thoroughly, then transfer them to a serving bowl. (See below: *Rinse the beans and lentils*.)

3. Slice the onion lengthwise into very thin slices. Seed the chili and slice it lengthwise into long, thin strips. Add the onion and chili to the serving bowl with the beans.

4. Halve the piece of cucumber lengthwise and seed (see below: *Seed the cucumber*). Cut each cucumber half into slices 1¼in (5mm) thick, then chop each slice into small pieces. Add them to the bowl with the rest of the vegetables.

5. Just before serving, mix in the harissa dressing (see below: *Dress at the last minute*). Taste and add more seasoning if needed.

KEYS TO PERFECTION

Rinse the beans and lentils

Rinse the beans and lentils to remove the thick, starchy liquid that clings to them. Pour them into a sieve to drain, rinse under cold running water, and drain well. Let dry completely before making the salad.

Seed the cucumber

Cut the cucumber in half lengthwise. Using a teaspoon, scoop out the seeds and discard; if the seeds are left in, the salad will be too wet. Keep the skin on, to help the pieces retain their shape.

Dress at the last minute

Pour the dressing over the salad and gently toss everything together. Do this just before serving; if added too early, the onion and cucumber will lose their crunch and the beans will become too soft.

2 red bell peppers

9 oz (250 g) pasta
shells (conchiglie)
(see opposite, box)

⅓ cup (75 ml) extra
virgin olive oil

finely grated zest
and juice of 1 lemon

salt and freshly ground
black pepper

1 tbsp mayonnaise

2½ oz (75 g) sun-dried
tomatoes, roughly chopped

8 cherry tomatoes, halved
or quartered

2 oz (60 g) black olives,
pitted and roughly
chopped

4½ oz (125 g) piece
of salami, cut into
bite-sized chunks

1 small red onion,
finely sliced

¼ cup chopped fresh
flat-leaf parsley

2 oz (60 g) pine nuts

7 oz (200 g) package feta
cheese, drained and cubed

¼ cup chopped fresh mint

MEDITERRANEAN PASTA SALAD

This multipurpose salad is good for buffet parties, picnics, and packed lunches, as it holds up well and can be made ahead to the end of step 3. Simply add the other ingredients just before serving.

1. Preheat the oven to 425°F (220°C). Line a baking sheet with aluminum foil. Halve the peppers and remove the cores and seeds. Place them, cut-side down, on the baking sheet. Roast for 30 minutes until the skins are blistered. Transfer the hot peppers to a plastic food bag, seal, and let cool.

2. Meanwhile, pour the pasta into a large pan of salted boiling water. Bring back to a boil, stir, and cook over medium–high heat for 7–8 minutes (or according to the package instructions) until al dente. Drain the pasta and mix it in a large bowl with the olive oil, lemon zest and juice, and seasoning (see below: *Boost the flavor*). Set aside to cool, stirring occasionally.

3. Remove the cooled peppers from the bag and peel off the skin. Roughly chop the flesh. Add it to the pasta with the mayonnaise, sun-dried and fresh tomatoes, olives, salami, onion, and most of the parsley. Toss well to mix, then check the seasoning.

4. Heat a small, nonstick frying pan until hot. Add the pine nuts and dry-fry over medium–low heat for a few minutes (see below: *Toast the pine nuts*). Gently fold the feta into the salad, then scatter the remaining parsley, mint, and toasted pine nuts on top. Serve the salad at room temperature.

KEYS TO PERFECTION

Boost the flavor

Cold pasta has a bland taste, so you need to dress the shells while they're still hot. The pasta will soak up the dressing, and the shapes will stay separate. Toss the pasta with the oil, lemon, and seasoning until glossy all over.

Toast the pine nuts

Toasting pine nuts enhances their flavor. They can burn easily, so stir and shake the pan constantly to prevent them from turning too dark. As soon as they're golden, take them out of the pan or they will continue to color.

CHOOSING AND USING PASTA SHELLS

Italian pasta shells are good for salads, because their shape helps trap the dressing. They come in many different sizes, from tiny ones (conchigliette) for soup to the jumbo conchiglioni, which are used for stuffing. For this recipe, you need to use small to medium-sized shells (conchiglie).

SERVES 4

5 oz (140 g) thin green
beans, stem ends trimmed

1 oz (30 g) Parmesan cheese

3½ oz (100 g) fresh baby
spinach leaves

2 Little Gem lettuces

For the dressing

1 tbsp white wine vinegar

1 tsp Dijon mustard

1 tsp granulated sugar

salt and freshly ground
black pepper

3 tbsp extra virgin olive oil

1 tbsp chopped fresh
tarragon

SPINACH, GREEN BEAN, AND LITTLE GEM SALAD

Choose a good-quality olive oil and vinegar for this light summer side salad. I also like to serve it at the end of a meal, with slim slices of Camembert or Dolcelatte instead of Parmesan for variety.

1. Make the dressing: put the vinegar, mustard, sugar, and some salt and pepper in a small bowl. Whisk together with a hand whisk. Gradually add the oil, whisking vigorously as you go, until it is all incorporated. (See below: *Make a classic French dressing.*) Taste and add more seasoning and sugar, if you wish. Set aside.

2. Slice the green beans in half lengthwise. Cook them in salted, boiling water for 2–3 minutes or until just tender. Drain and rinse under cold running water (so they retain their crunch), then drain again very well. Set aside. Make shavings of Parmesan using a vegetable peeler.

3. Tear any larger spinach leaves into manageable pieces, and leave the smaller ones whole. Tear the Little Gem lettuces into similar-sized pieces. Place the leaves in a large salad bowl and lay the beans on top of the leaves. Season with salt and pepper.

4. Stir the tarragon into the dressing, pour it over the leaves and beans, and gently toss together. Scatter the Parmesan shavings over the top.

KEYS TO PERFECTION

Make a classic French dressing

1 Whisk the vinegar, mustard, sugar, and seasoning until combined, then whisk more vigorously until thick and cloudy. The mustard will form an emulsion that will help to stop the dressing from separating.

2 Pour in the olive oil slowly in a thin, steady stream, whisking well, until the dressing looks creamy. If you pour in the oil too quickly, the dressing may separate. Add the tarragon at the last minute, or it will discolor.

PREPARE THE SALAD AHEAD

You can prepare the dressing (without the tarragon) up to 1 week ahead: store it in the fridge, then remix before using. The beans and leaves can be prepared 3–4 hours ahead, then covered and refrigerated until needed. However, it's vital not to put the dressing on the leaves and beans ahead of time, as they will quickly lose their crisp freshness. Do this just before you're ready to serve.

SERVES 4

6 oz (175 g) quinoa

1¾ cups (400 ml)
vegetable stock

4 scallions, trimmed,
halved lengthwise,
and thinly sliced

1¾ oz (50 g) mild
Peppadew peppers from
a jar, roughly chopped

1 tbsp lemon juice

2 tbsp extra virgin olive oil

3 tbsp chopped fresh
cilantro

2 tbsp chopped fresh mint

2 tbsp chopped fresh
flat-leaf parsley

3½ oz (100 g) pomegranate
seeds or ½–1 fresh
pomegranate

salt and freshly ground
black pepper

4½ oz (125 g) feta cheese

QUINOA SALAD WITH FETA, POMEGRANATE, AND FRESH HERBS

Using the tiny quinoa seed in a salad makes a great change from rice or couscous. It has many health benefits, and goes perfectly with dominant flavors, such as Peppadew peppers.

1. Rinse the quinoa (see below: *Make dry, fluffy quinoa*, step 1). Put it in a medium pan and pour in the stock, then bring to a boil and stir. Reduce the heat to medium–low and simmer, covered, for 20 minutes or until the water is absorbed. Once cooked, the grains will look plumper and almost translucent, and should still have a bit of bite.

2. Drain the quinoa in a fine-meshed sieve, then put it back in the pan. Leave it off the heat, covered, for 10 minutes. (See below: *Make dry, fluffy quinoa*, step 2.) Spread out the quinoa in a large shallow serving dish. Let cool.

3. Mix in the scallions and peppers, then stir in the lemon juice and oil. Gently stir in the cilantro, mint, parsley, and half the pomegranate seeds with their juice (see below: *Seed the pomegranate*). Season liberally with salt and pepper.

4. Crumble the feta over the salad. Scatter the remaining pomegranate seeds over the top and add an extra grinding of pepper.

KEYS TO PERFECTION

Make dry, fluffy quinoa

1 You must rinse quinoa in cold running water before cooking, as it has a bitter coating that can spoil its taste. Use a fine-meshed sieve for rinsing, as the quinoa grains are so tiny.

2 After cooking, drain the quinoa thoroughly to ensure the salad isn't watery. To make the quinoa dry and fluffy, return it to the hot pan, off the heat, cover with a lid, and leave it to dry off in the steam inside the pan.

Seed the pomegranate

If using fresh pomegranate, release the seeds by holding the halved fruit over a bowl and hitting the skin hard with a rolling pin. Spoon out any remaining seeds if necessary. Save any juice, as it adds a tangy flavor.

MARY'S TOP TIPS

Measure accurately

Treat yourself to a good set of digital scales and weigh accurately: use either imperial or metric measures; never mix the two. Measuring spoons are essential for baking, and check the capacity and dimensions of pans and baking dishes.

SERVES 4

2 red bell peppers, halved, cored, and seeded

2 yellow bell peppers, halved, cored, and seeded

8 oz (225 g) frozen fava beans

3 slices of Parma ham

For the dressing

2 tbsp extra virgin olive oil, plus 1 tsp for frying

2 tsp lemon juice

1 garlic clove, finely chopped

1 tbsp chopped fresh flat-leaf parsley

salt and freshly ground black pepper

ROASTED PEPPER AND FAVA BEAN SALAD WITH PARMA HAM

With its vibrant colors, this salad will enhance any table for a summer's lunch or light supper. Serve it at room temperature, with rustic bread on the side for dipping into the juicy dressing.

1. Preheat the oven to 425°F (220°C). Roast the peppers for 30 minutes or until well charred. Transfer them to a large plastic food bag, seal, and let cool. (See below: *Roast and skin the peppers*, steps 1 and 2.) While the peppers are cooling, cook the fava beans in a small pan of simmering water for 3 minutes. Drain and rinse under cold running water. Skin the beans by squeezing one end of each bean so it pops out of its skin.

2. Make the dressing: mix together the 2 tablespoons of oil with the lemon juice, garlic, and parsley. Season with salt and pepper. Pour 1 tablespoon of the dressing over the beans and toss together. Set aside.

3. Heat 1 teaspoon of the oil in a nonstick frying pan. Add the Parma ham and fry for 2–3 minutes or until crisp, turning often. Remove and drain on paper towels. Remove the peppers from the bag and peel off the skins (see below: *Roast and skin the peppers*, step 3). Slice the flesh into long strips.

4. Crumble the Parma ham into small pieces. Scatter the broad beans onto 4 large plates. Loosely arrange the pepper strips on top, drizzle over the remaining dressing, and scatter some of the crumbled ham over each salad.

KEYS TO PERFECTION

Roast and skin the peppers

1 Roasting brings out the natural sweetness of a pepper. Place the pepper halves, cut-side down, on a baking sheet lined with foil and roast in a hot oven until the skins are blackened and blistered.

2 While the peppers are still hot, place them in a large plastic food bag and seal the end tightly. This traps steam, which will help loosen the skin from the flesh, making the peppers easier to peel.

3 The peppers have a better texture and taste if the skin is removed. When the peppers are cool, pinch a little of the blistered skin and lift upward. The skin should come away easily from the flesh.

SERVES 10

1 lb 2 oz (500 g) green
cabbage

2 large carrots

7 oz (200 g) large
pink radishes

7 oz (200 g) snow peas

handful of fresh mint

handful of fresh cilantro

handful of fresh basil

3½ oz (100 g) roasted
cashews, chopped

For the dressing

1 fresh, medium-hot red
chili, seeded and finely
chopped

finely grated zest and
juice of 2 limes

6 tbsp sesame oil

¼ cup fish sauce (nam pla)

3 tbsp rice vinegar

2 tbsp granulated sugar

ASIAN-STYLE COLESLAW

*This is a great crunchy winter salad that is best made ahead,
so the dressing can flavor the vegetables. It keeps really well for
a few days. Its bold taste goes well with simple chicken or pork dishes.*

1. Finely shred the cabbage, carrots, radishes, and snow peas (see below: *Shred the vegetables finely*). Toss all the vegetables together in a large serving bowl until evenly mixed.

2. Coarsely chop the mint and cilantro, reserving a few whole leaves for the garnish. Add the chopped herbs to the vegetables in the serving bowl and toss thoroughly to combine.

3. Make the dressing by whisking all the ingredients together in a jug. Pour the dressing over the vegetables and, again, toss well to mix. Cover and chill for at least 1 hour, preferably longer—up to 12 hours.

4. Before serving, toss the salad well to bring up the dressing that has sunk to the bottom. Finely shred the basil and fold the shredded leaves into the salad with most of the chopped nuts.

5. To serve, scatter the remaining nuts and the reserved whole mint and cilantro leaves on top. Serve the coleslaw at room temperature.

KEYS TO PERFECTION

Shred the vegetables finely

1 Shred the vegetables as finely as possible using a very sharp knife. Peel off the outer cabbage leaves and cut the cabbage into wedges. Remove the core. Lay each wedge cut-side down and slice into fine shreds.

2 Cut the carrots in half crosswise, then lengthwise into very thin slices. Stack a few of the slices on top of each other, then slice the stack lengthwise into thin shreds. Cut the radishes into thin shreds.

3 Stack a few snow peas on top of each other and cut them on the diagonal into thin shreds. They look decorative sliced this way and are easier to eat in small pieces rather than when they're whole.

SERVES 4

Special equipment
*Ridged cast-iron
grill pan*

3 tbsp extra virgin olive oil

1 tbsp white wine vinegar

*salt and freshly ground
black pepper*

*about 1 tbsp olive oil,
for brushing*

*4 boneless, skinless
chicken breasts, about
5 oz (140 g) each*

*8 scallions, trimmed and
halved lengthwise*

*1 tsp chopped fresh
tarragon*

1 oz (30 g) arugula leaves

*1½ oz (45 g) lamb's
lettuce leaves*

For the avocado salsa

*2 medium, ripe avocados,
halved, pitted, and peeled*

1½ tbsp lime juice

*2 scallions, trimmed and
finely chopped*

¼ tsp Tabasco

*2 tsp chopped
fresh tarragon*

WARM CHICKEN SALAD WITH AVOCADO SALSA

This main meal salad is perfect for al fresco eating.
Grilling the chicken and scallions gives them extra flavor,
best highlighted when they're served warm on the dressed leaves.

1. Put the extra virgin olive oil and vinegar in a small bowl, mix together, and season with salt and pepper; set aside. Make the salsa: cut the avocado into chunky pieces, put in a bowl, then gently stir in the lime juice, chopped scallions, Tabasco, and the 2 teaspoons of tarragon. Season with salt and pepper and set aside. (See below: *Make a fresh green salsa*.)

2. Preheat the grill pan over high heat. Brush a little of the olive oil over both sides of the chicken breasts and season with salt and pepper. Lower the heat to medium–high and lay the chicken on the pan, with the plump, smooth-side down. Cook for 5 minutes or until the chicken is golden with charred grill marks, then turn and cook for another 5 minutes. Transfer the chicken to a board, cover loosely with foil, and set aside to rest.

3. Brush the halved scallions all over with the rest of the olive oil and season with salt and pepper. Lay them on the pan and cook for 2–3 minutes, so they get lightly charred all over (see below: *Grill effectively*).

4. To serve, stir the 1 teaspoon of tarragon into the oil and vinegar mix and toss the arugula and lamb's lettuce leaves with this dressing (see below: *Keep the leaves crisp*). Cut each warm chicken breast into 5 or 6 chunky slices. Serve the chicken on a pile of the leaves with the grilled scallions, and the avocado salsa on the side.

KEYS TO PERFECTION

Make a fresh green salsa

Mix the salsa very gently, as the avocado pieces can quickly become mushy if over-stirred. Don't make it too far ahead, as the avocado will turn brown, although the lime juice will slow down the discoloring process.

Grill effectively

When grilling, turn the scallions a few times so they soften quickly and don't burn. However, turn the chicken only once, so the grill markings don't get distorted. Serve them both warm.

Keep the leaves crisp

Toss the salad leaves with the dressing just before serving, otherwise they will wilt. The oil and vinegar can be mixed ahead of time, but add the tarragon right at the end or it will lose its color.

DESSERTS

SERVES 6

Special equipment
1 quart (1–1.2 liter) pudding basin or heatproof bowl; parchment-lined foil (see p64)

12 tbsp (175 g) butter (room temperature), plus extra for greasing

¼ cup golden syrup or light corn syrup

1 tbsp stem ginger syrup or light corn syrup

1 cup (175 g) dark brown sugar

3 large eggs

1 cup plus 2 tbsp (175 g) self-rising flour

1 tsp baking powder

½ tsp ground ginger

4 oz (115 g) ready-to-eat dried apricots, finely chopped

2 pieces of stem ginger or candied ginger, chopped

1 tbsp milk

For the custard
2 large eggs

1 large egg yolk

¼ cup (25 g) granulated sugar

1½ tsp cornstarch

2 tsp vanilla extract

1¼ cups (300 ml) milk

1¼ cups (300 ml) heavy cream

APRICOT AND GINGER SYRUP SPONGE WITH CREAMY CUSTARD

*This pudding is moist and sticky, and to spice up the flavor
I've mixed in some ginger. A jug of hot pouring custard (crème anglaise) is the
perfect accompaniment. Comfort food doesn't get much better than this.*

1. Generously grease the inside of the pudding basin or heatproof bowl. Put 3 tablespoons of golden syrup and the stem ginger syrup in the bottom of the basin and mix them together with a spoon.

2. Put the butter, brown sugar, eggs, flour, baking powder, and ground ginger into a large bowl and beat using an electric hand mixer or wooden spoon until the ingredients are evenly blended. Gently fold in the apricots and stem ginger, then the milk and remaining tablespoon of golden syrup. Spoon the batter into the basin and level the surface.

3. Cut a 12in (30cm) square of parchment-lined foil, grease the parchment side with butter, and make a pleat in the center. Place the square, buttered-side down, over the basin and tie securely with string. Use excess string to create a carrying handle. (See p250: *Wrap the pudding securely*.)

4. Place an upturned saucer in the bottom of a large, deep pan (this protects the base of the pudding from the pan's heat and prevents it from overcooking). Sit the basin on top of the saucer and pour boiling water into the pan until it comes one-third of the way up the basin.

Bring the water back to a boil over medium–high heat, then reduce the heat to a gentle simmer. Cover the pan and steam the pudding for 2¼ hours. (See p250: *Gently steam and serve the pudding*, step 1.)

5. Make the custard: whisk the eggs, egg yolk, granulated sugar, cornstarch, and vanilla extract in a heatproof bowl. Gently warm the milk and cream in a medium pan over low heat, then gradually whisk it into the egg mixture. Strain the mixture into the cleaned pan and heat gently, whisking constantly, until the custard thickens. (See p251: *Make silky-smooth custard*.) If you are not serving the custard immediately, prevent a skin from forming by pressing a sheet of plastic wrap directly onto the surface of the custard as soon as it is made; before serving, return it to the pan and reheat while whisking.

6. When the pudding is cooked, carefully lift the basin out of the pan, cut the string from the basin, and discard the parchment-lined foil. Invert the pudding onto a plate and let it stand for 5–10 minutes before cutting into wedges. (See p250: *Gently steam and serve the pudding*, step 2.) Serve with the hot custard in a pitcher.

KEYS TO PERFECTION
See pp250–251

KEYS TO PERFECTION

Wrap the pudding securely

1 Brush butter over the parchment side of the parchment-lined foil and make a pleat in it by folding over 1in (2.5cm) in the center. The pleat will allow the pudding to rise and expand during steaming; the butter will prevent the pudding from sticking to the paper as it rises.

2 Place the parchment, foil-side up, over the basin and press it firmly around and under the rim. Tie string tightly under the rim. This will prevent water from seeping into the basin during steaming, which would make the sponge soggy. Make a handle over the top of the pudding with a double length of string, knotting it securely to the string under the rim. Trim off the corners of the parchment-lined foil.

Gently steam and serve the pudding

1 As the pudding steams, keep the water at a gentle simmer—you may need to increase or reduce the heat. Check the water level every so often and add more boiling water if the level drops below one-third of the way up the basin. If there is not enough water the pudding won't steam properly, too much and it will bubble up beneath the foil and make the pudding soggy.

2 Remove the basin very carefully from the pan using the handle you made with the double length of string; take care, as the basin will be very hot. Remove the foil lid. Run a palette knife between the sponge and the basin to loosen the sides. Place an upturned, warmed plate over the pudding, then carefully turn them over together, holding firmly with a folded kitchen towel. Gently ease off the basin.

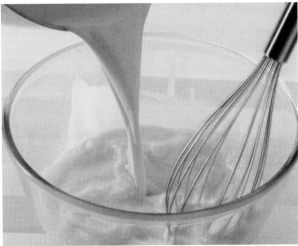

Make silky-smooth custard

1 Use a balloon whisk to whisk the eggs, egg yolk, granulated sugar, cornstarch, and vanilla together until evenly blended and no lumps of cornstarch remain. The extra egg yolk acts as a thickening agent and makes the custard a little richer, and the addition of a small amount of cornstarch to the mixture helps to stabilize the eggs and prevent them from curdling.

2 When mixing the warmed milk and cream with the eggs, the liquid must not be too hot, or the eggs may curdle. It should feel lukewarm when you dip your finger into it. After you've emptied the milk pan, rinse it before making the custard; you need to start with a clean pan, as any residue left from heating the milk and cream may catch or burn while the custard is cooking.

3 Strain the egg and milk mixture into the pan using a fine-mesh sieve. Straining is important, as it removes the stringy parts of the egg, which would spoil the texture of the custard if left in.

4 When cooking the custard, keep the heat low under the pan and be patient as you wait for the custard to thicken. It should be thick enough to coat the back of a wooden spoon. This stage can take as long as 10 minutes and you should watch it very carefully, whisking frequently. If you try to rush it by increasing the heat, the custard may split and curdle.

SERVES 8

Special equipment
Fluted tart pan with removable bottom, 9in (23cm) diameter and 1in (2.5cm) deep; baking beans

1¼ cups (275g) golden syrup or light corn syrup

1 tbsp molasses

finely grated zest of 1 orange

3 oz (85g) shredded unsweetened coconut

2 large eggs, beaten

2 tbsp orange juice

2½ oz (75g) pecans

clotted cream or crème fraîche, to serve

For the pastry

1 cup plus 2 tbsp (175g) all-purpose flour, plus extra for dusting

6 tbsp (85g) cold butter, diced

1 tbsp (15g) confectioners sugar

1 large egg yolk

252

MOLASSES AND PECAN TART

I've combined the best characteristics of a British dark treacle tart and an American pecan pie, to create a tart with a soft and slightly sticky filling made crunchy with a pecan nut topping.

1. Make the pastry: put the flour, butter, and confectioners sugar in a food processor. Process briefly until the mixture looks like breadcrumbs, then add the egg yolk and 1 tablespoon cold water. Process again until the mixture sticks together in clumps. Transfer to the work surface, then gather into a ball with your hands. Knead the pastry just 2 or 3 times to make it smooth.

2. Roll out the pastry on a lightly floured surface and use it to line the tart pan. Trim the pastry. Prick the base with a fork and chill for 30 minutes. Preheat the oven to 400°F (200°C). Place the lined tart pan on a baking sheet and bake blind for 15 minutes. Remove the paper and beans and bake for 5 more minutes. (See below: *Bake the pastry case blind*.)

3. Reduce the oven temperature to 350°F (180°C). Make the filling: mix the syrup and molasses together in a medium bowl. Stir in the orange zest and coconut, then the eggs and orange juice. Pour the syrupy mixture into the baked pastry case.

4. Break a few of the pecans into smaller pieces and leave the rest whole. Scatter the nuts all over the top of the filling. Bake for 25–30 minutes or until the filling is golden and set. Let cool in the pan before removing. Serve with clotted cream or crème fraîche.

KEYS TO PERFECTION

Bake the pastry case blind

1 Once you've lined the tart pan with the pastry, prick the base all over with a fork to prevent air bubbles from forming during baking. Chilling the pastry case will help to reduce shrinkage in the oven.

2 Line the bottom and sides of the pastry case with baking parchment, and weigh it down with baking beans. This ensures the sides don't collapse and the base doesn't puff up, keeping a good shape while the case bakes.

3 After 15 minutes' baking, remove the paper and beans and bake the empty case for another 5 minutes. You now have a case that is ready to be filled and baked again to give a crisp rather than soggy base.

SERVES 6

Special equipment
1–1½ quart (900 ml–1 liter)
metal pie pan, about
9 in (23 cm) diameter
and 1½ in (3.5 cm) deep

1¾ lb (800 g) tart apples,
such as Granny Smith

1 tbsp lemon juice

½ cup (100 g) granulated
sugar

2 tbsp cornstarch

½ tsp ground cinnamon

8 oz (225 g) blackberries

fresh cream, custard, or
vanilla ice cream, to serve

For the pastry

2¼ cups (350 g) all-purpose
flour, plus extra for dusting

12 tbsp (175 g) cold butter,
cut into small cubes

about 1 tbsp milk, to glaze

2 tsp granulated sugar,
to glaze

FALL FRUIT PIE

*Two classic fall fruits are combined in this generously filled pie.
It produces a fruity sauce, which thickens itself and coats the fruit as
it bakes. The pastry cooks best if you use a metal pie pan.*

1. Make the pastry: put the flour in a large bowl with the butter. Rub together with your fingertips until you have incorporated all the butter. Add about 6 tablespoons of cold water until the mixture holds together. Gently gather up, then pat into a ball. Wrap in plastic wrap and refrigerate for 30 minutes. Cut off just over half the pastry and leave the rest wrapped. Lightly flour the work surface and rolling pin. Roll out the pastry into a circle about 14in (35cm) across. (See p256: *Make a light pastry crust.*)

2. Carefully line the pie pan with the pastry (see p257: *Line the pan without stretching*). Place a baking sheet in the oven and preheat the oven to 425°F (220°C).

3. Quarter, peel, and core the apples, then cut them into slices about ¼in (5mm) thick. Put them in a large bowl and toss with the lemon juice. Mix the sugar with the cornstarch and cinnamon in a bowl, then toss with the apples. Add in the blackberries and briefly toss everything together. Be gentle when tossing, or the fruit will break up. Pour the fruit into the pastry-lined pan. (See p257: *Fill, cover, and seal the pie securely*, step 1.)

4. Make the top crust: roll out the remaining piece of pastry as before, into a 12in (30cm) circle. Brush the rim of the pastry lining the pan with a little milk. Place the folded pastry circle on the apples and unfold to cover the pie. Press the pastry edges down to seal, and trim off the excess with a small, sharp knife. Holding the knife horizontally and with its back to the cut edge of the pie, tap all around to secure the seal. Crimp the pie edge using your fingers. (See p257: *Fill, cover, and seal the pie securely*, step 2.) Cut a small slit in the center, about ¾in (2cm) long, to release steam.

5. Reroll the pastry trimmings and cut out pastry leaves. Brush the top crust with milk. Arrange the leaves in a circle around the steam hole. Brush the leaves with milk and sprinkle the top of the pie with the 2 teaspoons of sugar.

6. Put the pie pan on the heated baking sheet and bake for 15 minutes, then reduce the temperature to 350°F (180°C) and bake for another 30–35 minutes. Remove and let the pie sit for 5–10 minutes to allow the juices to settle before serving. Serve with cream, custard, or ice cream.

KEYS TO PERFECTION
See pp256–257

KEYS TO PERFECTION

Make a light pastry crust

1 It's important to keep utensils, hands, and ingredients cool for pastry. Use chilled butter straight from the fridge, otherwise it will be too soft to handle. Lightly rub the flour and butter together until it looks like fine breadcrumbs, lifting the mixture up as you rub in, which will aerate it, too.

2 Add just enough water to bind the mixture together. Start with the 6 tablespoons, adding only a few drops more if needed to bring it together, since too much water can cause the pastry to be tough. Work gently with your hands to bring together into a rough ball. To keep the pastry light, do not over-handle it.

3 Roll out just over half the chilled dough, flouring the work surface and the rolling pin first to prevent sticking. Don't use too much flour, or it will make the pastry dry. To prevent shrinkage later, roll the dough on one side only (so don't turn it over as you roll) and use short, sharp strokes in one direction only, giving a quarter turn between rollings so it rolls out evenly.

> ### GO EASY ON THE SUGAR FOR THE FILLING
>
> *Fruit baked in a pie with sugar can create a lot of liquid, so I combine some cornstarch with the sugar and cinnamon and toss the apples in the mixture, which helps to thicken the fruit juices that are released as the pie bakes. It's important not to add too much sugar, as this draws out juice from the fruit, and if there's too much it will overflow during baking. You can always offer extra sugar at the table if diners have a sweet tooth.*

Line the pan without stretching

1 When lining the pan, it's easy to stretch the pastry, which will cause it to shrink back in the oven. The best way I find to minimize stretching is to fold the rolled-out pastry in half, then in half again, to resemble a fan shape. I then carefully lay it in the pan with the point in the center. Use floured hands to prevent sticking.

2 Now unfold the pastry and ease it into the tin without stretching or pulling, so it fits snugly into the base and up the side. It's fine to have some pastry hanging over the edge, as it will get trimmed off later. Do not grease the pie pan before putting in the pastry. It is unnecessary and can cause the pastry to stick.

Fill, cover, and seal the pie securely

1 Fill the crust with the fruit mixture, mounding it up slightly in the center. Mounding the mixture keeps the fruit away from the pastry edge, so you can seal that easily when the top goes on. Also, it gives the pie a good shape. The fruit will settle as it softens, so without mounding the pie could end up with a dip in the center.

2 After you've sealed and trimmed the pie edge, and tapped around it with the back of a knife, crimp (or flute) the edge. Use your thumb and index finger of one hand to pinch the outer edge of the pastry while pushing the index finger of your other hand between them and upward slightly. Continue all around the pie edge at even intervals.

SERVES 4

2 large oranges
(preferably unwaxed)

¼ cup (60 g) granulated
sugar

4 thin slices peeled,
fresh ginger

1 lb 9 oz (700 g) pink
rhubarb, sliced into
pieces 2½ in (6cm) long

2 tbsp red currant jelly

plain yogurt or crème
fraîche, to serve

PINK RHUBARB AND ORANGE COMPOTE

*Young, slender, pink rhubarb gives this simple dessert
a rosy color and fresh flavor. Being more tender than the seasonal,
thicker-stemmed rhubarb, it just needs brief simmering.*

1. Peel 3 strips of rind from one of the oranges using a vegetable peeler and set aside, then squeeze the juice from the fruit. You should have about 5–6 tablespoons of juice. Pour the squeezed juice into a sauté pan or large frying pan, add in the sugar, and stir over medium–low heat until it has dissolved. Add the ginger slices and reserved orange rind.

2. Add the rhubarb to the pan and simmer for 2 minutes. Once the undersides start to soften, gently turn the rhubarb, then cover and simmer for another 5 minutes or until almost tender but still holding its shape, carefully pressing it down into the liquid. Remove it from the heat and let it sit in the liquid for 15 minutes, with the lid on. (See below: *Gently cook the rhubarb*, steps 1 and 2.) Discard the ginger and orange rind.

3. Peel the rind and white pith from the remaining orange using a small, sharp knife, then cut out the segments, reserving any juice. Transfer the rhubarb using a slotted spoon to a wide, shallow bowl. Add the orange segments.

4. Pour any reserved orange juice into the pan, then add the red currant jelly and stir over medium heat until it has melted. Increase the heat to medium–high and let the liquid bubble quite rapidly for 2–3 minutes. (See below: *Gently cook the rhubarb*, step 3.) Cool for 10 minutes, then pour over the fruit and let cool completely. Serve with yogurt or crème fraîche.

KEYS TO PERFECTION

Gently cook the rhubarb

1 Rhubarb can quickly collapse and lose its shape when cooking. Use a wide-based pan, so you can spread out the pieces, and don't stir, or they will break up; instead, turn them carefully using a slotted spoon.

2 Test the rhubarb with the tip of a knife. As soon as it's almost (but not quite) tender, remove it from the heat and let it sit for 15 minutes, covered. It will finish cooking in the hot liquid while retaining its shape.

3 Remove the rhubarb and reduce the liquid in the pan to create a light, shiny syrup. If you were to cook the rhubarb and the syrup together at this stage, the rhubarb would overcook and turn mushy.

SERVES 6

Special equipment
*1½–2 quart (1.7–2 liter)
baking dish, about
12 x 9in (30 x 23cm)
and 2in (5cm) deep*

*1 lb 10 oz (750 g) ripe red
plums (see p262, box)*

*2 large apples, about
1 lb 2 oz (500 g) total
(see p262, box)*

*2 cinnamon sticks
(see p262, box)*

⅓ cup (75 g) caster sugar

fresh cream, to serve

For the topping

*1 cup (150 g) all-purpose
flour*

*⅓ cup plus 1 tbsp (75 g)
semolina*

*3½ oz (100 g) cold butter,
cut into cubes*

*7 tbsp (60 g) granulated
sugar*

2 tbsp brown sugar

PLUM AND APPLE CRUMBLE WITH A SUPER-CRUNCHY TOPPING

My shortbread mix makes a buttery crumble topping with extra crunch. If preparation time is short, you can assemble the crumble without poaching the fruit and bake it for 10 minutes longer.

1. Preheat the oven to 350°F (180°C). Halve and pit the plums and quarter, peel, core, and thickly slice the apples. Put the fruit in a large, wide pan with the cinnamon sticks and granulated sugar and 2 tablespoons water. Place the pan over medium heat and bring the liquid to a simmer, stirring gently. Cover and poach the fruits for about 10 minutes, stirring occasionally. (See p262: *Poach the fruits before baking.*)

2. Remove the cinnamon sticks. Pour the poached fruit mixture into the baking dish. Spread out the mixture evenly, then set aside.

3. Make the topping: place the flour and semolina in a bowl and add the butter. Rub in the butter until the mixture has the consistency of breadcrumbs. Mix in the granulated sugar. Spoon the topping over the fruit in the dish, then sprinkle the brown sugar evenly over the top. (See p263: *Make a crunchy crumble topping.*)

4. Bake the crumble for 40 minutes, or until the topping is golden and the fruit juices are bubbling up around the edges. Allow to settle for 5–10 minutes before serving with fresh cream.

KEYS TO PERFECTION
See pp262–263

KEYS TO PERFECTION

Poach the fruits before baking

1 Poaching the fruits before covering with the topping makes a particularly juicy crumble. To halve the plums, run a small, sharp knife around the groove in each fruit, then twist the halves in opposite directions until they come apart. Push out the pit with your fingertips, or use the tip of the knife.

2 Cut the apples into quarters lengthwise, then peel off the skin and cut out the cores with a small, sharp knife. Cut each quarter into 4 thick slices.

3 A large, wide pan is best for poaching, as it enables the fruit to cook evenly without the need to stir too frequently. During poaching, the apples will start to break up. This is as it should be, and it helps to thicken the juices. As soon as the plums have started to soften, remove the pan from the heat.

FRUIT AND FLAVORINGS

Victoria plums are my favorite for cooking, because I like their lovely red color and sweet juiciness. Granny Smith apples are the perfect variety for a crumble. They soften down beautifully during baking and are just tart enough to balance the sweetness of the plums and sugar. Cinnamon gives the poached fruit a sweet, woody flavor and aroma. Cinnamon sticks vary in size. For this recipe, mine were about 3in (7.5cm) in length, but if yours are the very long ones, simply snap one in half.

Make a crunchy crumble topping

1 Stir the flour and semolina together in a large mixing bowl until they're evenly combined. Using half semolina to flour is a simple way to add texture and crunch to the baked crumble topping.

2 Using your fingertips, rub the cubes of butter into the flour and semolina. Do this very gently; never mash it with your fingers. The final texture should resemble breadcrumbs; don't make it too fine, or the topping will be soggy. Cold butter and cold fingertips are vital to prevent the mixture from becoming sticky. If necessary, hold your hands under cold running water to cool them, then quickly dry them.

3 Stir in the granulated sugar until it is evenly distributed. When making crumble, always add the sugar after working in the butter. If you add the sugar beforehand, the mixture will become too sticky to handle.

4 Spoon the crumble topping over the fruit in the dish, so that it forms an even layer, then top with brown sugar. Make sure that all the fruit is covered, especially around the edges. It's good to have a little juice bubbling up around the edges during baking, but too much juice will overflow and make the topping soggy.

MARY'S TOP TIPS

Stress-free entertaining

Take the stress out of entertaining by planning your menu carefully and preparing and cooking ahead. If serving a hot main course, provide a first course or dessert that you can make at least a day before. Use your freezer, too.

Special equipment
4 glasses, about 7 fl oz (200 ml) capacity

2½ cups (600 ml) heavy cream

3 tbsp whole milk

¼ cup (60 g) granulated sugar

1 vanilla bean

3 small leaves of fine leaf gelatin, each 4½ x 2½ in (11 x 6cm) (see p269, box)

or

.25 oz package (9 g/1 scant tbsp) unflavored powdered gelatin (see p269, box)

For the coulis

6 oz (175 g) raspberries, plus 5 oz (140 g) extra to serve

1 tbsp confectioners sugar

1 tsp crème de cassis

VANILLA PANNA COTTA WITH RASPBERRY COULIS

Traditionally, this dessert is set in molds and turned out, but for a change I have served it in glasses. I use heavy cream, as I find it gives a smoother texture than single or whipping cream.

Using gelatin leaves

1. Pour the cream and milk into a medium pan and stir in the granulated sugar. Split the vanilla bean and scrape out the seeds into the cream, then drop in the bean. Heat the cream and milk over low heat, stirring until the sugar has dissolved. Remove from the heat and let infuse for 5 minutes. (See p268: *Make a rich, creamy vanilla mixture.*)

2. Meanwhile, soak the gelatin leaves in cold water for 4–5 minutes, then squeeze well to remove any excess moisture. Stir the leaves into the hot cream until melted, then let the mixture sit for 5 more minutes to cool slightly. Remove the vanilla bean from the cream. (See p268: *Use gelatin for setting.*)

3. Carefully pour the cream mixture into the glasses. Let cool. Cover with plastic wrap and chill for about 6 hours or, preferably, overnight. (See p269: *Cover and chill the mixture.*)

4. Make the coulis: crush the raspberries with the confectioners sugar in a bowl, using a fork. Put a nylon sieve over a bowl and press the mixture through the sieve using a wooden spoon, then stir in the crème de cassis. (See p269: *Make a vibrant, smooth coulis.*)

5. To serve, spoon a little of the coulis on top of each panna cotta so that it covers the surface, then place 5 or 6 raspberries on top (the number will depend on the size of your glasses). Put the rest of the coulis in a small pitcher and serve it separately.

Using powdered gelatin

1. Pour the milk into a large heatproof bowl and sprinkle the powdered gelatin over the surface in an even layer. Let stand for 10 minutes to soften.

2. Meanwhile, pour the cream into a medium pan and stir in the sugar. Split the vanilla bean and scrape out the seeds into the cream, then drop in the bean. Warm the cream over low heat, stirring until the sugar has dissolved. Remove from the heat and left infuse for 5 minutes. (See p268: *Make a rich, creamy vanilla mixture.*) Remove the vanilla bean from the cream. Add the hot cream to the gelatin mixture and whisk to combine.

Continue from step 3, opposite.

KEYS TO PERFECTION
See pp268–269

Make a rich, creamy vanilla mixture

1 There are several ways of adding vanilla flavor to a dish, but for this dessert a vanilla bean gives the most fragrant taste. To extract the tiny black seeds, lay the bean flat on a board. Slice it in half through the center, sliding a small, sharp knife down the bean's length. Scrape out the seeds, then add them to the cream and milk. Drop the bean in, too, for added flavor.

2 Warm the cream and milk just until tiny bubbles start to appear around the edge of the pan. Boiling too rapidly, or for too long, will reduce the volume in the pan and spoil the flavor. Allowing the cream to just get hot enough to warm up the vanilla, then letting it infuse will bring out the vanilla flavor. Let the mixture infuse for 5 minutes before adding the gelatin.

Use gelatin for setting

1 To soften the gelatin leaves so they will melt completely, you need to soak them briefly in cold water before adding them to the hot liquid. Lay the gelatin leaves in a small, shallow dish and pour in enough cold water to cover them. Leave the gelatin in the liquid for 4–5 minutes only, no longer.

2 When the leaves are ready, they will look wrinkled and will be more pliable. Squeeze out excess water before dropping them into the hot cream. Keep stirring, so they melt evenly and completely. This is all done off the heat, as gelatin put into boiling liquid may not set later. Leave for 5 minutes, then remove the vanilla bean.

Cover and chill the mixture

Covering the panna cottas before chilling will protect their subtle vanilla flavor. Make sure they're cold first, then stretch a piece of plastic wrap over the top of each glass. If the desserts are covered while they're still warm, condensation will collect under the wrap and will drop onto the surface of the panna cottas. Chill for 6 hours, or overnight if possible.

Make a vibrant, smooth coulis

1 For the best flavor and color, choose raspberries that are just ripe—not too soft, not too firm. Put them in a bowl and crush them using a fork. Crushing the raspberries with the confectioners sugar helps to break them down and release their juices, making them easier to push through the sieve.

2 Press the raspberries firmly through a fine-mesh sieve set over a bowl, using the back of a wooden spoon to extract all their juices and as much pulp as will go through. A nylon sieve is best, as the acid in the fruit can react with metal. The coulis should be a thin, smooth purée. The crème de cassis, added at the end, gives depth of flavor.

SERVES 6

Special equipment
*Six 5 fl oz (150ml) ramekins;
cook's mini-blowtorch
(see p273, box)*

butter, for greasing

4 large egg yolks

*3 tbsp (45g) granulated
sugar*

½ tsp vanilla extract

*1¼ cups (300ml)
half and half*

*1¼ cups (300ml)
heavy cream*

*2½ tsp instant coffee
granules*

*¼ cup (50g) turbinado
sugar*

CAPPUCCINO CRÈME BRÛLÉE

The addition of a little coffee makes this rich, creamy dessert rather special. Measure the coffee carefully, as the flavor should be subtle. Any shape of ramekin will set off these brûlées perfectly.

1. Preheat the oven to 325°F (160°C). Lightly grease the ramekins with butter. Break the egg yolks into a large bowl, add in the granulated sugar and vanilla, and beat with a wire whisk to combine.

2. Put the half and half and cream in a medium pan and heat until scalding. Remove from the heat and stir in the coffee until it dissolves, then let the mixture cool slightly for about 2 minutes. Pour the cream mixture into the egg yolk mixture and stir thoroughly to combine. Strain the custard and pour it into the prepared ramekins. (See p272: *Make a silky-smooth custard.*)

3. Place the ramekins in a roasting pan and pour hot water into the pan until it comes halfway up the sides of the ramekins. Bake for 25–30 minutes, then remove the ramekins from the roasting pan and let cool. Cover and chill in the fridge overnight (or up to 2 days ahead). (See p272: *Gently cook and chill the custards.*)

4. Sprinkle the turbinado sugar evenly over the tops of the custards. Use the blowtorch to caramelize the sugar, being careful not to burn it. (See p273: *Make a crunchy brûlée topping.*) Serve as soon as the caramel has cooled and become brittle.

KEYS TO PERFECTION
See pp272–273

KEYS TO PERFECTION

Make a silky-smooth custard

1 When heating the cream, make sure you take it off the heat just before it comes to a boil, at the point when you can see small bubbles appearing around the edge of the pan. Add the slightly cooled cream and coffee mixture to the egg yolks in a steady stream, beating all the time with a wire whisk.

2 For an ultra-smooth texture, strain the custard into a heatproof liquid measuring cup before carefully pouring it into the greased ramekins, distributing the mixture equally.

Gently cook and chill the custards

1 Pour enough hot water into the roasting pan so it comes halfway up the sides of the dishes. The water bath ensures that the egg mixture cooks gently and is less likely to curdle.

2 The custards should have a slight wobble when removed from the oven. If overcooked, they will become too firm and air bubbles will develop, which will spoil the texture. Cool the custards completely before covering and putting in the fridge. If still warm when covered, the tops will get speckled with drops of condensation.

Make a crunchy brûlée topping

1 Sprinkle demerara sugar over the custards, to a thickness of about ⅛in (3mm). Make sure that you cover the custard evenly, using the back of a teaspoon to pat the sugar down over the surface. I prefer to use turbinado sugar for the topping, as I find that it gives a much tastier, crunchier caramel topping than white sugar.

2 Light the blowtorch and, holding it a few inches above the sugar, keep it moving continuously in a circular motion. As soon as the sugar melts and turns golden brown in one area, move it to another immediately. Do not leave the blowtorch over one particular area for too long, or the sugar will burn.

3 The melted sugar cools quite quickly and becomes brittle. Serve soon after being caramelized. If left to stand for too long after using the blowtorch, the caramel begins to dissolve to the point where it will start to turn to liquid. The brûlée can be cracked open with a teaspoon.

HOW TO MAKE THE TOPPING USING A BROILER

It's best to use a blowtorch to caramelize the sugar, as broiling is slightly slower and can start to overcook the softly set custard. However, if you don't have a blowtorch, you can use a preheated, very hot broiler instead. Put the ramekins as close to the broiler as possible and broil for about 5 minutes. After broiling, chill the brûlées for 2–3 hours before serving, so the caramel can soften slightly: this makes it easier to crack when eating (it is not necessary if you've used a blowtorch).

Special equipment
Small, fine paintbrush

1¾ cups (400 ml)
heavy cream

½ cup (100 g) granulated
sugar, plus extra for frosting

finely grated zest of
½ lemon

¼ cup lemon juice

3 tbsp limoncello

4–8 fresh mint leaves

egg white, for brushing

4 tsp full-fat crème fraîche

LEMON AND LIMONCELLO POSSET

The Italian liqueur, limoncello, brings a unique taste and added zest to a wonderfully simple, traditional British pudding. Serve with thin pieces of shortbread or amaretti biscuits.

1. Pour the cream into a medium pan and add the sugar and lemon zest. Heat slowly over low heat, stirring, until the sugar has dissolved completely. Increase the heat slightly and simmer gently for 3 minutes, stirring occasionally. Remove the pan from the heat and stir in the lemon juice and limoncello. Strain into a pitcher. (See below: *Super-smooth mixture.*)

2. Pour the mixture into 4 small glasses or coffee cups and let cool completely. Cover and chill for a few hours, or overnight, until set.

3. Meanwhile, sugar-frost the mint leaves. Lightly beat the egg white with a fork until slightly foamy, then brush it over both sides of the leaves (see below: *Crisp, frosted leaves*). Sprinkle with granulated sugar, gently shaking off any excess. Lay the leaves on a board and set aside for at least 1 hour or until dry and crisp.

4. To decorate and serve each chilled posset, scoop some crème fraîche into a teaspoon. Gently scrape the bowl of a second teaspoon inside the bowl of the first, pressing as you go, so you scoop the contents from the first spoon to the second. Transfer the crème fraîche back to the first spoon in the same way. Repeat, scooping back and forth until you have a smooth oval "quenelle" shape. Place it on top of a posset and top with 1 or 2 frosted mint leaves.

KEYS TO PERFECTION

Super-smooth mixture

1 Keep the heat low at first, so the sugar dissolves rather than crystallizes, and stir; when you no longer hear the sugar "crunch" on the bottom of the pan, increase the heat.

2 For a really smooth, silky texture, pour the mixture through a fine-mesh sieve into a large measuring cup. This will make it easier to pour into the serving glasses or cups.

Crisp, frosted leaves

Make sure the mint leaves are dry before you start and use a clean, fine paintbrush to apply the egg white. Use the egg white sparingly; if too heavily coated, the leaves will droop.

SERVES 8

Special equipment
*Swiss roll pan, 12 x 9in
(30 x 23cm) and ¾in (2cm)
deep; small piping bag
(optional)*

butter, for greasing

*6 oz (175 g) plain dark
chocolate (about 50%
cocoa solids)*

6 large eggs, separated

*⅔ cup (175 g) granulated
sugar*

2 tbsp cocoa powder

*1¼ cups (300 ml)
heavy cream*

*¼ cup Baileys Irish
Cream liqueur*

*confectioners sugar, sifted,
for dusting*

For the icing

*⅓ cup (50 g) confectioners
sugar, sifted*

2 tsp heavy cream

*2–3 tsp Baileys Irish
Cream liqueur*

CHOCOLATE AND IRISH CREAM ROULADE

This is one of my all-time favorite, make-ahead party desserts.
It freezes beautifully (uniced), then you simply thaw it in the fridge
overnight and drizzle the icing on top just before serving.

1. Preheat the oven to 350°F (180°C). Lightly grease the Swiss roll pan with butter and line with parchment paper. It helps to make a small diagonal snip in each corner of the parchment paper, about 1¼in (3cm) long, so the paper fits snugly into the corners of the pan.

2. Break the chocolate into pieces and place in a heatproof bowl set over a pan of gently simmering water. The base of the bowl must not touch the water. Heat until just melted, then remove from the heat, stir, and let the chocolate cool slightly (see p278: *Make a light cake*, step 1).

3. Meanwhile, place the egg whites in a large bowl and whisk using an electric hand mixer on high speed until fluffy and stiff, but not dry.

4. Place the granulated sugar and egg yolks into another large bowl and whisk on high speed until light, thick, and creamy, about 1½ minutes. Pour in the cooled chocolate and stir until blended. Add two large spoonfuls of the egg whites to the chocolate mixture and mix gently, then fold in the remaining egg whites. Sift the cocoa and fold it into the mixture. Pour the mixture into the prepared pan and level the surface (see p278: *Make a light cake*, step 2).

5. Bake for 20–25 minutes or until the cake is well risen and firm on top. Remove the cake from the oven and set aside, leaving it in its pan, until cold (expect it to dip and crack a little).

6. Place the cream in a bowl with the Baileys Irish Cream liqueur and whip until thick enough to just hold its shape. If insufficiently whipped it will be too runny to spread; if over-whipped, it will become too thick to spread evenly.

7. Lightly dust a large piece of parchment paper with confectioners sugar. Turn the cake out onto the parchment and carefully peel off the lining paper. Spread the surface of the cake with the whipped cream, leaving a bare rim of about ¾in (2cm) all the way around the edges. With one of the short ends near you, make a score mark ¾in (2cm) in from this edge, being careful not to cut right through. Starting at this point, tightly roll up the roulade. Transfer the roulade to a serving platter or board. (See pp278–279: *Roll a neat roulade*.)

8. Make the icing: put the confectioners sugar in a bowl, then mix in the cream and enough Baileys Irish Cream liqueur to give a smooth consistency. Drizzle the icing over the top of the roulade, or pipe it using the small piping bag.

KEYS TO PERFECTION
See pp278–279

KEYS TO PERFECTION

Make a light cake

1 As soon as the chocolate has melted, take the pan off the heat so the chocolate doesn't overheat, or it will become too stiff; it needs to be a pourable consistency. Stir, lift the bowl off the pan, and let the chocolate cool until it feels tepid. If the chocolate is too hot when stirred into the egg yolks, it will start to cook them.

2 Pour the cake mixture into the buttered and lined Swiss roll pan. The mixture should be light and airy now that the egg whites have been added. Ease it into the corners and smooth the surface level using a spatula. Do this very gently, so that you don't squash out the air you have just whisked in.

Roll a neat roulade

1 Let the roulade cake cool completely before you take it out of the pan. Run a small palette knife around the inside of the parchment paper in the pan to loosen the cake, so you can turn it out easily without it breaking.

2 Gently turn the cake out onto a large sheet of parchment paper that has been lightly dusted with confectioners sugar. Carefully loosen the parchment that surrounds the cake and peel it off, making sure you don't take the cake with it.

Roll a neat roulade (continued)

3 Using a palette knife, spread the cream evenly over the roulade, so you will get a uniform spiral of cream in each slice. Rather than spread the cream right up to the edges, leave a gap of about ¾in (2cm) all around, or the cream will start to ooze out as you start rolling.

4 Use a sharp knife to make a score mark ¾in (2cm) in from a short edge, and cut about halfway through the cake on the score line. This will be a useful starting point when you start rolling and will give you a tighter, neater roulade.

5 Roll the cut edge over tightly to start with, using the baking parchment to help keep it all tight by gently pulling it up and over the roll. Don't worry if the cake cracks—that is quite normal and will be part of the roulade's charm.

6 Keep rolling, again using the parchment to help by pulling it up and over as you roll. After rolling, make sure the join is underneath, as this will keep the roll secure, then transfer the roulade to a serving platter using a large, wide spatula or two smaller spatulas.

MAKES ABOUT 20 FILLED MERINGUES

Special equipment
Large piping bag; ½in (10mm) plain piping nozzle

3 large egg whites

⅔ cup (175 g) granulated sugar (preferably golden)

For the filling

20 raspberries, about 4 oz (115 g) in total

about 10 tsp lemon curd

about 10 tbsp full-fat crème fraîche

RASPBERRY CRUSH MINI MERINGUES

These are perfect little mouthfuls for a dessert treat.
You can make the mini meringues up to two weeks ahead, store
them in an airtight tin, and fill them just before serving.

1. Preheat the oven to 250°F (130°C). Cut out 2 pieces of parchment paper to fit 2 large baking sheets. Draw about 20 circles, approximately 1¾in (4.5cm) diameter, on each sheet of parchment. (See p282: *Pipe even rounds*, step 1.)

2. Put the egg whites in a large bowl and whisk using an electric hand mixer on full speed until stiff and resembling a cloud. Start to add the sugar a tablespoon at a time, whisking well between each addition, until it has all been mixed in. The finished meringue mixture should look stiff and glossy. (See p282: *Make a smooth, glossy meringue mixture.*)

3. Dab a small bit of the meringue mixture on each corner of the baking sheets and gently press the parchment on top, face down (so the pencil marks are underneath). Fit the piping bag with the piping nozzle. Spoon the rest of the meringue mixture into the bag (pipe half at a time if your bag is not big enough for all the mixture). Pipe about 40 small meringues onto the lined baking sheets. (See pp282–283: *Pipe even rounds*, steps 2–4.)

4. Bake for 1 hour. Turn the oven off, open the oven door so it is slightly ajar, and leave the meringues in the oven until they are completely cold, for about another 1 hour. (See p283: *Bake crispy meringues.*)

5. To fill each pair of meringues, crush a raspberry on a small plate using a fork. Spread one flat side of a meringue with about ½ teaspoon of the lemon curd. Carefully spoon the crushed raspberry over the curd. Spread the flat side of another meringue with about ½ tablespoon of crème fraîche and sandwich the two together. (See p283: *Make neat meringue sandwiches.*) Repeat with the remaining meringues and filling. Do this no more than about 1 hour before serving, or the meringues will go soft.

KEYS TO PERFECTION
See pp282–283

KEYS TO PERFECTION

Make a smooth, glossy meringue mixture

1 Take the eggs out of the fridge about 30 minutes before you need them, as you'll get more volume from the whites if they're at room temperature. Make sure you separate the eggs really carefully to prevent any yolk from mixing with the whites. Whisk the egg whites in a large, clean bowl, using the electric hand mixer on full speed. The mixture will become stiff and create soft peaks if the beater is lifted.

2 Immediately start to whisk in the sugar, 1 tablespoon at a time. Whisk well between each addition, so the sugar is incorporated fully, otherwise the meringue may collapse during baking, or "weep" beads of sugar. When all the sugar has been added, the meringue will look smoother and very glossy and will stand in taller, stiffer peaks. Pipe the mixture right away, or the mixture will start to deflate.

Pipe even rounds

1 To ensure the meringues are of an equal size when piped, draw about 40 circles in total, about 1¾in (4.5cm) in diameter and ¾–1in (2–2.5cm) apart, in pencil on the sheets of parchment paper. Use a round shape as a guide, such as a pastry cutter or small pot. Do this before you make the meringue mixture, or it may deflate.

2 Before piping, dab a little of the raw meringue mixture in the corners of the baking sheets, then press the parchment paper onto them. Lay the parchment face down, so the penciled circles are underneath but still visible. The parchment will stick to the baking sheets and be kept firmly in place when piping.

Pipe even rounds (continued)

3 To fill the piping bag more easily, sit it in a measuring cup and fold the ends of the bag over the top of the cup. Spoon in the meringue, without overfilling the bag. Lay the bag on the worktop, and tap it down very gently with the side of your hand to remove any air bubbles. Twist the end of the bag to seal.

4 Hold the bag vertically, about 1in (2.5cm) above the baking sheet, and pipe rounds just inside the pencil lines, gently squeezing the mixture out into a smooth round with an even pressure as you lift the bag up. To finish, lightly push the nozzle down into the meringues, then quickly lift it off to give a small peak.

Bake crispy meringues

It's important to allow the meringues long enough in the oven, so they can cook to the perfect texture. When done, they should be pale and crisp if tapped with a finger. They will also come away easily and cleanly from the parchment paper. If they're still sticking, keep them in the oven a bit longer. Leaving them in the turned-off oven with the door slightly ajar enables them to dry out without overcooking.

Make neat meringue sandwiches

When spreading the lemon curd, crushed raspberry, and crème fraîche on each meringue, go almost but not right to the edge, otherwise the mixture will ooze out when you sandwich the meringues together. It's important to use full-fat crème fraîche rather than a low-fat variety, as full-fat will retain its thick, creamy consistency better after the meringues have been filled.

SERVES 8

Special equipment
*Round springform pan or
loose-bottomed cake pan,
8in (20cm) diameter and
2¼in (5.5cm) deep*

1 lb 9 oz (700 g) full-fat
cream cheese (room
temperature)

½ cup (125 g) granulated
sugar

1 tbsp all-purpose flour

1 tsp vanilla extract

1 tsp finely grated
lemon zest

1 tsp lemon juice

2 large eggs

3½ fl oz (100 ml) full-fat
sour cream

For the base

4 tbsp (60 g) butter, plus
extra for greasing

8 graham crackers, about
4–4½ oz (115–125 g), broken
into large pieces

For the topping

¼ cup (50 g) granulated
sugar, plus 1 tsp to serve

10 oz (300 g) blueberries

3½ fl oz (100 ml) full-fat
sour cream

CHEESECAKE WITH BLUEBERRY TOPPING

You can't beat a simple, rich cheesecake with a crumb base and a classic sour cream topping. To make this one extra special, I've included a lightly cooked, fresh blueberry sauce for spooning over.

1. Preheat the oven to 325°F (160°C). Lightly grease the springform or cake pan with butter. Line the bottom with parchment paper.

2. Make the base: put the graham crackers in a plastic food bag, seal the bag, and crush the crackers with a rolling pin. Melt the butter in a medium pan. Remove from the heat and stir in the crumbs. Pour the buttery crumbs into the pan and press the mixture evenly over the bottom. Place the pan on a baking sheet and set aside. (See p286: *Make a crispy base.*)

3. Make the filling: put the cream cheese in a large bowl and beat using an electric hand mixer on low speed until creamy. Gradually beat in the sugar, then the flour. Next, beat in the vanilla and lemon zest and juice, then the eggs, one at a time. Briefly beat in the sour cream. Pour the filling over the base. (See p286: *Make a smooth, creamy filling.*)

4. Bake the cheesecake for 40 minutes, then turn off the oven and leave the pan in the oven (with the door closed) for 2 hours. Remove from the oven, then loosen the cheesecake from the side of the pan using a palette knife. When completely cold, chill the cheesecake in its pan for at least 6 hours, preferably overnight. (See p287: *Chill the baked cheesecake.*)

5. Make the topping: put the sugar in a medium, heavy-bottom pan with 1 tablespoon of water. Heat over low heat for several minutes until the sugar has dissolved. Increase the heat and let it bubble for less than a minute, without stirring, until syrupy and a very pale gold color. Remove the pan from the heat and stir in half the blueberries, then return to the heat and let the berries cook briefly in the syrup for 1–1½ minutes to release their juices. Take the pan off the heat and stir in the rest of the blueberries. Let cool. (See p287: *Make a syrupy blueberry topping.*)

6. To serve, mix the teaspoon of sugar into the sour cream. Remove the cheesecake from the pan, then slide it onto a serving plate, removing the lining paper as you do. Spread the sour cream smoothly over the top, as near to the edge as you can. Chill for 20–30 minutes. Use a large, sharp knife to slice, then place a spoonful of the blueberries on top of each slice and serve the rest separately.

KEYS TO PERFECTION
See pp286–287

KEYS TO PERFECTION

Make a crispy base

1 Lay the bag of graham crackers on a flat work surface and pound them with a rolling pin, or run a rolling pin over the crackers until crushed—or a combination of both. You're aiming for fine crumbs, as this will give the cheesecake base a better texture than if it consisted of large lumps, and makes the cheesecake easier to slice.

2 After combining the crumbs with melted butter, press them down firmly onto the bottom of the pan using the back of a metal spoon, or use your fingers to smooth and pat it down—whichever you find easiest. Try to make the crust the same thickness all over, so you have a firm, even base for the filling.

Make a smooth, creamy filling

1 Take the cream cheese out of the fridge at least 2 hours before making the cheesecake, so you can mix it quickly and smoothly without over-beating. Use an electric hand mixer on a low speed throughout the mixing. Beat the ingredients together to remove lumps, but be careful not to over-beat, or you'll mix in too much air and create bubbles in the mixture.

2 After you've filled the pan with the mixture, jiggle it gently to settle the filling evenly, and then burst any air bubbles that rise to the surface with the back of a teaspoon.

Chill the baked cheesecake

1 After baking, the cheesecake will appear to be very soft and wobbly in the center and slightly puffy at the side. So it doesn't overcook, finish the cooking slowly by leaving it in the turned-off oven. As the cheesecake cools, a small crack or two may appear on the surface, but don't worry if this happens—it will be covered with the sour cream topping later.

2 Loosen the cheesecake from the pan by running a small palette knife around the inside of the pan. Releasing the side of the cheesecake from the pan (but keeping it in its pan while it continues to cool) makes it easier to remove and helps prevent cracking across the middle. When completely cool, put the cheesecake in the fridge, in its pan, to chill. This improves the texture.

Make a syrupy blueberry topping

1 When making the syrupy base for the fruit topping, keep the heat low to start with, or the sugar will crystallize (you don't want it to bubble at this stage). Once the sugar has dissolved, increase the heat to medium–high, so the mixture can bubble and become syrupy; don't stir. It will take 35–40 seconds to reach a syrupy consistency; if you cook it too long, the syrup will turn to caramel.

2 As soon as the bubbles start to turn a very pale golden color, remove the pan from the heat and stir in half the blueberries. The syrup may stiffen, but don't worry—it will loosen again when it is reheated. Return the pan to the stove and cook gently, stirring, until the blueberries are just starting to burst and release their juices. Take the pan off the heat again and stir in the remaining blueberries.

SERVES 4

Special equipment
*2 freezerproof containers:
large and shallow, about
2½ quart (2.8 liter) capacity;
smaller and deeper, 1 quart
(1–1.2 liters) capacity*

⅔ cup (175 g) granulated
sugar

1 lb 5 oz (600 g) blackberries,
plus a few extra to serve

3 tbsp elderflower cordial

1 tbsp lemon juice

BLACKBERRY AND ELDERFLOWER SORBET

For a light end to a meal, sorbet is ideal, and it keeps for up to a month in the freezer. Fresh blackberries give an intense flavor and color, and the elderflower adds a refreshing note.

1. Put the sugar and 1¼ cups (300 ml) of water into a large pan and heat gently over low heat until the sugar dissolves, stirring occasionally with a wooden spoon. Increase the heat and bring to a boil. Boil fairly rapidly for 2 minutes over medium heat.

2. Add the blackberries, and when the liquid gently bubbles reduce the heat and simmer for about 2 minutes to soften. Remove from the heat and let cool. Pour the mixture into a food processor and process to a thin purée. Sieve the mixture into a bowl. (See below: *Make a smooth, fruity mixture*.)

3. Stir in the elderflower cordial and strain the lemon juice into the bowl. Let stand until completely cold.

(The sorbet mixture can be made up to a day ahead and kept covered in the fridge.)

4. Pour the mixture into the large container, cover, and freeze for 2–3 hours. Spoon the partially frozen mixture into a food processor and process. Transfer the puréed mixture into the smaller container, cover, and freeze for about 8 hours or overnight. (See below: *Check the consistency*.)

5. About 30 minutes before serving, transfer the sorbet to the fridge to soften slightly. Serve in scoops topped with a few extra blackberries.

KEYS TO PERFECTION

Make a smooth, fruity mixture

1 As soon as the blackberries have softened slightly, take the pan off the heat. They need to be soft enough to purée, but not so soft that they break up and start to lose their color and flavor.

2 Sieving the base will give you a super-smooth texture. Place a small, fine-mesh sieve (ideally nylon) over a bowl and press the fruit through with the back of a wooden spoon. Discard the seeds and pulp left in the sieve.

Check the consistency

After the first freeze, the sorbet should be turning mushy. Processing the mixture will break down the ice crystals and the sorbet will be smooth, thick, and slushy. After the final freeze, it will be firm.

SERVES 4

Special equipment
*Freezerproof container,
about 1 quart (1–1.2 liters)
capacity*

4 large egg yolks

*½ cup (115 g) granulated
sugar*

*1¼ cups (300 ml)
whole milk*

¾ cup (200 ml) heavy cream

½ cup (100 g) mascarpone

1 tsp vanilla extract

*8 oz (225 g) strawberries,
hulled and chopped*

*2 tbsp strawberry or
raspberry jam or conserve*

MASCARPONE AND STRAWBERRY RIPPLE ICE CREAM

This luxurious ice cream, with ripples of fresh strawberry purée running through it, can be made easily without a machine. Both the ice cream and extra sauce can be frozen for up to a month.

1. Make a rich custard: put the egg yolks and sugar in a large heatproof bowl and whisk using a balloon whisk until thick, light, and fluffy, and the mixture leaves a trail when the whisk is lifted. Gently warm the milk in a medium pan over low heat until hand-hot, then gradually whisk the milk into the egg mixture.

2. Pour the mixture back into the pan (rinse it out first so the mixture doesn't burn) and heat gently over low to medium–low heat, whisking all the time, until the mixture is thick enough to coat the back of a spoon (this can take about 10 minutes). Do not boil, or the eggs will curdle.

3. Pour the custard into a heatproof bowl and let it cool slightly, then cover the surface of the custard with plastic wrap (to prevent a skin from forming). Refrigerate for several hours until completely cold, preferably overnight.

4. Pour the heavy cream into a large bowl and lightly whisk using a wire whisk. Stir 2 tablespoons of the custard into the mascarpone, to loosen. Slowly stir the chilled custard into the heavy cream, then the mascarpone/custard mix and the vanilla extract. Pour into the freezerproof container and freeze for about 3 hours. (See p292: *Make a smooth, creamy base.*)

5. Meanwhile, put the strawberries in a large bowl with the jam and blend using a handheld blender to a smooth purée. Press through a fine sieve into a bowl and chill until needed. (See p293: *Add the fruity ripples*, step 1.)

6. Once the ice cream is starting to freeze around the edges of the container, stir it well. Freeze again for another 2–3 hours or until more thickly frozen. Stir, then transfer the ice cream to a food processor and process briefly. Put the ice cream back in the freezerproof container and freeze for another 1–2 hours. (See pp292–293: *Freeze the ice cream.*)

7. Stir the ice cream, then pour in just under half the purée (a little at a time) and gently swirl it into the ice cream so it ripples through rather than being completely mixed in (see p293: *Add the fruity ripples*, step 2.)

8. Freeze for another 3 hours or until firm enough to scoop. If the ice cream becomes quite firm (that is, if it has been frozen for several days), take it out of the freezer and bring to room temperature for 10 minutes before serving, to make scooping easier. Serve with the rest of the sauce.

KEYS TO PERFECTION
See pp292–293

KEYS TO PERFECTION

Make a smooth, creamy base

1 As this recipe is made by hand rather than in an ice-cream maker, I like to lightly whisk the heavy cream to create extra lightness. You don't want to whisk too stiffly, just briefly until it's light and floppy and holds a soft shape. Stir the chilled custard into the cream, then the mascarpone and vanilla. As the mascarpone is quite thick, it will blend in more easily if you mix a little of the custard into it first.

2 Pour the custard and cream mixture into a rigid freezerproof container with a capacity of about 1 quart (1–1.2 liters). You want the mixture to almost fill the container, leaving about ¼in (5mm) for expansion during freezing. If there is too much space between the lid and the surface of the ice cream, ice crystals will start to form.

Freeze the ice cream

1 When the ice cream starts to freeze around the edges of the container, use a fork to scrape the partly frozen crystals from the edge and mix them in with the softer ice cream in the middle. Stir until the mixture is well blended and smooth.

2 When making ice cream by hand, I've found that processing it in a food processor after it has been in the freezer for a few hours gives it a really good texture. Stir the ice cream a couple of times before processing, and don't process it for long—just enough to make it smooth and so more of the ice crystals are broken down.

USING AN ICE-CREAM MAKER

If you prefer to use an ice-cream maker instead of making the ice cream by hand, there is no need to whisk the heavy cream. Simply stir it into the chilled custard with the mascarpone and vanilla. Once the ice cream has been churned, transfer it to a freezerproof container and ripple the sauce through as described below, before returning it to the freezer to finish freezing.

Freeze the ice cream (continued)

3 Since putting the ice cream in the processor softens it, return it to its container and freeze for another hour or two, until it's thick enough to ripple the strawberry sauce through. The ice cream is ready to be rippled once it feels quite thick when stirred, but not too solidly frozen.

Add the fruity ripples

1 The strawberries must be dry before you purée them, or the sauce will be too runny. Use a handheld blender, as this works best for a small amount. I've sweetened with jam rather than sugar, to deepen the color and intensify the fruity flavor. After puréeing, press through a nylon sieve, using the back of a wooden spoon to extract as much of the pulp as you can; this will help thicken the sauce.

2 Use just under half the sauce for the ripples (the rest can be served with the ice cream), pouring or spooning it over the top in batches, then stirring gently through with a dessert spoon (in between pourings) to create swirls of sauce all through the ice cream. If you add too much too quickly and stir it in too vigorously, you will lose the effect of the ripples.

CAKES, COOKIES, AND BREAD

⅔ cup (115 g) all-purpose
flour, plus extra for dusting

6 tbsp (85 g) butter
(room temperature),
cut into small pieces

1¾ oz (50 g) aged cheddar
cheese, finely grated

1 oz (30 g) Parmesan
cheese, finely grated

¼ tsp paprika

1½ tsp poppy seeds

1 large egg yolk

CHEESE AND POPPY SEED STRAWS

These buttery, savory straws are always popular. They're best eaten within a day or two, while still crisp, but if you keep any for longer they can be revived in a medium oven for 3–4 minutes.

1. Put the flour and butter in a large bowl and rub them together lightly with your fingertips until the mixture resembles breadcrumbs. Stir in the cheddar, 1 tablespoon of the Parmesan, the paprika, and the poppy seeds.

2. Stir the egg yolk into the dry ingredients using a butter knife. Work everything together with your hands to form a dough, but don't over-handle. Wrap the dough in plastic wrap and chill for 10–15 minutes.

3. Meanwhile, preheat the oven to 375°F (190°C). Line a large baking sheet with parchment paper.

4. Roll out the dough on a lightly floured surface to make a rectangle about 8 x 7in (20 x 18cm) and ¼in (5mm) thick. Scatter the remaining Parmesan over the top. Cover with a piece of plastic wrap and press the cheese into the dough using a rolling pin. (See below: *Shape neat straws*, steps 1 and 2.)

5. Cut the dough rectangle in half across, then cut each half lengthwise into 12 strips. Carefully lay the strips on the lined baking sheet. (See below: *Shape neat straws*, step 3.)

6. Bake for about 15 minutes or until golden. Remove and transfer the straws to a wire rack to cool completely.

KEYS TO PERFECTION

Shape neat straws

1 Roll out the chilled dough. Keep the sides of the rectangle as straight as you can as you roll, so you can get as many neat straws as possible. Lightly trim the edges after rolling, if necessary.

2 Scatter Parmesan over the dough. Cover with plastic wrap to prevent sticking, then press and roll gently so the cheese is pressed in; don't let the rectangle get any bigger or the dough will be too thin. Remove the plastic.

3 Use a sharp knife to cut the dough into neat strips, then use a long palette knife to transfer the strips to the lined baking sheet. The parchment makes it easier to remove the baked straws without breaking them.

MAKES 12

Special equipment
12-cup muffin tin;
12 paper cupcake liners

6 tbsp (85 g) butter

1 cup plus 6 tbsp (250 g)
self-rising flour

1 tsp baking powder

⅓ cup (45 g) ground
almonds

1½ tsp ground cinnamon

½ cup (115 g) granulated
sugar

2 large eggs

9 oz (250 g) plain, full-fat
yogurt

1 tbsp whole or low-fat milk

6 oz (175 g) fresh
raspberries

1 Braeburn or Gala apple,
about 5½ oz (150 g),
peeled and chopped
into ½in (1cm) pieces

For the glaze

2 tbsp granulated sugar

1 tbsp orange juice

RASPBERRY AND APPLE MUFFINS

Fruity and lightly spiced, these muffins make a tempting mid-morning snack and go surprisingly well with cheese at lunchtime. They're best eaten fresh, but will keep for up to two days.

1. Preheat the oven to 400°F (200°C). Line each cup of the muffin tin with a paper liner. Warm the butter in a small pan over low heat until it melts, then set aside to cool.

2. Place the flour, baking powder, ground almonds, cinnamon, and sugar in a large bowl and stir to combine. In a medium bowl beat the eggs and stir in the yogurt, milk, and cooled melted butter. Stir this mixture into the flour mixture, then add the raspberries and apple and stir briefly. (See below: *Make a light mixture*.)

3. Spoon the mixture into the liners. Bake for about 25 minutes or until well risen and firm to the touch.

4. Meanwhile, make the glaze: warm the sugar and orange juice in a small pan over low heat, just until the sugar has dissolved, then increase the heat and let the mixture bubble for about 30 seconds so it turns a bit syrupy—not too long, or it will get too sticky.

5. Remove the muffins from the oven. Leave them in the tin for 1–2 minutes, then transfer them to a wire rack. While they are still warm, brush the top of each muffin with the glaze. Let cool.

KEYS TO PERFECTION

Make a light mixture

1 Stir the wet ingredients into the dry ones quickly, gently, and briefly; overmixing will result in tough muffins. Stop stirring as soon as it is combined. The mixture should feel light and soft.

2 Add in the fruit and stir 3 or 4 times only. If you add the raspberries too soon, or keep stirring after they've been added, they will start to break down, which will make the mixture too wet.

Special equipment
*12-cup shallow muffin tin;
12 paper cupcake liners;
large piping bag;
medium star (size 8) nozzle*

*2 tsp instant coffee
granules*

*8 tbsp (115 g) butter (room
temperature) or baking
spread (at least 70% fat)*

*½ cup (115 g) granulated
sugar*

*⅔ cup (115 g) self-rising
flour*

1 tsp baking powder

2 large eggs

*1½ oz (45 g) walnut halves,
finely chopped*

For the icing

*2 tsp instant coffee
granules*

*1⅔ cups (350 g)
confectioners sugar,
plus extra for dusting*

*12 tbsp (175 g) butter
(room temperature)*

*6 walnut halves, halved
lengthwise*

COFFEE AND WALNUT BUTTERFLY CAKES

The combination of coffee and walnut is always popular.
For these small cakes I've used the all-in-one method, which really
simplifies cake-making and, I think, makes it much more foolproof.

1. Preheat the oven to 350°F (180°C). Line each cup of the muffin tin with a paper liner. Stir the coffee with 2 teaspoons of hot water in a small bowl until the granules have dissolved. Set aside to cool.

2. Place the butter, granulated sugar, flour, and baking powder in a large bowl. Add the eggs and the cooled coffee mixture and beat well using an electric hand mixer or a wooden spoon until smooth. Stir in the walnuts. Divide the mixture equally among the liners. (See p302: *Light, all-in-one mixture.*) Bake for 15–20 minutes or until well risen and firm on top. Remove the cakes from the tin and let cool on a wire rack.

3. Make the icing: stir the coffee and 2 teaspoons of hot water in a small bowl until the granules have dissolved, then let cool. Sift the confectioners sugar into a large bowl, add the butter and the coffee mixture, and beat using an electric hand mixer or a wooden spoon until smooth and well blended (see p303: *Smooth, swirled icing*, step 1).

4. Cut a circle out of the top of each cake and cut each circle in half. Set aside. Spoon the icing into the piping bag fitted with the nozzle, and pipe the icing into the center of each cake. (See p303: *Smooth, swirled icing*, steps 2–4.)

5. Place the reserved semicircles on top of each cake to represent butterfly wings. Place a walnut quarter between the "wings" and dust with confectioners sugar.

KEYS TO PERFECTION
See pp302–303

KEYS TO PERFECTION

Light, all-in-one mixture

1 Because everything is beaten together, the butter must be soft enough to blend in easily, so leave it out of the fridge for 2–3 hours, or overnight, before using. Measure all the ingredients carefully and level off the teaspoon measure of baking powder with the back of a knife. If too much is added, it can make the cakes dry.

2 After adding the eggs and coffee mixture, beat using an electric hand mixer. Set it at a slow speed initially, then increase the speed once the flour has been absorbed. You can use a wooden spoon to beat the ingredients instead, but it will take a little longer (about 2 minutes with an electric whisk, or 3 minutes with a wooden spoon).

3 As you beat, keep turning the bowl and scrape the sides with a flexible spatula to make sure that all the ingredients are beaten in evenly. The mixture will start to look paler, creamier, and slightly glossy. It will also be soft enough to drop off the beaters when you lift them up.

4 Use a teaspoon and a butter knife to transfer the mixture to the paper liners. Put the same amount of mixture into each liner, so the cakes bake evenly and end up the same size.

Smooth, swirled icing

1 Sift the confectioners sugar into a large bowl in order to remove any lumps. This will give the icing a more even texture, which will make it easier to pipe. After the butter and coffee mixture have been mixed in, the finished icing should have a smooth, fluffy consistency.

2 Using a small, sharp knife, cut a circle from the top of each cake, about 2in (5cm) in diameter and 1in (2.5cm) deep. Cut it at an angle, so you end up with a cone-shaped hole that is large enough for you to pipe the icing into. Cut each circle in half to make "butterfly wings" to decorate the tops of the cakes.

3 Before filling the piping bag with icing, insert the nozzle and fold back the top of the bag so it doesn't get messy as you fill. Carefully spoon the icing into the bag, twist the top tightly, and press the bag lightly to get rid of any trapped air bubbles.

4 To pipe, hold the bag upright over the hole in the center of each cake, then gently squeeze the top of the bag to pipe the icing in a steady stream, guiding the nozzle around the hole to make neat swirls. Repeat for the other cakes.

MAKES 16–18

Special equipment
*3in (7.5cm) plain
round cutter*

½ cup (75g) semolina or
ground rice

1 cup (140g) all-purpose
flour, plus extra for dusting

⅓ cup (75g) light
brown sugar

¼ cup (25g) cocoa powder

12 tbsp (175g) butter
(room temperature),
cut into cubes

3½oz (100g) dark
chocolate chips

CHOCOLATE CHIP SHORTBREAD COOKIES

Buttery and very rich, few can resist these delicious cookies. Semolina brings a lovely crunch, and mixing in cocoa powder with chocolate chips makes the chocolate flavor all the more intense.

1. Put the semolina in a large bowl with the flour, sugar, and cocoa powder. Add the butter and rub it in with your fingertips. Work the dough together with your hands, stir in the chocolate chips, then press the dough until it forms a smooth, round ball. (See below: *Make a rich, buttery dough.*)

2. Roll out the dough on a lightly floured surface to a ¼in (5mm) thickness (you can roll half at a time if you find it easier to handle). Using the cutter, cut the dough into cookies. (See below: *Roll and cut carefully.*) Gather up the trimmings, reroll, and cut out more cookies.

3. Lay the cookies on 2 large baking sheets. Chill until firm, about 30 minutes. Meanwhile, preheat the oven to 325°F (160°C).

4. Bake for 20–25 minutes or until the cookies start to look very slightly darker at the edges. Remove from the oven and leave on the baking sheets for a few minutes, then transfer to a wire rack to cool completely.

KEYS TO PERFECTION

Make a rich, buttery dough

1 Bring the butter to room temperature before making the dough, for easy blending and rolling. Using your fingertips, rub the butter into the dry ingredients until the mixture resembles fine breadcrumbs.

2 Stir in the chocolate chips just as the dough mix is starting to come together. That way they won't melt from being over-handled. Press and knead the mixture until it forms a smooth ball.

Roll and cut carefully

Before rolling, make sure the surface is lightly dusted with flour; too much will dry out the dough and make it too crumbly. A plain cutter cuts through the chocolate chips more easily than a fluted one.

MAKES 24

Special equipment *baking dish, 12 x 9in (30 x 23cm) and 1½in (4cm) deep*

12 tbsp (175g) butter, cut into large cubes, plus extra for greasing

3 cups (275g) rolled oats

3½oz (100g) roasted chopped hazelnuts

2 tsp ground cinnamon

½ cup (200g) brown sugar

¼ cup (75g) light corn syrup

4½oz (125g) dried figs

FIG AND NUT BARS

These bars are wonderfully crisp on top and beautifully moist inside. As they hold together well, they're perfect for lunch boxes. They will keep for at least a week stored in an airtight container.

1. Preheat the oven to 325°F (160°C). Grease the baking dish. Line the bottom with parchment paper. Put the oats, hazelnuts, and cinnamon into a large bowl and stir well using a wooden spoon until combined.

2. Put the butter, sugar, and corn syrup into a medium pan. Place the pan over medium–low heat and stir until all the ingredients are melted together and smooth. Remove the pan from the heat.

3. Holding each fig by its stalk over the pan, snip the fruit into about 10 small pieces using kitchen scissors. Discard the stalks. Stir the figs into the melted mixture, then pour the melted mixture into the large bowl containing the dry ingredients and stir until everything is evenly combined.

4. Spoon the mixture into the prepared dish and level the surface (see below: *Even baking*). Bake for 35 minutes. At the end of this time, the top will be golden brown and just firm to the touch. Don't be tempted to cook for longer, as the bars will be too crisp—they continue to firm up as they cool.

5. Remove the dish from the oven and let it rest for 10 minutes, then mark into bars. Let it cool completely before cutting the bars and removing them from the dish (they will break if taken out too soon). (See below: *Neat bars*.)

KEYS TO PERFECTION

Even baking

Spread the mixture over the bottom of the dish using the back of a metal spoon. Ease it into the corners and press down firmly to make it level for even baking.

Neat bars

While the mixture is warm, mark out 24 bars with a sharp knife. Run the tip around the edge of the dish, then cut about halfway through the mixture. Finish cutting when the bars have cooled completely.

MAKES 18

Special equipment
*8in (20cm) square cake pan,
2in (5cm) deep; small
paintbrush*

*8 tbsp (115g) butter,
plus extra for greasing*

*1¾oz (50g) whole,
blanched almonds,
coarsely chopped*

1¾oz (50g) pine nuts

3 tbsp light corn syrup

*7oz (200g) dark chocolate,
chopped into small pieces*

2 tsp cocoa powder

*3½oz (100g) dried apricots,
chopped*

*10oz (300g) soft amaretti
biscuits*

*edible gold leaf,
to decorate*

CHOCOLATE AND AMARETTI BARS

These no-bake bars are lovely to have with coffee at the end of a meal. The edible gold-leaf decoration looks elegant, but you can top them with shavings of chocolate instead, if you prefer.

1. Grease the cake pan with butter and line the bottom with parchment paper. Heat a medium, nonstick frying pan, pour in the almonds and pine nuts, and dry-fry over medium heat for about 3 minutes or until golden, turning often so they brown evenly. Transfer to a small bowl and set aside.

2. Put the butter, corn syrup, and half the chocolate into a large heatproof bowl set over a pan of gently simmering water; the base of the bowl should not touch the water. As soon as the chocolate has melted, remove the bowl from the pan. Stir in the cocoa, then the apricots and dry-roasted almonds and pine nuts. Coarsely crumble in the amaretti biscuits (see below: *Crunchy base*). Stir just to combine.

3. Spoon the mixture into the pan and press down with a palette knife to level the surface. Cover and put in the fridge to set for at least 3 hours, or overnight. Remove the pan from the fridge. Put the remaining half of chocolate into a heatproof bowl set over a pan of gently simmering water, and when melted remove the bowl from the pan. Pour the chocolate over the top of the bar base, spread it thinly over the surface, and let it set for 30 minutes to 1 hour (see below: *Even chocolate topping*).

4. Cut into 18 bars using a sharp knife, remove from the pan, and decorate each bar with edible gold leaf (see below: *Elegant finish*).

KEYS TO PERFECTION

Crunchy base

When adding the amaretti to the chocolate mixture, crumble the biscuits quite coarsely, and try to have a mixture of sizes and textures—crumbly and chunky—for variety. Stir them in gently so they don't break up.

Even chocolate topping

Smooth the melted chocolate topping evenly over the biscuit base using a palette knife, then let the topping set so it will cut cleanly when sliced. Don't return the bars to the fridge, or the chocolate will lose its sheen.

Elegant finish

Edible gold leaf is paper-thin and extremely delicate. Use the tip of a small, sharp knife to cut a tiny piece away from the sheet, then use a small paintbrush to apply it from the knife's tip onto the chocolate once it has set.

Special equipment
*Baking dish, 12 x 9in
(30 x 23cm) and 1½in
(4cm) deep*

*16 tbsp (225 g) butter
(room temperature),
plus extra for greasing*

*1¼ lb (550 g) cooking
apples, such as
Granny Smith*

juice of ½ lemon

*¾ cup (225 g) light
brown sugar*

*2 cups (300 g)
self-rising flour*

2 tsp baking powder

1 tsp ground cinnamon

4 large eggs

1 tbsp whole or low-fat milk

confectioners sugar, to dust

SPICED DORSET APPLE CAKE

As well as being a good coffee- or tea-time cake, this makes a comforting dessert, served warm with whipped cream or crème fraîche. I often make it in the fall, when I have a glut of apples.

1. Preheat the oven to 350°F (180°C). Grease the baking dish with butter and line with parchment paper. Quarter, peel, core, and thinly slice the apples, and put them in a shallow dish. Pour in the lemon juice and toss gently together. (See below: *Soft, juicy apples.*)

2. Put the butter, brown sugar, flour, baking powder, ½ teaspoon of the cinnamon, the eggs, and milk in a large bowl. Beat thoroughly using an electric hand mixer for about 2 minutes (or use a wooden spoon for about 3 minutes) until smooth and light.

3. Spoon half the mixture into the prepared dish and spread it out evenly. Lay half the apple slices on top and sprinkle with the remaining ½ teaspoon of cinnamon. Spoon the remaining cake mixture on top and carefully

level the surface. Scatter the rest of the apple slices over the cake mixture and press them lightly into the surface. (See below: *Defined layers.*)

4. Bake for 40 minutes or until well risen and golden brown on top. The cake will feel spongy but firm, and will be starting to come away slightly from the edges of the dish. Also, the apples should be soft. Let the cake cool in the dish for 10 minutes, then loosen the sides with a small palette knife and turn out the cake, peel off the parchment paper, and let cool on a wire rack. Sift confectioners sugar over the top of the cake.

KEYS TO PERFECTION

Soft, juicy apples

It's important to slice the apples very thinly. If they're too thick, they won't soften enough when baked. Tossing them in lemon juice helps stop them from turning too brown, as well as giving flavor and extra juiciness.

Defined layers

1 When spreading the second half of the cake mixture over the apples and cinnamon, do so gently using a palette knife to ensure the apple slices beneath aren't disturbed, thus retaining the layered effect.

2 Spread the apples evenly over the cake mixture and lightly press them in. You don't need to be too neat when layering the apples; in fact, the top looks more interesting if you scatter the apples in a random pattern.

MARY'S TOP TIPS

Get the timing right

Timing is crucial, particularly when baking, so it's worth investing in a timer (preferably digital) and always preheat the oven when specified. All ovens vary, so be vigilant and make a note of timings for next time.

SERVES 20

Special equipment
*Springform pan, 8in (20cm)
diameter and 3in (7.5cm)
deep; fine skewer*

7 oz (200 g) natural glacé
cherries, rinsed, thoroughly
dried, and quartered

6 oz (175 g) raisins

14 oz (400 g) currants

12 oz (350 g) golden raisins

5½ oz (150 g) dried
cranberries

3½ oz (100 g) dried apricots,
chopped to the same size
as the cherries

⅔ cup (150 ml) sherry, plus
extra for "feeding"

finely grated zest of
2 oranges

18 tbsp (250 g) butter
(room temperature),
plus extra for greasing

1 cup (250 g) light
brown sugar

4 large eggs

1 tbsp molasses

½ cup (75 g) self-rising flour

1 cup 175g (6oz)
all-purpose flour

1½ tsp pumpkin spice

1¾ oz (50 g) blanched
almonds, chopped

50 g (1¾ oz) Brazil nuts,
chopped

MY FAVORITE FRUIT CAKE

*Rich, dark, and temptingly moist, this is based on a Victorian recipe
and makes the perfect Christmas, birthday, or christening cake.
You can either decorate it or enjoy it just as it is.*

1. Place all the dried fruit in a large container with a tight-fitting lid, pour in the sherry, and add the orange zest. Stir well. Cover and let the fruit soak for 3 days, stirring every day. (See p317: *Moist, rich, golden brown cake*, step 1.)

2. Grease the bottom and side of the springform pan and line with a double layer of greased parchment paper (see p316: *Grease and line the cake pan*). Preheat the oven to 275°F (140°C).

3. Put the butter, sugar, eggs, and molasses in a very large bowl and beat well using an electric hand mixer to combine. Don't worry if the mixture looks curdled at this stage. Add both the flours and the pumpkin spice, and stir thoroughly using a large metal spoon until blended. Stir in the soaked fruit (half at a time if it is easier), then the nuts. Spoon the mixture into the prepared pan and level the surface with the back of the spoon.

4. Bake in the center of the oven for 4–4½ hours (checking the color after 2 hours) or until the cake feels firm and is a rich golden brown color. Remove and let the cake cool in the pan. When cold, pierce the top of the cake at intervals with the skewer and "feed" with 2 tablespoons of sherry. (See p317: *Moist, rich, golden brown cake*, steps 2–4).

5. Remove the cake from the pan but keep the lining paper on (to keep the cake moist). Wrap the cake in a double layer of parchment paper and again in aluminum foil. Store in a cool place for up to 3 months, skewering and "feeding" once a week with sherry.

KEYS TO PERFECTION
See pp316–317

KEYS TO PERFECTION

Grease and line the cake pan

1 As this fruit cake bakes for several hours, you need to line the springform pan with a double layer of parchment paper, or the cake may burn around the edges. To make a lining for the bottom of the pan, sit the base on a double thickness of parchment and draw around the circumference onto the paper in pencil. Cut just inside the pencil line.

2 To line the side, cut a strip of double thickness parchment that is long and deep enough to go all around the tin, allowing a small overlap for the ends. Make a fold, about 1in (2.5cm) wide, along one of the long sides. Cut slightly slanting lines into the folded strip at about 1in (2.5cm) intervals.

3 Place the lining paper for the side inside the greased tin, so the snipped strips sit snugly on the base. Lay the parchment circles for the bottom of the tin over the snipped part of the side strip, then grease all the parchment paper well using a pastry brush and a little butter. Make sure the butter is at room temperature, so it is soft enough to spread easily.

MAKE THE FRUIT CAKE WELL IN ADVANCE

This cake is best made 2 months before you want to serve it, although you can make it up to 3 months or as little as 3 weeks ahead. If it's eaten too early, it will be crumbly. Wrap it in a double layer of parchment, then in foil; never put foil directly in contact with a fruit cake, as the acid in the fruit can cause the foil to corrode, impairing the flavor of the cake. Store the cake in a cool place, such as a fridge or cool cupboard, as it may turn moldy in a warm kitchen.

Moist, rich, golden brown cake

1 You must allow 3 days before making the cake for marinating the dried fruit in sherry. This is essential to plump up and flavor the fruit. If you reduce the soaking time, there will be a surplus of liquid, which will alter the texture of the finished cake. Leave to marinate at room temperature, and turn the fruit in the liquid every day.

2 Inspect the cake after it has been in the oven for 2 hours: it may be the desired color by then, but the cake will not yet be cooked. If it's already a rich golden brown at this stage, lay a piece of foil loosely over the top. This will protect the top of the cake as it finishes cooking and prevent it from getting too dark.

3 After 4 hours, the cake may be done. To test if it's cooked, insert a fine skewer into the center of the cake. When withdrawn, the skewer should be clean and dry, not wet and sticky. If it's still sticky, return the cake to the oven to bake for a bit longer.

4 When the cake has cooled, pierce the top at intervals with the skewer and drizzle it with 2 tablespoons of sherry. To ensure a wonderfully moist cake with lots of flavor, I repeat this "feeding" process about once a week.

SERVES 12

Special equipment
2lb (900g) loaf pan, about 8½ x 4½in (21.5 x 11cm) and 2½in (6cm) deep, 1 quart (1.2 liter) capacity

8 tbsp (115g) butter (room temperature) or baking spread (at least 70% fat), plus extra for greasing

2 very ripe bananas, about 7oz (200g) total peeled weight

½ cup (150g) light brown sugar

2 large eggs

1¼ cups (225g) self-rising flour

1 tsp baking powder

2 tbsp whole or low-fat milk

2½oz (75g) pecans, chopped

For the icing and decoration

¼ cup (25g) confectioners sugar

2 tsp honey

10–12 pecan halves, about ¾oz (20g)

BANANA LOAF WITH HONEY ICING

This is a great way to use up ripe bananas, including black-skinned ones. The riper they are, the better the flavor of this loaf. You can keep very ripe bananas in the freezer until you're ready to bake.

1. Preheat the oven to 350°F (180°C). Grease the loaf pan and line with parchment paper (see below: *Line the loaf pan*).

2. Mash the bananas (see below: *Optimum flavor and texture*). Put the butter, brown sugar, eggs, flour, baking powder, and milk in a large bowl and beat using an electric hand mixer for 1 minute (or 2 minutes with a wooden spoon) until blended. Add the banana and beat for 30 seconds or until mixed in. Stir in the chopped pecans. Spoon the mixture into the prepared tin. Level the top.

3. Bake for about 1 hour or until well risen and golden brown. Check after 45 minutes. If the top is browning too much, lay a piece of foil over it.

To see if the loaf is done, insert a skewer in the middle; it should come out clean.

4. Let the loaf cool in the pan for a few minutes. Run a palette knife around the edge of the pan, turn out the loaf, peel off the lining paper, and finish cooling on a wire rack. When the loaf has cooled completely, sift the confectioners sugar into a bowl and stir in the honey and ½ teaspoon cold water to make a runny icing. Drizzle this over the cake and lay the pecan halves down the middle.

KEYS TO PERFECTION

Line the loaf pan

To prevent the loaf from sticking, grease and line the pan: sit the pan on parchment paper and draw around the base, then cut just inside the lines. Lay the paper in the bottom of the pan. You don't need to line the sides.

Optimum flavor and texture

Use very ripe bananas and mash them with a fork until broken down and pulpy. Make sure you have about 7 oz (200 g) of mashed banana. Too little will result in a lack of flavor, too much and the cake may have a heavy texture.

LOAF PAN SIZES AND CAPACITY

2 lb (900 g) loaf pans can vary in size and be thinner, fatter, or deeper than the one I have used for this recipe. Provided your pan has the same volume capacity (1 quart/1.2 liters), you will have the right amount of mixture for the loaf. However, if the dimensions are different you may have to adjust the cooking time. For instance, if your pan is slightly shallower but longer than the one used here, the loaf may bake a bit more quickly. Conversely, if it is shorter and deeper, it may take longer.

SERVES 15

Special equipment
*2 springform pans,
8in (20cm) diameter
and 1¾in (4.5cm) deep*

*16 tbsp (225 g) butter
(room temperature) or
baking spread (at least 70%
fat), plus extra for greasing*

*1 cup (225 g)
granulated sugar*

*1¼ cups (225 g)
self-rising flour*

2 tsp baking powder

4 large eggs

edible red food paste

For the filling

*2½ cups (350 g)
confectioners sugar*

*12 tbsp (175 g) butter
(room temperature)*

¼ tsp vanilla extract

4 tsp whole or low-fat milk

6 tbsp lemon curd

**For the glacé icing and
decoration**

*2 cups (275 g)
confectioners sugar*

*edible colored food pastes:
red, mint green, and yellow*

*15 candy-coated
chocolate candies
(5 pink, 5 green, 5 yellow)*

PASTEL RAINBOW CAKE

There are many versions of the multilayered rainbow cake.
This is my simple one, which is perfect for all sorts of occasions.
I like subtle colors, but you can make it as bright as you like.

1. Preheat the oven to 350°F (180°C). Grease the springform pans and line the bottoms with parchment paper. Put the butter, granulated sugar, flour, and baking powder in a large bowl. Add the eggs and beat well using an electric hand mixer for about 2 minutes (or use a wooden spoon for about 3 minutes) until smooth and light.

2. Divide the mixture equally in half. Spoon one half of the mixture into one of the prepared pans. Color the other half pale pink with the red food paste (add it bit by bit until you're happy with the shade) and spoon it into the other pan. Level the surfaces. Bake both cakes for about 25 minutes. Cool for 2 minutes, then loosen the sides and let rest for 10 minutes. Turn the cakes out, carefully remove the pan bases and lining paper, and let cool on a wire rack. (See p322: *Evenly layered, beautifully baked cakes*, steps 1 and 2.)

3. Make the filling: sift the confectioners sugar into a large bowl, add the butter, vanilla, and milk, and beat together using an electric hand mixer (or wooden spoon) until soft, smooth, and well blended.

4. When the cakes are cold, cut them in half. Place a white sponge layer, cut-side facing up, on a flat serving plate or a cake stand. Spread with 2 tablespoons of the lemon curd, then with one-third of the filling. Lay a pink sponge layer on top and, again, spread with 2 tablespoons of lemon curd and one-third of the filling. Repeat with another white layer of sponge and the remaining lemon curd and filling. Finish with a pink layer of sponge on top, with the base uppermost to give a flat top. (See p322: *Evenly layered, beautifully baked cakes*, steps 3 and 4.)

5. Make the glacé icing: sift the confectioners sugar into a bowl. Stir in 7 teaspoons cold water, then adjust if necessary with a few more drops of water to make a thickish, spreadable icing. Make 3 small piping bags from parchment paper. Set out 3 small bowls and put 1 tablespoon of the icing into each. Using the colored food pastes, color one batch pink, one pale green, and one yellow. Spoon each batch of icing into separate piping bags and fold over the tops to seal. (See p323: *Smooth icing and pastel decoration*, steps 1–3.)

6. Check the consistency of the remaining white icing and add a drop more water if needed. Spread it evenly over the top of the cake. While it is still soft, quickly pipe squiggly lines all over using each of the colored icings. (See p323: *Smooth icing and pastel decoration*, step 4.) Stick alternate colored candies upright all around the top edge. Let the icing set before slicing.

KEYS TO PERFECTION
See pp322–323

KEYS TO PERFECTION

Evenly layered, beautifully baked cakes

1 To make sure you have an equal amount of cake batter for each pan, weigh each half of the mixture before you add the edible red food paste. If they weigh exactly the same, the cakes will be of the same depth, giving you attractive, even layers when cut. Gradually add the food paste to half the batter until you get the shade you like.

2 After dividing the mixture equally between the prepared pans, smooth the surfaces with a palette knife to level, so the cakes cook evenly. Bake the cakes side by side in the oven for even cooking. Don't be tempted to open the oven door before 20 minutes, or the cakes will sink. When done, the cakes will shrink away from the sides of the pans and the tops will spring back if pressed.

3 The cakes need to be halved evenly for the layering to look its best. Let the baked cakes cool completely before slicing, as they will be more crumbly and difficult to cut if warm. Mark a guide-line in the center of the side of each cake with a large serrated knife, then continue working your way around the cake. Carefully slice through the cake on the guideline to produce two even halves.

4 When spreading the buttercream filling over the surface of the cakes, make sure you do so evenly using a palette knife or round-bladed knife. If it's spread unevenly, the cake layers will be uneven, too. As you spread the filling, try not to disturb the lemon curd layer underneath; you don't want it to get mixed in with the icing.

Smooth icing and pastel decoration

1 Adding just the right amount of water to the icing is key. You want just enough so the icing is smooth and runny, but not so runny that it will run down the sides of the cake. If you lift the spoon out of the bowl, the icing should fall in a slow, steady stream. When piping, the icing needs to be firm enough to hold its shape (if it's too runny, the lines will not be well defined) but soft enough so it flows easily.

2 When adding coloring to the icing (and the batter), it's best to add it cautiously; if too much is added the colors can quickly become very vivid. Dip a wooden toothpick into the food paste and dab in just a little to start with. More can be added to deepen the color, but it's hard to take it away if too much is used. Stir so it blends in well, otherwise you'll have streaks of color in the icing.

3 For perfect lines, use a piping bag. For each bag, cut out a piece of parchment paper 8in (20cm) square. Fold it in half to make a triangle. With the long, folded edge near you, take one corner up to the tip of the triangle, then bring the other corner across and wrap it around the back to make a pointed bag. Fold over tightly to seal. Snip off the tip to make a small piping hole.

4 After spooning the icing into the piping bags, fold the top of each bag over the icing so it can't leak out. Taking one filled bag at a time, hold it upright between your fingers and use your thumbs to press the icing out in a steady trail, moving the bag around over the top of the cake so the icing falls in squiggly lines. Repeat with the other icing bags so the lines overlap all over the cake to give a colorful pattern.

SERVES 24

Special equipment
1½ quart (1.7 liter) tube pan, 9in (23cm) diameter and 3in (7.5cm) deep; fine skewer

16 tbsp (225g) butter (room temperature) or baking spread (at least 70% fat), plus extra for greasing

1 cup (225g) granulated sugar

1½ cups (275g) self-rising flour

1 tsp baking powder

4 large eggs

2 tbsp whole or low-fat milk

finely grated zest of 3 limes

3½ oz (100g) blueberries

For the glaze

6 tbsp lime juice (from 3–4 limes)

⅔ cup (175g) granulated sugar

LIME AND BLUEBERRY RING DRIZZLE

*Fresh limes and juicy blueberries add a lovely flavor, color,
and texture to this cake. To get maximum juice from the limes,
microwave them all together for 30–60 seconds before squeezing.*

1. Preheat the oven to 350°F (180°C). Grease the tube pan. Cut about 8–10 strips of parchment paper, each 6 x 1in (15 x 2.5cm), and use them to line the pan (see below: *Line the tube pan*).

2. Place the butter, granulated sugar, flour, and baking powder in a large bowl. Add the eggs, milk, and lime zest and beat using an electric hand mixer for about 2 minutes (or 3 minutes with a wooden spoon) until smooth.

3. Spoon half the mixture into the pan and level it, then scatter the blueberries over the top, keeping them away from the edge of the pan (this makes them less likely to stick). Spoon the rest of the mixture over the blueberries, and spread it evenly with a palette knife to cover the fruit.

4. Bake for 35–40 minutes or until well risen and the top springs back when lightly pressed. While the cake bakes, make the glaze: mix the lime juice with the granulated sugar and set aside. Let the cake cool in its pan for a few minutes, then loosen the side with a palette knife. Turn it out onto a wire rack set over a cookie sheet, and peel off the lining strips.

5. While the cake is still warm, prick all over with the skewer. Stir the glaze, then spoon it over the warm cake. Let it cool completely. (See below: *Glaze the warm cake*.)

KEYS TO PERFECTION

Line the tube pan

To prevent the cake from sticking to the tube pan, line it with 8–10 parchment strips. Lay the strips at equal intervals, starting from the top of the inner funnel, down to the bottom of the pan, and up the side.

Glaze the warm cake

1 As the tube pan is deep, it's best to skewer very small holes all over the warm cake before glazing, so the glaze can soak in. Use a fine skewer (sometimes called a "cake tester") so the holes aren't too big.

2 Spoon the glaze over the cake slowly (or it will run off) and let it drizzle down and soak in before spooning over more. Rub it down the sides with the spoon. Glaze while the cake is still warm; if cool, the glaze will not soak in.

SERVES 10

Special equipment
*2 springform pans,
8in (20cm) diameter
and 1¾in (4.5cm) deep*

*14 tbsp (200g) butter
(room temperature) or
baking spread (at least 70%
fat), plus extra for greasing*

½ cup (50g) cocoa powder

¼ cup whole or low-fat milk

3 eggs

1 cup (175g) self-rising flour

1 tsp baking powder

1 tsp ground ginger

*1 cup (250g)
granulated sugar*

*2 pieces of candied ginger,
finely chopped*

For the filling and topping

*1¾ (225g)
confectioners sugar*

*8 tbsp (115g) butter
(room temperature)*

*2 tbsp stem ginger syrup
or light corn syrup*

1 tbsp whole or low-fat milk

*2 pieces of candied ginger,
finely shredded*

GORGEOUS GINGER AND CHOCOLATE CAKE

Mixing together chocolate and a hint of ginger creates an intriguing blend of flavors in this moist, rich cake. To make sure the ginger doesn't sink, it's important to chop it finely.

1. Preheat the oven to 350°F (180°C). Grease the springform pans and line the bottom of each with parchment paper. Put the cocoa powder into a large, heatproof bowl. Stir in 6 tablespoons boiling water, then add the milk. Mix to make a smooth paste (see below: *Smooth mixture*).

2. Add the remaining cake ingredients and combine using an electric hand mixer for 1–2 minutes only (or 3 minutes with a wooden spoon); do not overmix, or the cake may not rise.

3. Divide the cake mixture equally between the prepared pans and level the tops. Bake for 25–30 minutes or until the cakes shrink away from the side of the pan and spring back when lightly pressed in the center. Let the

cakes cool for a few minutes in their pans, then turn them out and peel off the paper. Turn the cakes right side up and let cool on a wire rack.

4. Make the filling and topping: sift the confectioners sugar into a large bowl. Add the butter, candied ginger syrup, and milk, and beat together using an electric hand mixer (or wooden spoon) until well blended. Transfer one of the cakes to a serving plate and spread half the icing over the top. Place the second cake on top of the filling and cover the top with the remaining icing. (See below: *Evenly iced cakes.*) Use the palette knife to draw large "S" shapes to give a swirl effect, then decorate the edge with the shredded candied ginger.

KEYS TO PERFECTION

Smooth mixture

Cocoa powder can be lumpy, so mix it to a smooth paste with boiling water, then milk before adding the remaining ingredients. Use a wooden spoon to break up any lumps.

Evenly iced cakes

Make sure the butter for the icing is at room temperature, so it will spread easily. Use equal amounts of icing between the layers and on top of the cake, and cover right to the edges.

BUYING AND USING COCOA POWDER

This cake looks and tastes very chocolatey, but it doesn't actually contain any chocolate—it's made with cocoa powder. Buy a good-quality cocoa powder, preferably an organic one. This will be darker than the less expensive varieties, and will ensure that your cake has a deep, rich chocolate color and flavor.

MAKES 1 LOAF

Special equipment
2 lb (900g) loaf pan, about
8½ x 4½in (21.5 x 11cm)
and 2½in (6cm) deep,
1 quart (1.2 liters) capacity
(see p318, box)

4 tbsp (50g) butter

3 oz (85g) raisins

1¾ oz (50g) natural glacé
cherries, rinsed, dried,
and chopped

1 oz (30g) currants

2½ cups (450g) white
bread flour, plus extra
for dusting

7g packet easy-blend
(fast-action) dried yeast

1 tsp salt

1½ tsp pumpkin spice

1 tsp ground cinnamon

¼ cup (50g) light
brown sugar

⅔ cup (150ml) whole or
low-fat milk

1 large egg, beaten

sunflower oil, for greasing

For the crosses and glaze

2 tbsp all-purpose flour

2 tsp granulated sugar

HOT CROSS BUN LOAF

For this recipe the fruit and flavorings are similar to those in traditional hot cross buns, but I've made one large loaf instead, which is quicker. Try it fresh or toasted—it's utterly delicious.

1. Melt the butter and let it cool. Mix the raisins, cherries, and currants in a large bowl and set aside. Combine the bread flour, yeast, salt, spices, and sugar in a separate large bowl. Heat the milk with 5 tablespoons water until hand-warm. Make a well in the flour mixture and pour in the cooled butter and beaten egg. Add the warm milk and water in a steady stream, while mixing everything together with a butter knife. Gather the dough into a ball. (See p330: *Make a rich, fruity dough*, step 1.)

2. Turn out the dough onto a lightly floured surface and knead for 8–10 minutes or until smooth and elastic. Lay the dough on top of the dried fruit mix in the bowl and knead together to combine. To finish working in the fruit, turn the dough onto the work surface again and knead for 1–2 minutes. Shape the dough into a round and place it in a large, lightly oiled bowl. Cover with plastic wrap and leave in a warm place for about 1½ hours or until doubled in size. (See p330: *Make a rich, fruity dough*, steps 2–4.) Lightly grease the loaf pan and line the bottom with parchment paper.

3. Turn the risen dough out onto the work surface and knead it just 3 or 4 times. Divide the dough into 4 equal pieces. Shape each one into an oval. Place each piece in the pan in a line. (See p331: *Get the best shape*.) Cover

with a clean tea towel and leave in a warm place to rise for about 50 minutes to 1 hour or until the dough reaches about 2in (5cm) above the top of the pan. Preheat the oven to 450°F (230°C).

4. For the crosses, make a small piping bag out of parchment paper (see p323: *Smooth icing and pastel decoration*, step 3). Mix the all-purpose flour with 4½ teaspoons cold water in a small bowl to make a smooth paste, then spoon it into the piping bag. When the dough has risen, pipe a cross on top of each piece. (See p331: *Decorate the loaf*, step 1.)

5. Bake for 5 minutes, then reduce the temperature to 425°F (220°C) and bake for another 15 minutes, covering the top loosely with foil when the top is golden brown. Bake for 5–10 minutes more. The loaf is done when it feels firm.

6. Make the glaze: mix the granulated sugar with 1 teaspoon cold water. Loosen the sides of the loaf with a small, round-bladed knife, then turn out of the pan. Peel off the parchment paper and place the loaf on a wire rack. Brush the glaze over the top of the loaf while it is still warm. (See p331: *Decorate the loaf*, step 2.) Slice when the loaf has cooled completely.

KEYS TO PERFECTION
See pp330–331

KEYS TO PERFECTION

Make a rich, fruity dough

1 The dough for this loaf is enriched with butter, milk, and egg. Add the milk and water to the flour, butter, and egg in a slow, steady stream, and as you pour stir the mixture to combine well using a butter knife. The dough is ready when it comes together to form a ball; it should feel quite soft and slightly sticky.

2 To make the dough elastic, knead it for 8–10 minutes on a lightly floured work surface. Push down with the heel of your hand into the ball of dough and stretch it out away from your body, then bring the end of the dough back over the top and press it down in the middle. Give a quarter turn and repeat.

3 To incorporate the fruit into the kneaded dough, lay the dough on top of the fruit in the bowl. Knead from the outside into the center, so everything starts to get evenly mixed in. Once you've worked in as much of the fruit as you can, turn the dough out and finish kneading in any stray pieces of fruit for 1–2 minutes more. To keep the dough light and the fruit intact, don't knead too much at this stage.

4 Let the dough rise until it has doubled in size. Generally, if the dough is left in a warm place, this will take about 1½ hours, but the timing can vary depending on the temperature of the room, so keep checking. Bread will rise at its best pace in a warm environment—about 77°F (25°C) is ideal—rather than one that is too hot or too cold.

Get the best shape

1 Divide the risen dough into 4 equal-sized pieces by cutting it with a sharp knife. Weigh each piece of dough to make sure they're all of equal weight. Weighing will give a more accurate result than dividing by eye, and will give you the best shape for the finished loaf.

2 Form each piece of dough into a plump oval shape by rolling it on the work surface with your hands so it's the width of the pan, checking that each piece is the same length. Again, this will give the best shape to your loaf. Position the ovals in the pan so they fit snugly next to each other in a line.

Decorate the loaf

1 When mixing the paste for the crosses, add enough water so the mixture is liquid enough to pipe yet is able to hold its shape. If too much water is added, the crosses will be less defined. So that the crosses cover each entire domed piece of the loaf, start to pipe each line where the dough meets the rim of the pan and take it over the top of the dough until it touches the rim on the other side.

2 For a perfect finish, brush the sugar glaze over the top of the loaf while it is still warm. The warmth of the dough will help the glaze to set and give the loaf a glossy sheen.

MAKES 1 LOAF

*2 tbsp (20 g) butter
(room temperature),
plus extra for greasing*

*1¼ cups (225 g) all-purpose
flour, plus extra for dusting
and sprinkling*

*1 cup (225 g)
whole grain flour*

1 tsp baking soda

1 tsp salt

1¾ cups (400 ml) buttermilk

IRISH SODA BREAD

This traditional bread is made without yeast, so it's perfect for days when you want a loaf on the table quickly. The buttermilk provides a soft-textured dough with a unique flavor.

1. Preheat the oven to 400°F (200°C). Lightly grease a baking sheet with a little butter.

2. Put both flours in a large bowl. Add the butter and rub it in with your fingertips. Stir in the baking soda and salt. Pour in the buttermilk and 2 tablespoons of hand-warm water. Briefly mix the ingredients (see below: *Make a light-textured dough*, step 1). The dough should be very soft and sticky, but still easy to shape. Add another tablespoon of water if needed.

3. Turn out the dough onto a lightly floured surface and gather into a neat round, about 8in (20cm) in diameter (it needn't be too smooth). Place the loaf on the baking sheet and cut a ½in (1cm) deep cross in the top. (See below: *Make a light-textured dough*, steps 2 and 3.) Sprinkle the top of the loaf with a little white flour.

4. Bake for 30–35 minutes or until risen and golden brown. Tap the base of the loaf to see if it is cooked: it should sound hollow. Transfer to a wire rack to cool. The soda bread is best eaten very fresh, but if wrapped well it will keep for 1 or 2 days.

KEYS TO PERFECTION

Make a light-textured dough

1 A few turns using your hands are all that is required to make sure the buttermilk and water are blended in. Throughout the process, don't over-handle the dough; the less you handle it, the lighter the bread will be.

2 Shape the dough into a round with your hands. Just lightly gather it together into a ball, then gently pat it out to a circle about 8in (20cm) across. As there is no yeast in this mixture, it doesn't require any kneading.

3 Using a sharp knife dipped in flour to prevent sticking, cut a cross on the loaf, about ½in (1cm) deep. As the loaf bakes, the cross will open out, enabling the bread to cook through to the center.

MAKES 1 LOAF

2 cups (300 g) whole
grain flour

¾ cup (200 g) bread flour,
plus extra for dusting

1½ tsp salt

7g packet easy-blend
(fast-action) dried yeast

2 tbsp (30 g) butter
(room temperature),
cut into small pieces

6 tbsp mixed seeds,
such as sesame, sunflower,
flaxseed, and pumpkin

sunflower oil, for greasing

SEEDED WHOLE GRAIN TWIST

I've learned from Paul Hollywood that when making bread it's good to have a slightly wet, sticky dough, as it produces better results. This loaf contains a mix of seeds for added texture and flavor.

1. Mix both the flours, salt, and yeast together in a large bowl. Add the butter and rub it in with your fingertips. Stir in 5 tablespoons of the seeds. Make a well in the center of the flour mixture and pour in 1¼ cups (300 ml) hand-warm water. Mix everything together to make a dough. Gather the dough into a ball. (See p336: *Make a soft, pliable dough*, step 1.)

2. Turn the dough out onto a lightly floured surface and knead for 8–10 minutes or until smooth and elastic. Put the dough in a large, lightly oiled bowl and cover with plastic wrap. Let rise in a warm place for about 1½ hours or until the dough doubles in size. (See p336: *Make a soft, pliable dough*, steps 2–4.)

3. Line a large baking sheet with parchment paper. When the dough has risen, gently knead it on the lightly floured work surface 3 or 4 times (no more, as too much handling now will reduce the dough's lightness).

4. Cut the dough into 2 equal-sized portions and roll the pieces into "ropes" about 16in (40cm) long. Lay one on top of the other to make an "X," then twist them together tightly. Tuck the ends under and press to seal. (See p337: *Create an evenly shaped twist.*)

5. Lay the loaf on the prepared baking sheet and cover with a clean kitchen towel. Let sit for 40–50 minutes or until doubled in size. Preheat the oven to 450°F (230°C).

6. Uncover the loaf and brush the top with cold water. Sprinkle the remaining 1 tablespoon of seeds over the twists and gently press in. Bake the loaf for 10 minutes, then reduce the oven temperature to 425°F (220°C) and bake for another 20 minutes. (See p337: *Bake a crisp crust.*) Place on a wire rack to cool.

KEYS TO PERFECTION
See pp336–337

KEYS TO PERFECTION

Make a soft, pliable dough

1 Add the hand-warm water to the ingredients in the bowl in a steady stream, mixing as you do so with a round-bladed knife. It's crucial to measure the water accurately and add the full amount. If you don't add enough initially and the dough is too dry, it's harder to add more water later. Once all the water is added and the dough has come together, feel the texture: it should be soft, moist, and sticky.

2 Gather the dough into a ball, turn it out onto a lightly floured work surface, and begin to knead. The process of kneading makes the dough more elastic, and you need to do it for 8–10 minutes at this stage for a well-textured loaf. Use the weight of your body to push down with the heel of your hand into the ball of dough, then stretch it away from your body.

3 Bring the end of the stretched-out dough back over the top and press it down in the middle. Give a quarter turn and repeat. Get into a smooth rhythm. As you knead, the dough will start to feel less sticky but still soft and smooth. Add more flour to the work surface only if the dough is sticking to it; too much extra flour may dry out the dough. Put the dough into an oiled bowl (the oil will prevent sticking).

4 Let the dough rise in a warm place, but not too hot or it could dry out the dough. Rising is important to improve the bread's structure and flavor. You want the dough to reach double its original size and look and feel very light and spongy. This will usually take about 1½ hours, but keep checking, as it depends on the temperature of the room.

Create an evenly shaped twist

1 Weigh each half of dough to make sure they're the same weight, to give you an evenly shaped twist. Using the palms of your hands, roll each half to make two long "ropes." If the dough sticks and is difficult to roll, rub a tiny amount of olive oil onto the surface to help it grip.

2 Lay both dough strands to form an "X" on the work surface. Taking hold of the bottom two ends, twist them over each other 2 or 3 times to make a tight twist. Taking hold of the whole loaf from the middle, carefully turn it over and twist the other 2 ends in the same way. This will give you a plump rather than long, thin twist. Tuck both ends under very slightly and press down to seal.

Bake a crisp crust

1 Before putting the twist in the oven, make sure the oven has preheated to the correct temperature (otherwise the loaf may continue to rise and the sides may split) and that the dough has risen to twice its previous size (but no more, or it may collapse). Just before baking, brush the loaf lightly with water, to create a crisp crust, and scatter over the reserved seeds, pressing them in gently.

2 When the loaf is baked it should be golden brown and firm. I tap it on the base to check if it's ready. It should have a hollow drumlike sound. If it doesn't, return the loaf to the oven for a few more minutes.

MAKES 1 LOAF

Special equipment
*Terracotta flowerpot,
6in (15cm) diameter and
5¼in (13cm) deep*

*2 cups (375g) bread flour,
plus extra for dusting*

*1½ tsp easy-blend
(fast-action) dried yeast*

1 tsp salt

*2 tbsp (20g) butter
(room temperature),
cut into small pieces*

*1½ oz (45g) aged cheddar
cheese, coarsely grated*

*1½ oz (45g) Parmesan
cheese, coarsely grated*

2 tbsp snipped fresh chives

sunflower oil, for greasing

1 egg, beaten

CHEESE AND CHIVE FLOWERPOT LOAF

Using a terracotta flowerpot as a mold for this cheese loaf gives it an interesting and unusual shape. Buy a new, clean flowerpot, season it (see below, box), and keep it just for baking bread.

1. Mix the flour, yeast, and salt in a large bowl. Rub in the butter with your fingertips. Combine the cheeses, reserving ½ oz (15 g) for the top. Add the rest to the bowl with the chives. Make a well and add 1 cup (240 ml) of hand-warm water in a steady stream, mixing with a butter knife to make a soft dough, adding a little extra water if required. Gather the dough and knead on a lightly floured surface for 8–10 minutes or until smooth and elastic. Shape into a round, put it in a large, lightly oiled bowl, cover with plastic wrap, and leave in a warm place for 1½ hours or so, until at least doubled in size.

2. Brush the seasoned flowerpot inside with oil and line (see below: *Line the pot*). Knead the dough 3 or 4 times, form it into a sausage shape about 7in (18cm) long and narrower at one end, and put it in the pot. Cover with a kitchen towel and leave for 45–55 minutes or until the dough has risen to about 1½in (4cm) above the pot. (See below: *Let the dough rise*.)

3. Move the oven shelf to its lowest position. Preheat the oven to 450°F (230°C). Brush the loaf top with the egg and sprinkle with the reserved cheese. Place the pot on a baking sheet and bake for 5 minutes, then reduce the oven temperature to 425°F (220°C) and bake for another 30 minutes. When the loaf is firm on top, remove it from the oven and let it sit in the pot for 2–3 minutes. Remove it from the pot, carefully peel off the baking parchment, and let cool on a wire rack.

KEYS TO PERFECTION

Line the pot

Cut out a circle of parchment paper to fit the bottom of the pot and a strip to fit around with a slight overlap. Cut the strip in half. Line the bottom, then sides. Oil where the strips overlap.

Let the dough rise

Put the dough in the flowerpot with the narrow end facing down and let rise. The dough should rise above the pot before you put the loaf in the oven.

SEASON THE FLOWERPOT

Before you use the pot for the first time you need to "season" it. To do this, wash it thoroughly and dry well, then brush it all over generously, inside and out, with sunflower or vegetable oil. Place the pot on a baking sheet and put it in an oven preheated to 450°F (230°C) for 1 hour. Be careful when you remove the pot, as it will be very hot. After baking the bread, just wipe the inside of the pot rather than wash it.

MAKES 10

2¾ cups (500 g) bread flour, plus extra for dusting

7g packet easy-blend (fast-action) dried yeast

1½ tsp salt

3 tbsp (45 g) butter (room temperature), cut into small pieces

sunflower oil, for greasing

1 egg, beaten

about 1 tsp poppy seeds, for sprinkling

LITTLE COTTAGE ROLLS

A large, cottage-style loaf is traditional, but here I've used the same shape to make daintier, individual rolls. They're the ideal size for serving with soup or cheese, and freeze really well, too.

1. Combine the flour, yeast, and salt in a large bowl. Add the butter and rub it in with your fingertips. Make a well in the flour mixture and pour in about 1¼ cups (300 ml) hand-warm water in a steady stream, while mixing together with a butter knife. Gather the dough together, adding a few more drops of water, if needed. Turn the dough out onto a lightly floured surface and knead for 8–10 minutes or until smooth and elastic. Put it in a large, lightly oiled bowl, cover with plastic wrap, and let rise for about 1½ hours or until doubled in size. Line 2 large baking trays with parchment paper.

2. Turn the dough out onto the work surface and knead 3 or 4 times. Cut the dough into 10 equal-sized pieces. For each piece of dough, cut off one-third with a sharp knife, then shape both the smaller and larger portions into balls. Put the larger balls on the baking sheets and sit the smaller balls on top. Flour the handle of a wooden spoon and push it through the center of each stacked roll. (See below: *Make neat rounds*, steps 1 and 2.) Cover with a kitchen towel and let rise in a warm place until doubled in size, for 40–45 minutes.

3. Preheat the oven to 450°F (230°C). Brush the rolls with the egg and sprinkle with poppy seeds (see below: *Make neat rounds*, step 3). Bake for 5 minutes, then reduce the temperature to 425°F (220°C). Bake for another 10 minutes or until the rolls are golden and firm and sound hollow when tapped on the underside. Cool on a wire rack.

KEYS TO PERFECTION

Make neat rounds

1 Sit the large balls well apart on the baking sheets, so they can rise without touching, otherwise they will lose their shape. Place the smaller balls on top of the larger ones.

2 To secure the top ball to the bottom one, and prevent it from toppling over in the oven, push a floured wooden spoon handle right through the center of both balls.

3 When the rolls have doubled in size, for a glistening glaze brush them all over with beaten egg using a pastry brush, then add a light sprinkling of poppy seeds.

INDEX

A

almonds
   chocolate and amaretti bars 308
   grilled trout with chicory and
      almonds 66
   raspberry and apple muffins 298
amaretti biscuits: chocolate and
   amaretti bars 308
anchovies: chicken Caesar
   salad crostini 28
apples
   fall fruit pie 254–7
   pheasant breasts with
      apple and cider 120
   plum and apple crumble with
      super-crunchy topping
      260–63
   raspberry and apple muffins 298
   spiced Dorset apple cake 310
apricots
   apricot and ginger syrup sponge
      with creamy custard 248–51
   chicken tagine 108–11
   chocolate and amaretti bars 308
   my favorite fruit cake 314–17
arrabbiata sauce, pork
   chops with 144
artichokes: cooking methods
   186–8
arugula
   caramelized red onion and
      arugula tartlets 50–53
   warm chicken salad with
      avocado salsa 244
Asian-style coleslaw 242
Asian-style fish parcels 62–5
asparagus
   asparagus with soft poached
      egg and buttery crumbs 46–9
   cooking methods 188–9
   pan-fried scallops with warm
      tomato dressing 36
   summer vegetable soup 18
   tender-crisp asparagus 48
avocados: warm chicken salad
   with avocado salsa 244

B

baby corn: cooking methods
   186–7
bacon
   my new spaghetti carbonara
      170
   pheasant breasts with apple
      and cider 120
   venison cottage pie 122–5
balsamic glaze, vine tomato and
   shaved fennel salad with 228
banana loaf with honey icing 318
banana shallots 134
basil: Asian-style coleslaw 242
bass: sea bass with creamy
   lemon sauce 90
basting chicken 98
beans
   eggplant, butter bean, and
      chorizo tapa 32
   cooking methods 186–7
   lentil and chili bean salad 230
   rinsing beans 230
bean sprouts
   classic pad Thai 182
   my special egg-fried rice 180
   pan-fried tuna with mixed pea
      stir-fry 80
béchamel sauce 166–8
beef
   browning 132
   cannelloni with double cheese
      sauce 166–9
   chargrilling 134
   filet of beef, buying and
      cooking 128
   peppered filet of beef 128
   ribeye steak with caramelized
      shallots 134
   searing 128
   steak and Guinness pie 130–33
beer: steak and Guinness
   pie 130–33
beets: cooking methods 188–9
biscuits
   cheesecake with blueberry
      topping 284–7
   chocolate chip shortbread
      cookies 304

blackberries
   blackberry and elderflower
      sorbet 288
   fall fruit pie 254–7
blanching green vegetables 194
blind baking pastry shells 252
blueberries
   cheesecake with blueberry
      topping 284–7
   lime and blueberry ring
      drizzle 324
boiling vegetables 194
bok choi
   Asian-style fish parcels 62–5
   cooking methods 186–7
braising vegetables 194
bread
   breadcrumbs 48
   cheese and chive flowerpot
      loaf 338
   chicken Caesar salad crostini 28
   hot cross bun loaf 328–31
   Irish soda bread 332
   little cottage rolls 340
   seeded whole grain twist 334–7
broccoli
   broccolini, sugarsnap
      pea, and pancetta stir-fry 196
   cooking methods 186–7
   penne with cherry tomato
      sauce 164
   stir-fried duck 116–19
   using in stir-fries 118
broccolini
   broccolini, sugarsnap pea,
      and pancetta stir-fry 196
   penne with cherry
      tomato sauce 164
   stir-fried duck 116–19
   using in stir-fries 118
broiling vegetables 206
browning
   chicken 110
   meat 132
Brussels sprouts
   Brussels sprouts with
      hazelnuts 208
   cooking methods 186–7
butter, tarragon 96–9

ACKNOWLEDGMENTS

About the author

For more than four decades, Mary Berry CBE has brought her unfussy approach to cooking and baking into British homes. Her role as judge on *The Great British Baking Show* from 2010 to 2016 endeared her to the hearts of North American viewers. She is a highly respected and bestselling author with more than 80 cookbooks to her name and more than 6 million in sales worldwide—her name has become a byword for honest, reliable recipes that anyone can follow. Mary Berry is the author of several DK books including *Baking with Mary Berry* and *Cooking with Mary Berry*.

Mary Berry would like to thank

For the 2014 UK edition: As ever, I have a wonderful team working with me on my book. Huge thank yous to Angela Nilsen and Jeni Wright, who worked with us to create perfect recipes with true dedication—thank you for your amazing hard work. My thanks also to Polly Boyd, who has edited this book with a fine-tooth comb, making sure every letter and photo is in place; Mary-Clare Jerram at DK for always being the most devoted commissioner; Peter Luff, Nicola Powling, and Karen Constanti for the design; and Dawn Henderson and Christine Keilty for overseeing the project. For the lovely food photography I would like to thank William Reavell and Stuart West, and home economists Jane Lawrie, Emma-Jane Frost, Nico Ghirlando, and Carol Tennant. Thanks are also due to lovely photographer Georgia Glynn Smith for the action photos of me—what a talent and delight to have on shoot.

Finally, and most important of all, to Lucy Young, who has been my assistant for 30 years and liaises with everyone above … I now refer to *her* as the boss!

DK would like to thank

For the 2014 UK edition: Angela Nilsen and Jeni Wright, who worked with Mary Berry to develop and perfect the recipes; Lucy Young for recipe consultation; Geoff Fennell and Penny Stock for art direction; Liz Hippisley for recipe styling; Laura Buscemi, Mandy Earey, Anne Fisher, and Vicky Read for design assistance; Steve Crozier and Karen Constanti for retouching; Isabel de Cordova for wardrobe styling; Jo Penford for hair and make-up; Elizabeth Clinton, Sarah Edwards, Kate Fenton, and Jenny Volich for hand modeling; Vanessa Bird for indexing.

For the 2021 US edition: Saffron Stocker for new design concept; Kate Curnes Ramos for North American recipe adaptations; Adam Brackenbury for image repro work.

A note about ingredients

Baileys is a trademark of R & A Bailey & Co; Guinness is a trademark of Diageo Ireland; Peppadew is a trademark of Piquante Brands International (Proprietary) Limited.